Activity Theory, Authentic Learning and Emerging Technologies

Although emerging technologies are becoming popular for teaching, learning and research, the relationship between their use and transformative effects on higher education remains largely unexplored. This edited collection seeks to fill this gap by providing a nuanced view, locating higher education pedagogical practices at the intersection of emerging technologies, authentic learning and activity systems.

Providing numerous case studies as examples, *Activity Theory, Authentic Learning and Emerging Technologies* draws on a wide range of contexts to illustrate how such a convergence has the potential to track transformative teaching and learning practices in the higher education sector. Chapters provide the reader with a variety of transformative higher education pedagogical practices in southern contexts, theorised within the framework of Cultural-Historical Activity Theory (CHAT) and tool mediation, while using authentic learning as a pedagogical model upon which this theoretical framework is based.

The topics covered in the book have global relevance, with research paying particular attention to South Africa, Australia and New Zealand, where the authors are based. The book will be of interest to educators, researchers and practitioners in higher education, as well as those interested in emerging technologies in education more generally.

Vivienne Bozalek is Professor of Social Work and Director of Teaching and Learning at the University of the Western Cape, South Africa.

Dick Ng'ambi is Associate Professor and Master's Programme Convenor in the School of Education, University of Cape Town, South Africa.

Denise Wood is Professor of Learning, Equity, Access and Participation at Central Queensland University, Australia. She is also an Extraordinary Professor in the Faculty of Education, University of the Western Cape, South Africa.

Jan Herrington is Professor of Education in the School of Education, Murdoch University, Australia.

Joanne Hardman is Senior Lecturer in the School of Education, University of Cape Town, South Africa.

Alan Amory is Professor and Director of the Centre for Academic Technologies, University of Johannesburg, South Africa.

Routledge Research in Higher Education

Developing Creativities in Higher Music Education
International perspectives and practices
Edited by Pamela Burnard

Academic Governance
Disciplines and policy
Jenny M. Lewis

Refocusing the Self in Higher Education
A phenomenological perspective
Glen L. Sherman

Activity Theory, Authentic Learning and Emerging Technologies
Towards a transformative higher education pedagogy
Edited by Vivienne Bozalek, Dick Ng'ambi, Denise Wood, Jan Herrington, Joanne Hardman and Alan Amory

Activity Theory, Authentic Learning and Emerging Technologies

Towards a transformative
higher education pedagogy

**Edited by Vivienne Bozalek,
Dick Ng'ambi, Denise Wood,
Jan Herrington, Joanne Hardman
and Alan Amory**

 Routledge
Taylor & Francis Group

LONDON AND NEW YORK

First published 2015
by Routledge
2 Park Square, Milton Park, Abingdon, Oxon OX14 4RN

and by Routledge
711 Third Avenue, New York, NY 10017

Routledge is an imprint of the Taylor & Francis Group, an informa business

British Library Cataloguing in Publication Data
A catalogue record for this book is available from the British Library

Library of Congress Cataloging in Publication Data
Activity theory, authentic learning and emerging technologies : towards a
transformative higher education pedagogy / edited by Vivienne Bozalek
[and five others].

    pages cm — (Routledge research in higher education)

    1. Educational technology—South Africa   2. Educational technology—
Australia.   3. Education, Higher—South Africa.   4. Education,
Higher—Australia.   I. Bozalek, Vivienne.
LB1028.3.A287 2014
371.33—dc23

                      2014015062

ISBN: 978-1-138-77859-7 (hbk)
ISBN: 978-1-315-77182-3 (ebk)

Typeset in Baskerville
by RefineCatch Limited, Bungay, Suffolk

Contents

Figures

Tables

Contributors

Najma Agherdien is an Instructional Designer at the e-Learning Support and Innovation Unit, University of Witwatersrand. Her involvement includes professional development of staff, presentation of workshops, research related activities and on-going support and consultation. She holds a Masters in Computer-based Education (Cum Laude) and is currently doing a PhD in Higher Education Studies. Najma is the recipient of an award for 'best paper in innovative pedagogies in higher education'. Her research interests include teaching and learning in higher education, educational technology, curriculum and academic development.

Alan Amory is Professor and Director of the Centre for Academic Technologies at the University of Johannesburg, South Africa. Alan was the recipient of the South African Government's Innovation Fund Award to investigate the use of computer video games in learning, which has been recognised as pioneering work in the field. More recently he received funding from the Department of Arts and Culture to investigate the relationship between education, computer video games and gender. Alan is an NRF-rated scientist for his research in the use of games in teaching and learning, use of technological tools to support tool-mediated knowledge constructions, and the use of Activity Theory to understand these phenomena.

Veronica Barnes studied Industrial Design at the Cape Peninsula University of Technology (CPUT), where she also obtained her MTech: Design. An Industrial Design lecturer for 13 years at CPUT, Veronica obtained a National Higher Diploma: Higher Education & Training in 2011. As an educator, she explores innovative pedagogies and technologies. Her research areas include critical thinking skills, industrial design education, authentic learning, digital storytelling, non-traditional students, and Universal Design for Learning. She has presented papers at conferences including HELTASA and DEFSA (Design Educators' Forum of South Africa). She first published in the *South African Journal of Higher Education* in 2011. Her paper on non-traditional student learning was presented at the 5th International Digital Storytelling Conference, Turkey, 2013. She is co-authoring a chapter for the edited collection: *Engaging Student Learning in Non-Traditional Formats*.

Aaron Bere is an IT Lecturer specialising in software development in the School of Information Technology at the Central University of Technology in South Africa. His work has been published in the *British Journal of Educational Technology* and appeared at international peer-reviewed conferences. His research interest is the use of mobile technologies to support the digital inclusion of previously disadvantaged groups in South Africa.

Vivienne Bozalek is Professor of Social Work and the Director of Teaching and Learning at the University of the Western Cape (UWC), South Africa. Prior to this she was Chairperson of the Department of Social Work, University of the Western Cape. She holds a PhD from Utrecht University. Her areas of research, publications and expertise include the use of post-structural social justice and the political ethics of care perspectives, critical family studies, innovative pedagogical approaches in Higher Education, and feminist and participatory research methodologies. She has co-edited two books – one entitled *Community, Self and Identity: Educating South African Students for Citizenship* with Brenda Leibowitz, Ronelle Carolissen and other colleagues (2013), and another volume entitled *Discerning Hope in Educational Practices* with Brenda Leibowitz, Ronelle Carolissen and Megan Boler (2014).

Cheryl Brown is a Senior Lecturer in the Centre for Educational Technology at the University of Cape Town, South Africa. She completed her PhD in Information Systems in 2011 focusing on what technology means to students and how this influences the way they use technology at university. Her research is focused on digital literacy and identity particularly among first-year university students. She teaches in the Centre's postgraduate program in Information and Communication Technologies in Education and is member of the University's First Year Experience Advisory Committee.

Anita Campbell is a first-year mathematics specialist interested in innovative ways to engage students. Her Master's degree assessed alternative ways of remediating first-year students' algebra difficulties. Subsequent research topics have included the design of optimal ways of arranging cooperative learning, voluntary tutoring as a means of reconstructing identities, just-in-time revision using online quizzes, the benefits of using guest lecturers and the development of a database of student-made video explanations in multiple languages. She taught at the University of KwaZulu-Natal, Pietermaritzburg, for 12 years and is currently a lecturer in the academic support programme for engineering students at the University of Cape Town.

Lindsay Clowes is an Associate Professor in the Women's & Gender Studies Department at the University of the Western Cape. She has taught in Europe, America and Africa and holds a PhD in historical studies from the University of Cape Town. She is an NRF-rated scholar. Drawing on feminist and queer theory as well as discursive psychology, sociology and Critical Men's Studies, her work problematises power inequalities and the ways in which human choices are constrained by subject positions structured around biological sex, gender, sexuality, race and class.

Thomas Cochrane is an Academic Advisor and Senior Lecturer in Educational Technology at AUT University's Centre for Learning and Teaching (CfLAT). His research interests include mobile learning, Web 2.0, and communities of practice. His PhD thesis was entitled: 'Mobilizing learning: transforming pedagogy with mobile Web 2.0'. Thomas has managed and implemented over 45 mobile learning projects, with a recent focus upon Android and iOS smartphones and the iPad as catalysts to enable student-generated content and student-generated learning contexts, bridging formal and informal learning environments. He has written over 100 peer-reviewed publications, and has been invited to present keynote speeches at several international educational technology conferences.

Carina de Kock received her B.Cur degree at the University of Stellenbosch and specialised in Theatre nursing. She currently holds the position of Nurse Educator at a private hospital group where she trains future Nursing and Operating Department Assistants students. She received her MPhil in Health Professions Education in April 2014.

Dorothea Mathudi Dimpe is a lecturer at Tshwane University of Technology, Faculty of Science, Department of Food Technology Biotechnology. She taught Microbiology I in 2012. Her research interests include planning to improve students' academic performance and increase student participation, interaction and engagement in the learning process in class and after hours.

Daniela Gachago is a lecturer in the Educational Technology Unit at the Center for Higher Education Development at the Cape Peninsula University of Technology. Her research interests lie in the use of emerging technologies to improve teaching and learning in higher education, with a particular focus on social media and digital storytelling for social change.

James Garraway is an Associate Professor at the Center for Higher Education Development at the Cape Peninsula University of Technology and has a PhD in higher education studies. His main research focus is on the relationship between university and work learning and knowledge but he also publishes in the field of academic staff development. He has published in international and local peer-reviewed journals and books. He currently works at the Centre for Higher Education at the Cape Peninsula University of Technology in South Africa in curriculum and staff development and heads up the Work-integrated Learning Research Unit (WILRU).

Chivaugn Gordon is the Head of undergraduate Obstetrics and Gynaecology education at the University of Cape Town, where she obtained her medical degree. She has Diplomas in both HIV Management and Mental Health, which are her areas of clinical interest. She is currently enrolled in an MPhil in Health Sciences Education at the University of Stellenbosch. Her research interests in medical education include undergraduate teaching and learning in matters concerning lesbian, gay, transgender and intersex patients; teaching on gender-based violence; and primary health care service learning in the context of student volunteerism.

Joanne Hardman is a Senior Lecturer in Educational Psychology at the School of Education (UCT). A Commonwealth Scholar, she obtained her PhD in Education at UCT. She has published numerous articles, reports and book chapters in her field of research interest, developmental psychology and Cultural-Historical Activity Theory. She is an NRF rated scientist and Fellow of Bath University (UK). While she is a member of numerous local and international societies, it is her membership of the Cultural-Historical Approaches to Children's Development and Childhood Society that currently informs much of her research. In 2012 she edited *Child and Adolescent Development in South Africa: A Socio-cultural Perspective* (Oxford University Press). She is currently involved in a collaborative EU-funded project in the School of Education (UCT) that seeks to understand differential attainment in underprivileged schools. At the tertiary education level her research focuses on using technology to facilitate students' access to academia, predominantly through mediating textual access by developing students' questioning capacity.

Jan Herrington is a teacher and researcher at Murdoch University, Australia. She teaches in the educational technology area in the School of Education, including a compulsory first-year unit in the Bachelor of Education called Living and Learning with Technology. In addition to using design-based research, her main area of research is in authentic learning, and her recently published book *A Guide to Authentic e-learning* (with Thomas C. Reeves and Ron Oliver) was winner of the AECT Outstanding Book of the Year Award in 2010. She was a Fulbright Scholar in 2002 at the University of Georgia, USA. She is currently Chair of the Executive Committee of the EdMedia World Conference on Educational Media and Technology.

Eunice Ivala is the coordinator of the Educational Technology Unit, Fundani Centre for Higher Education and Development, at the Cape Peninsula University of Technology (CPUT), South Africa. Previously she was a project manager at the Media in Education Trust Africa, an educational specialist at the South African Institute for Distance Education and a lecturer at the University of KwaZulu-Natal. She holds a BEd Honours degree from the University of Nairobi, Kenya; an MEd degree in Computer-Based Education from the University of Natal, Durban, South Africa; and a PhD in Culture, Communication and Media Studies from the University of KwaZulu-Natal, South Africa. Her research focus is in ICT-mediated teaching and learning in developing contexts.

Roisin Kelly-Laubscher is a lecturer and NRF rated researcher in the Department of Biological Sciences at the University of Cape Town. She runs the first-year Biology course for the extended science degree program. She has a PhD in Physiology and is currently completing a postgraduate diploma in higher education at the University of Cape Town. She is interested in academic development and the use of technology in teaching. She has published papers in many peer-reviewed scientific journals and presented her work at both scientific and teaching and learning conferences.

Rita Kizito currently works as a Teaching and Learning Specialist at the University of the Western Cape. She holds a PhD in Curriculum Studies from Stellenbosch University and has been involved in education-related work for the past 32 years, 11 of which have been in the field of curriculum and learning design and development. She has published and presented in over 10 journals and studies related to teaching and learning and was the recipient of the O Houle Adult Education scholarship award for a period of two years (2001–2003). Her latest publication is her dissertation book: *Using Realistic Mathematics Education to Design Learning Activities: RME as an Instructional Design Perspective for Introducing the Derivative-Integral Relationship via Distance Education.*

Lotte Latukefu is a lecturer and researcher in the Faculty of Law, Humanities and the Arts at the University of Wollongong. She holds a PhD in Music Education from the University of Wollongong and Master of Music from the Manhattan School of Music (NY). Lotte has published extensively on collaborative learning in higher music education. She maintains a busy singing career and since 2006 has premiered nationally and internationally 15 new Australian compositions.

Brenda Leibowitz is the Chair of Teaching and Learning in Higher Education in the Faculty of Education at the University of Johannesburg. She was previously Director of the Centre for Teaching and Learning at Stellenbosch University. She completed her PhD at the University of Sheffield on students' acquisition of academic literacy. Her research interests include the scholarship of teaching and learning, the professional development of academics, academic literacy and social justice in higher education. She is currently a co-editor of the *International Journal for Academic Development.* She serves on the executive committee of the Higher Education Learning and Teaching Association of Southern Africa (HELTASA) and convenes the national CHE-Heltasa Teaching Excellence Awards committee.

Walter Liebrich studied Biology at the University of Ulm, where he completed his PhD in Natural Sciences in 1989. He has been with Stellenbosch University since 2002. He is an HPCSA-registered Medical Biological Scientist. His interest in teaching comes from his involvement in postgraduate training of Medical Scientists and Pathology Registrars. In this role he has developed an online course in Clinical Immunology. He has also been e-learning co-ordinator in the Stellenbosch University Rural Medical Partnership Initiative (SURMEPI) since 2011. To strengthen his educational background, Walter has started studying towards an MPhil in Health Science Education in 2012. He is currently busy with his practical project 'Expert evaluation of an online course in clinical immunology'.

Noel Lindsay is the Academic Director of Singapore Operations and Director of the Entrepreneurship, Commercialisation and Innovation Centre, at the University of Adelaide where he is the Professor of Entrepreneurship and Commercialisation. Noel's research interests include social entrepreneurship, where he is interested in how entrepreneurship in disadvantaged communities can help empower individuals in those communities, and business entrepreneurship, including cultural differences in the decision-making processes and behaviour of entrepreneurs and venture investors in different societal systems.

Nomakhaya Mashiyi is employed at the University of the Western Cape as a Teaching and Learning Specialist in the EMS Faculty. She has extensive teaching experience in the field of education which spans high school, teacher training, Technikon and university. She is interested in how ICT-mediated support for academic staff can enhance teaching and learning. Her research interests also include multilingualism and graduate attributes.

Ilse Meyer qualified in 1983 with a BSc in Physiotherapy from Stellenbosch University. Thereafter, she gained experience in private practice, different hospital settings and in community service. In 2013, she completed her Master's in Philosophy in Health Science Education. At present, she is working in the Division of Physiotherapy, Stellenbosch University, as a Clinical Co-ordinator. Her special interest is the clinical education of physiotherapy students in a variety of clinical placements.

Makinti Minutjukur is the Director of the Pitjantjatjara Yankunytjatjara Education Committee (PYEC) in the Anangu Pitjantjatjara Yankunytjatjara Lands in remote northwest South Australia.

Veronica Mitchell facilitates several courses and levels of students in the Health Sciences Faculty at the University of Cape Town, South Africa. She is registered for Doctoral studies related to her work with undergraduate medical students in Obstetrics. Her recent research for the Master of Philosophy in Higher Education Studies highlighted the value that students' experiences can bring to curricular design. Her background is a Bachelor of Science in Physiotherapy. As an educator fostering social justice in healthcare, she explores ways to empower students towards transformative learning. She has published websites as Open Educational Resources on the University of Cape Town's OpenContent repository.

Jolanda Morkel is a registered architect and Senior Lecturer in the Department of Architectural Technology in the Faculty of Informatics and Design at the Cape Peninsula University of Technology, where she teaches in design studios, currently in a blended part time programme specifically designed for non-traditional students. Her research interests include design and design education, specifically related to studio-based learning. The focus of her current doctoral work is the online design learning conversation. Jolanda has published a number of conference proceedings on the use of technology in design learning, and co-authored two book chapters in the field of design.

Vickel Narayan is a teaching and learning consultant at the Centre for Teaching and Learning at Auckland University of Technology, New Zealand. He has a keen interest in Web 2.0 technologies and its potential to engage students and teachers in the teaching and learning process. Vickel is particularly interested in exploring mobile Web 2.0 tools for creating, nurturing and maintaining virtual communities, social connectedness, fostering social constructivism, student-generated context and context. He is also interested in Virtual Worlds, particularly the pedagogical implications of their use in education.

Dick Ng'ambi is an Associate Professor and a leading researcher in mobile learning in resource-constrained environments. He works at the School of Education at the University of Cape Town (UCT), South Africa. He is currently the co-ordinator of a postgraduate programme in educational technology, and a convener of a doctoral programme in the School of Education. He has published over 70 papers in journals and peer-reviewed conferences, and delivered presentations and keynotes at several conferences. He is a rated researcher by the National Research Foundation. He holds a PhD in Information Systems from UCT, a Master's degree in Computer Science from Birmingham, UK, and a Bachelor of Science degree in Mathematics from the University of Zambia. His research interests are in low-cost technologies with high-educational impact, emerging technologies, co-production of knowledge and open educational resources (OER).

James Oldfield teaches and coordinates Information Systems and Applications and Accounting Information Systems at Unitec Institute of Technology in New Zealand. His current research interests are in the use of Web 2.0 Tools and Mobile Learning. His research has specifically focused most recently on the use of iPad and similar devices in authentic learning environments in education and educational games.

Patient Rambe holds a PhD in Educational Technology from the University of Cape Town, South Africa. He is currently a Postdoctoral Research Fellow in the Department of Computer Science and Informatics at the University of the Free State. He is a former Assistant Director in the Office of International Academic Projects in the Office of the Vice Chancellor at the same university. Patient's work has been published in the *British Journal of Educational Technology*, the *Australasian Journal of Educational Technology*, the *South African Computer Journal* and other peer-reviewed international conferences. He has published in the following research areas: student engagement using social media in higher education, mobile learning in resource-poor environments and technology-mediated identity formation of previously disadvantaged students. His research interest is the innovative pedagogical uses of social media in resource-constrained environments.

Michael Rowe is a Senior Lecturer in the Department of Physiotherapy at the University of the Western Cape, with an interest in the use of emerging technologies to change teaching and learning practices. His PhD research evaluated the use of technology-mediated approaches that can be used to create blended learning environments for the clinical context. He continues to conduct research into the integration of digital technology in the classroom.

Tamara Shefer is Professor in the Department of Women's and Gender Studies and Deputy Dean of Teaching and Learning in the Faculty of Arts at the University of the Western Cape. Her research has been primarily on gendered power relations in heterosexual relationships and she has also published in the areas of HIV/AIDS, gender-based violence, masculinities, racism, and the politics of higher education and authorship. She has co-edited five books including *The Gender of Psychology* (2006, UCT Press, with Boonzaier and Kiguwa), *From Boys to Men* (2007, UCT Press, with Ratele et al.) and most recently *Books and/or Babies: Pregnancy and Young Parenting in Schools* (2012, HSRC Press, with Morrell and Bhana).

Sibongile Simelane is a DEd candidate in the Faculty of Humanities, Department of Mathematics and Science at Tshwane University of Technology. She began her DEd study in 2010. Her research interests include technology-enhanced teaching and learning, online learning, training and empowerment, e-assessment and innovative and emerging technologies in teaching and learning.

Anna Stetsenko was a Research Scientist at Moscow State University and also at the Institute of General and Educational Psychology of the Russian Academy of Education; a Postdoctoral Research Fellow at the Max Planck Institute for Human Development and Education in Berlin, Germany; an Invited Visiting Fellow at the Centre for Cultural Studies in Vienna, Austria; and Assistant Professor in the Department of Developmental Psychology, University of Bern, Switzerland. Currently Anna is Associate Professor and Head of the PhD Program in Developmental Psychology, The Graduate Center of the City University of New York. Anna has been active in developing the socio-cultural activity theory and its implications for the issues of human development and learning. The focus of her empirical research is on children's and adolescents' social development (e.g., gender, self-concept, motivation) with an emphasis on how this development is shaped by their interactions and activities within socio-cultural contexts. Anna is on the editorial boards of and has served as consultant editor to leading scientific journals.

Deirdre Tedmanson lectures in social analysis, human service project management and community development in the School of Psychology, Social Work and Social Policy at the University of South Australia. She uses participatory action and qualitative research methods in her research which focuses on social policy and social justice issues, human service organisations, alternative care for children and Indigenous community development; social, emotional mental health and well-being and social enterprise development. Ms Tedmanson has been a Chief Investigator on an Australian Research Council (ARC) Linkage project and also received an ARC Discovery grant for research with remote Indigenous communities in central Australia.

Simone Titus is a lecturer in the Department of Sport, Recreation and Exercise Science at the University of the Western Cape and holds a Master's Degree in Sport, Recreation and Exercise Science. Her research interests are in the area of emerging technologies in higher education and how ICT tools can be used to enhance student engagement. She has a keen interest in sport and gender, specifically dealing with gender bias in sport. She has published a monograph entitled: *The Experiences of Female Sport Administrators: Gender Bias in the Workplace.* She is currently doing her PhD on game-based learning through the use of emerging technologies in higher education.

Katrina Tjitayi is the Anangu School Improvement Coordinator for the Anangu Pitjantjatjara Yankunytjatjara Lands schools and she is also a graduate of the University of South Australia's Anangu Tertiary Education programme.

Bruce Underwood is an experienced educator who has spent 25 years working with Indigenous people as an adult educator and classroom teacher. While currently located in Adelaide, South Australia, Bruce co-ordinates the Anangu Tertiary Education Program (AnTEP) a community-based remote area tertiary education program for people living in the Anangu Pitjantjatjara Yankunytjatjara Lands (APY Lands) in the northwest corner of South Australia. Bruce travels extensively in the APY Lands, and has a detailed understanding of issues and strategies related to working effectively with Anangu adults in remote communities. His main interests are in remote area Indigenous education and the use of technology in remote areas.

Irina Verenikina lectures in educational psychology in the Faculty of Social Sciences, University of Wollongong. He holds a PhD in Educational Psychology from the Russian Academy of Education and is a Full Member of the Australian Psychological Society. In 2002–2008 Dr Verenikina represented Australia and New Zealand as a member of the Executive Committee of ISCAR (International Society for Cultural Research and Activity Theory). Currently he is Chair of the Triennial ISCAR Congress to be held in Sydney, Australia, in 2014. His research interests relate to the application of socio-cultural psychology and activity theory to teaching and learning.

Kathy Watters is an associate of the Directorate of Teaching and Learning and the Division for Lifelong learning at the University of the Western Cape. She holds a BA (Speech and Hearing Therapy) from the University of Witwatersrand and an MPhil in Adult Education from the University of Cape Town, South Africa. Her research interests include adult literacy, adult basic education, further education, lifelong learning, use of emerging technologies in higher education and more recently social entrepreneurship.

Denise Wood is Professor of Learning, Equity, Access and Participation at Central Queensland University, Australia. She is also an Extraordinary Professor in the Faculty of Education at the University of the Western Cape, South Africa. Denise's research focuses on the potential of new media technologies such as participatory Web 2.0 and 3D virtual learning environments to enhance the educational and social participation of young people with disabilities, as well as exploring the pedagogical potential of these environments to engage learners in the higher education context. She is currently leading several national funded research projects focusing on improving the accessibility of online technology enhanced learning and improving pathways to education and employment for learners from special equity groups. Her research involves collaboration with not for profit community organisations and national and state governments in Austrlia, as well as in the Western Cape, Gauteng and Limpopo Provinces of South Africa.

Foreword

Anna Stetsenko

Theories come alive and grow in their applications to new research tasks and problems that arise across diverse contexts and research fields, in novel locations, and against the background of emerging novel challenges, circumstances, and conditions. Cultural-historical activity theory, with its venerable and long legacy dating back several decades, and unlike many competing theoretical frameworks also developed during the early to mid-twentieth century, has been fortunate to be coming alive, again an again, in diverse contexts, problem areas, and applications. Its growth and development have been so substantial over the years, and especially during the past approximately two decades, that we can now speak of various research schools and orientation spawned within the overall framework developed by the first activity theorists Lev S. Vygotsky, Alexei N. Leontiev, and Alexander R. Luria. Although not without some complications and 'growth pains' which inevitably accompany any rapid process of development, such as theoretical and methodological disagreements among various research directions within CHAT, these are causes for celebrating the rich legacy and viability of this tradition. These are also causes for taking the time to reflect on its strengths and future prospects yet also its conundrums and contradictions that necessarily mark any vibrant and expanding framework.

The present edited volume is a wonderful example of CHAT coming alive in many new ways – especially geographically, extending this theory to the southern hemisphere, and also in a novel application at the intersection with authentic learning and emerging technologies, with both points well reflected upon by the volume's editors. Remarkable is also the explicit intention to grapple with the notions and phenomena of change and transformation, in an important shift away from the insufficiently dynamic traditional portrayals of human development and learning. This theme is brought to the fore in several chapters and follows well with the earlier efforts by various scholars (including myself) to provide not only a thoroughly dynamic, situated, culturally mediated, and contextualized account of human development and learning – in line with the perennial themes in CHAT – but also, to more explicitly integrate and explain the phenomena of agency, innovation, ambiguity, and imagination. This shift represents a significant expansion of the cultural-historical research into the new territories. At the same time, in a dialectical combination of continuity and change, this shift also indicates a revival of the initial impetus which characterized CHAT in its early years and which faded with time due to the influence of the top-down ideology and other pressures stemming from its particular historical and geographic location. That initial impetus had to do not only with studying what exists but also, and most crucially, with exploring and creating the conditions of possibility for development and learning to be reaching out into the new zones of proximal development and their uncharted territories.

Indeed, the original CHAT was conceived during the turbulent time of an unprecedented sociopolitical turmoil and change and reflected the extraordinary dynamism and challenges of its time. In actively and agentively contributing to ongoing social transformations, in a direct link to creating new radical alternatives in the conditions of social existence, especially education, this project de facto challenged traditional models of science steeped in the ethos of adaptation. This was a model for a social science devoted not to the narrowly understood objective, that is, disinterested and impartial, experimentation but to creating knowledge as part and parcel of larger scale projects that self-consciously commit to and participate in creating new forms of social life and communal practices. What CHAT offered was a radical approach to doing science that served as an antidote to many received notions in challenging the taken for granted assumptions and established canons especially at the worldview level assumptions about ontology and epistemology of human ways of doing, knowing, and being. However, a number of these breakthrough suggestions remained, in large part, only implicitly articulated and insufficiently explored. One of such suggestions was precisely about the status of change as playing the role of an ontological and epistemological principle in defining human development and learning. Conceptualizing change was an enormously difficult undertaking that entailed many challenges associated with overcoming the ballast of traditional substance ontologies that defined the world to consist of fixed elements and incorrigible structures. The implicit assumption that fuelled worldview level developments in the early CHAT tradition was that the world is constantly changing, and moreover, that it is changing through human collaborative practices which bring about changes not only in the material conditions of existence but also in the ways that people themselves come to know, to act, and to be. This approach entailed a novel model of personhood positing human beings as agentive actors implicated in the changing dynamics of the world rather than passive recipients of outside stimuli or undergoers of chemical reactions in the brain. This approach contained a relational ontology that broke with the static notions of human development and learning constituted by adaptation to the established order and, moreover, offered an outline for a transformative worldview in which people develop and learn while moving beyond the status quo and contributing to ongoing community practices.

Many of these early themes raised or at least outlined by CHAT (de facto very much ahead of their time and thus, as if in peering into the future) have been abandoned in later developments of CHAT which for a while remained stalled due to mounting reactionary political and socio-cultural trends. Yet we are witnessing the revival of these themes and the present volume illustrates this trend.

This is likely in response to the changing landscape and context in which human development and learning are embedded and which shape these processes in significant ways. As the world is evidently changing more rapidly than during any previous period in the past, presenting us with increasingly dynamic and overlapping matrices of socio-cultural and political-economic relations, the models and theories of human development begin again to take up the challenges of reflecting this rapid dynamism, creativity, and instability. The goal of developing transformative pedagogy, for example, is clearly suited for meeting such challenges in offering adequate theoretical groundings for novel educational models. Such models not only fit in with the presently given world but prepare learners to be agentive social actors who participate in and contribute to creating new realties and social conditions of collective life. It is no coincidence that the present volume, having taken CHAT to new territories – literally and figuratively – that are particularly dynamic as for example, in South Africa, is positioning itself to be opening up new theoretical frontiers as well. The next step in this direction is to consider how such conceptual advances necessitate further critical scrutiny of a plethora of concepts and methodologies so that the broader transformative worldview that underpins transformative pedagogy is explored and developed in the fullness of a paradigmatic shift that this worldview entails.

Preface

The book was developed as part of a national research project entitled *Emerging ICTs in Higher Education* funded by the National Research Foundation (NRF) in South Africa. The project, which was funded for a three year period (2011–2013), focused on the use of emerging technologies to enhance teaching and learning in South African higher education institutions (HEIs), using Cultural-Historical Activity Theory (CHAT) as a theoretical framework. The project team members consisted of a group of educators from eight South African higher education institutions and one from an Australian higher education institution. In the first year of the project, a survey of all South African HEIs was conducted, followed by a series of in-depth interviews with a sample of innovative higher educators from ten of the South African HEIs. During the course of the project, it became apparent that the work of Jan Herrington on authentic learning was a useful tool for analysing the ways in which emerging technologies had been used to improve teaching and learning in HEIs. Project team members then made contact with Jan Herrington to invite her to be part of a colloquium on Authentic Learning and Emergent Technologies, organised in the final year of the project, by doing a keynote address at the colloquium.

The Authentic Learning and Emerging Technologies colloquium took place at the University of the Western Cape in March 2013, and papers were invited from a larger audience in South Africa who were researching in the area of interested. The chapters which are written in this volume were developed, to a large extent, from the presentations at this colloquium held in Cape Town, South Africa. Jan Herrington and Alan Amory were approached to be editors of the proposed book, in addition to project members Vivienne Bozalek, Dick Ng'ambi, Denise Wood and Joanne Hardman. In addition to these papers, these editors approached other experts in the field to contribute chapters to augment the collection. The role of the community of enquiry in the research project provided the opportunities for apprenticeship with emerging researchers and more experienced scholars, and for scaffolding of sharing of knowledge, expertise and exemplars in a transparent and accountable ways. The writing process thus involved opportunities for co-constructing knowledge between these authors and the sharing of examples of practice through the lens of activity theory.

The main thrust of this book is that although emerging technologies are becoming popular for teaching, learning and research in higher education, there is little transformative effect that these technologies are having on the practices in higher education. This edited collection fill this gap by providing a more nuanced view, locating higher education pedagogical practice at an intersection of emerging technologies, authentic learning and activity systems.

Acknowledgements

This book would not have been possible without the support of many people, some of whom we explicitly acknowledge here and others too numerous to list. We thank the National Research Foundation (NRF) for the provision of financial assistance to run the research project on Emerging Technologies in South African Higher Education Institutions. This edited collection is one of the numerous outcomes from this NRF-supported outcomes. We would like to make it clear that the opinions expressed and conclusions arrived at in this edited collection are those of the editors and authors and cannot to be attributed to the NRF.

We are very grateful towards the generous academics and higher education researchers and practitioners who agreed to peer review the chapters in this book. We acknowledge the following people for doing this: Peter Smagorinsky, Ritva Engeström, Elizabeth Henning, Geoff Lautenbach, Arona Dison, Cathy Hutchings, Jurg Bronnimann, Henk Huigser, Sue Gregory, Helen Farley, Shirley Walters, Judy Jurgëns, Lynn Quinn, Birgit Schreiber, Nasima Badsha, Chris Winberg, Sherran Clarence, Ronelle Carolissen, Nick Rushby, Gilly Salmon, Moragh Paxton, Yusef Waghid, Laura Czerniewicz, and Sioux McKenna.

Finally, we would like to acknowledge the other team members of the NRF Emerging ICTs in Higher Education project and the research respondents for making it possible to conduct the research which gave fruition to this edited collection.

Introduction

Vivienne Bozalek, Dick Ng'ambi, Denise Wood,
Jan Herrington, Joanne Hardman and Alan Amory

Although emerging technologies (ETs) are becoming popular for teaching, learning and research in higher education, the relationship between their use and transformative effect on higher education remains largely unexplored. Thus, many of the current conceptions view ETs as tools in 'how to' manuals, remaining at the level of simplistic discussions that are generally under-theorised. This edited collection seeks to fill this gap by providing a more nuanced view, locating higher education pedagogical practice at the intersection of ETs, authentic learning (AL) and activity systems. In so doing, this book provides accessible explanations of each of these areas, followed by practical examples and case studies drawn from a wide range of contexts, which illustrate how such a convergence has the potential to influence transformative teaching and learning practices in the higher education sector.

There is currently a knowledge gulf between activity theorists, pedagogical models, and emerging technologies. While these three knowledge domains are discussed in the literature as separate knowledge areas, there has been a dearth of work that has attempted to bring the three together. The leading studies in the field are drawn predominantly, though not exclusively (see, for example, Russell & Schneiderheinze, 2002) from Finland (see, for example, Impedovo, Ritella, & Ligorio, 2013) as well as the other work done by the Centre for Research on Activity Development and Learning (CRADLE) (www.helsinki.fi/cradle/index.htm). There is, however, very little comparable work undertaken in Africa that seeks to weave these knowledge domains together. Notable for our purposes here is the work of Ritva Engeström et al. (2014) on transforming pedagogical practices with technology using the change laboratory methodology that has emerged from Engeström's (2007) activity systems model. This work, carried out in Botswana, used change laboratories to effect pedagogical transformation in schools where novel technology was introduced (Virkuunen & Newnham, 2013). While this work speaks to the power of merging these three knowledge domains, it is the only study of its kind in Africa that has published results in international journals. The current book draws impetus from this work and seeks to develop a picture of how Cultural-Historical Activity Theory (CHAT) can be used in the southern hemisphere to talk to pedagogical transformation in higher education with the introduction of novel technology. Unlike Engeström et al. (2014), this book does not present case studies that use change laboratories. For our purposes, we use Engeström's (1987) systems model as a mechanism with which to take 'snapshots' of cases across time, in order to track pedagogical transformation with emerging technologies.

This text, then, addresses the perceived gap in the literature by providing in-depth engagement with activity theory, authentic learning and emerging technologies in the southern hemisphere – more particularly in South Africa, Australia and New Zealand. Thus, our edited collection occupies a unique niche of leveraging the current fragments of innovative uses of *emerging technologies*, with a pedagogical model of *authentic learning*, in the context of an established methodological perspective of *activity systems theory*, in the context of *higher education*. It therefore advances what is currently known, demystifying and operationalising theories at the same time as laying a useful foundation for teaching with emerging technologies to achieve transformative learning outcomes.

The chapters provide the reader with a range of transformative higher education pedagogical practices in southern contexts theorised within the framework of Cultural-Historical Activity Theory (CHAT), using Authentic Learning as a pedagogical model, which aligns well with this theoretical framework. The book is comprised of four Parts: the first provides an emphasis on the theoretical position of CHAT, the second on Authentic Learning (AL), the third on Emerging Technologies (ETs), and the fourth presents case studies, involving these three areas of concentration in this edited collection. Parts I–III begin with an accessible introduction on the section theme – CHAT, AL and ETs, followed by chapters which elaborate on the themes in different disciplines and geopolitical contexts. Part IV consists of three chapters, each of which is devoted to the three themes of CHAT, AL and ETs and which consist of a number of case studies in each chapter which exemplify through practical examples how these themes have been applied in higher education contexts.

The book has an international focus, with a particular focus on South Africa, Australia and New Zealand – all different countries within the southern hemisphere with their peculiar histories, economies and cultures. Although the book draws substantially from these three regions, it builds on internationally accepted theoretical perspectives of activity theory, authentic learning and emerging technologies. This dual focus of southern perspective examples, looked at in the light of globally accepted theories, makes the book appealing to an international audience. These particular southern contexts – South Africa, Australia and New Zealand – provide a novel perspective which is not yet been fully explored in other texts of this general area of interest, given their northern focus. Although the primary focus is higher education, the examples may be useful for the education sector more generally.

The authors of the chapters and case studies in this collection include international experts, as well as emerging researchers and practitioners in CHAT, AL and ETs, across different disciplinary fields. The book opens with a Foreword from the eminent CHAT scholar, Anna Stetsenko. In addition, the editors provide an Introduction and a Conclusion, which synthesises the significant findings from a review of the literature and the case studies presented in each chapter to provide a focus on transformative higher education pedagogy, which draws on Activity Theory, authentic learning, and the role of emerging technologies in transformative teaching, learning and research practices. The collection triangulates both primary and secondary research. Since it is an edited collection, a number of different studies are included, some of which are empirical and others which are case study-based and accessible to higher educators wishing to apply these theoretical approaches to their own teaching, learning and research practice.

Structure of the book

The book is divided into four Parts. In Chapter 1 of Part I, Joanne Hardman and Alan Amory provide an introduction to CHAT, in which they explain how a CHAT framework provides a descriptive language capable of illuminating teaching with emerging technologies (ETs) in higher education institutions (HEIs). The importance of Vygotsky's work for understanding how learning and teaching are *culturally* and *socially* located and Vygotsky's notion of tool mediation are foregrounded in the chapter. Building on Vygotsky's original triadic view of human activity, Engeström's Activity Theory model provides a useful tool for analysis for the chapters that follow in this Part. The authors introduce first, second and third generation Activity Theory, indicating the potential of this framework as a theoretical heuristic provided by CHAT. This chapter provides the reader with a framework for viewing the subsequent chapters in Part I, as well as illuminating the case studies in Chapter 13 which focus on CHAT, and the Conclusion which examines how CHAT can be used to develop analyses illustrating how higher education pedagogies can be regarded as transformative. The case studies in Chapter 13 illustrate how different novel technologies potentially impact on pedagogy in higher education. While one case study draws solely on CHAT, other cases link CHAT to the notion of authentic learning as a transformative pedagogy, showing how technology can be used to achieve this object.

Chapter 2 by James Garraway and Jolanda Morkel is a good example of what Stetsenko (2008) is proposing as an active transformative stance towards learning where people come to learn and are human through actively transforming the world through their goals, focusing on social justice ideals. It reports on an architecture course where students who were involved in community service were strongly motivated to learn, as the experience afforded more opportunity than one in an office to contribute to changing the lives of others.

Chapter 3 by Denise Wood et al. provides an example of how cultural historical activity theory can be used to theorise indigenous education in Australia. The chapter makes use of third generation Activity Theory, looking at the three Activity Theory systems that students are involved in: the university, their community and their teaching practice, and how contradictions in these systems can lead to transformation.

Chapter 4 by Dick Ng'ambi and Cheryl Brown reports on how Activity Theory guided the design of well-integrated authentic learning activities that mediated learning in a blended postgraduate course. Thus, the chapter provides a good example of how the affordances of emerging technologies can be appropriated to design authentic learning tasks that mediate learning within a learner's Zone of Proximal Development (ZPD) through a 'most knowledgeable other' in a postgraduate course.

Part II of the book concentrates on the pedagogical model of Authentic Learning, with Chapter 5 providing an introduction to this model by one of the eminent authors in this field, Jan Herrington. In Chapter 5, she outlines nine elements associated with authentic learning environments and briefly discusses some of the common misconceptions regarding the concept of authentic learning. She makes the point that, while emerging technologies may be fruitfully used in designing authentic tasks, the use of the technologies in themselves does not necessarily lead to authenticity in design.

The chapters which follow from South Africa and Australia (Chapters 6, 7 and 8) show how the principles of authentic learning can provide a useful heuristic to illustrate examples of good pedagogical practice using ETs in higher education. While Chapter 5 describes the *theory* associated with authentic learning, the remaining chapters in Part II illustrate its use in *practice* – in an undergraduate Women's and Gender Studies research module, and a postgraduate Health Science Education module. Using a form of apprenticeship coaching, Chapter 6 by Brenda Leibowitz et al. describes the learning tasks used in a module entitled 'Education Research for Change', where students and teachers work collaboratively to write a publishable paper as they learn research methods. In Chapter 7, by Tamara Shefer and Lindsay Clowes, students act as junior researchers as they develop a research study and write a full research report, with the support of writing coaches. And finally, in Chapter 8, by Noel Lindsay and Denise Wood, an intercontinental entrepreneurship curriculum focusing on creative problem solving is examined from an authentic learning perspective.

Part III foregrounds the potential use of ETs for transformative pedagogical practice in higher education. The introductory chapter of this section (Chapter 9) by Dick Ng'ambi and Vivienne Bozalek, provides the reader with a basic understanding of how ETs have been conceptualised and written about in higher education. This chapter elaborates on the characteristics of ETs and on their context-specific nature, examining various definitions of ETs, and settling on the characteristics of ETs, as a preferred interpretation of ETs in higher education. It also relates ET to the other parts of the book – CHAT and AL – and shows how these intersect. In the chapters that follow, various aspects of ETs are focused on in different higher education contexts. In Chapter 10, by Vivienne Bozalek, Daniela Gachago and Kathy Watters, in-depth interviews with South African educators are analysed in terms of how they have used ETs in their pedagogy and how the context makes a difference to what they do. Their sensitivity to their students' needs is highlighted in their attempts to promote graduate attributes in South African students, particularly in resource-constrained environments. Chapter 11, by Thomas Cochrane, Vickel Narayan and James Oldfield, is an example of how ETs are currently been used in New Zealand (NZ) higher education pedagogies. This chapter looks at three case studies of mobile technologies in the NZ context to illustrate AL and how it can be achieved across a wide variety of instances. They argue that it is difficult to operationalise AT, therefore it is of limited value. They use the nine principles of AL plus six critical success factors, including the following:

1   the pedagogical integration of the technology into the course and assessment;
2   lecturer modelling of the pedagogical use of the tools;
3   creating a supportive learning community;
4   appropriate choice of mobile devices and Web 2.0 social software;
5   technological and pedagogical support;
6   creating sustained interaction that facilitates the development of ontological shifts, both for the lecturers and the students.

The final chapter in Part III, Chapter 12, by Denise Wood, examines how three-dimensional virtual learning environments (3DVLEs) and Second Life (SL), in particular, in a final year media arts course at the University of South Australia, can support transformative learning. The analysis draws on CHAT to look at the affordances of SL for an AL task for communication skills and for cultural diversity skills that they could apply to work after graduating. The students were required to operate in complex systems giving rise to contradictions which gave potential for expansive learning.

Part IV consists of three chapters, each with a number of case studies focusing on CHAT, AL and ETs respectively. Chapter 13, by Joanne Hardman et al., reports on six case studies that use CHAT and the notion of tool mediation to track peda-gogical transformation with technology. Case study 13.1 illustrates how a novel technique for teaching can lead to self-directed learning and draws its theoretical impetus from neo-Vygotskian approaches to mediation. Case studies 13.2, 13.3 and 13.4 indicate how CHAT can serve as a framework for understanding teach-ing with technology, pointing to the impact that blogging can potentially have on transforming pedagogy. Case studies 13.5 and 13.6 situate their studies in an AL pedagogical model, showing how the use of technology can affect pedagogical transformation, provided that the tasks are authentic. These chapters illustrate how CHAT provides a useful heuristic capable of illuminating teaching with ETs in higher educational settings in case studies from different southern contexts.

The usefulness of AL and its associated principles as an heuristic is further illustrated in, Chapter 14, by Jan Herrington et al., which presents three examples that feature shorter case studies of authentic learning principles in a range of contexts, specifically: obstetrics education, physiotherapy education, and sports science education.

Chapter 15, by Dick Ng'ambi et al., comprises four case studies using different emerging technologies: Facebook, mobile phones to access learning management systems and videos as well as mobile instant messaging applications such as What's App. These case studies show how ETs can be used to expand the teaching and learning space, crossing boundaries between formal and informal learning to enhance student engagement and motivation. ETs were also reported to be useful for collaborative activities and appropriation of peer-generated content.

The book concludes with a chapter written by the editors, which synthesises the Parts to contemplate on how the ideas and applications thereof could suggest a possible transformative model for higher education pedagogy.

References

Centre for Research on Activity, Learning and Development. Available at: www.helsinki.fi/cradle/.

Engeström, Y. (1987). *Learning by expanding: An activity-theoretical approach to developmental research.* Helsinki: Orienta-Konsultit.

Engeström, Y. (2007). Enriching the theory of expansive learning: Lessons from journeys toward coconfiguration. *Mind, Culture and Activity, 14*(1–2), 23–39.

Engeström, R., Batane, T., Hakkarainen, K., Newnham, D. S., Nleya, P. Senteni, A., & Sinko, M. (2014). Reflections on the use of DWR in intercultural collaboration. *Mind, Culture and Activity*, 21(2), 129–147.

Impedovo, M., Ritella, G., & Ligorio, M. B. (2013). Developing codebooks as a new tool to analyze students' eportfolios. *International Journal of ePortfolio, 3*(2), 161–176.

Russell, D. L., & Schneiderheinze, A. (2005). Understanding innovation in education using activity theory. *Educational Technology and Society, 8*(1), 38–53.

Stetsenko, A. (2008). From relational ontology to transformative activist stance. *Cultural Studies of Science Education, 3*, 471– 491.

Virkkunen, J., & Newnham, D. (2013). *The change laboratory: A tool for collaborative development of work and education.* Amsterdam: Sense Publishers.

Part I

Activity Theory

1 Introduction to Cultural-Historical Activity Theory and tool mediation

Joanne Hardman and Alan Amory

Introduction

South Africa faces an educational crisis that has seen its schooling population placed last on international benchmarking tests in crucial areas such as mathematics and science (Howie, 2001; Evans, 2013). The effect of poor educational attainment at a school level is felt in higher education settings, where lecturers are faced with students who have not been sufficiently prepared to engage with academia (Hardman & Ng'ambi, 2003). In a bid to effect pedagogical change to meet the needs of diverse students, some lecturers have turned to the use of emerging technologies as developmental tools to assist students in accessing academia successfully. The project that informs this book seeks to investigate what emerging technologies are utilized in higher education in South Africa and Australia as well as developing an understanding of how these technologies potentially can affect pedagogical change. While some cases referred to in the book are drawn from Australia, the primary context for this book is South Africa, a country characterized by a turbulent history that continues to influence students' developmental trajectories today. This is a multicultural country with 11 national languages, steeped in a history of unequal access to educational opportunities; clearly, to understand the subtleties of any transformative process in this country requires a theoretical framework capable of speaking to cultural and historical influences. To this end, the book adopts a Cultural-Historical Activity Theory framework (CHAT) as a foundation for understanding change as culturally and historically informed. Part I of this book introduces CHAT against the background of three case studies that utilize this framework in order to understand the potentially transformative nature of emerging technologies in higher education. All the cases reported in Part I of this book aim to understand teaching/learning with technology as culturally situated, historically informed, complex activity systems, imbued with power and control, which directs how emerging technologies are taken up as developmental tools. This introductory chapter outlines a brief history of the ideas that inform CHAT. As the focus of Part I of this book is on understanding pedagogy with emerging technology, the introductory chapter focuses its argument on understanding pedagogy as an activity system.

Vygotsky and mediation: towards a theory of pedagogy as an *activity system*

Operating from a Marxist conceptualization of psychology as emerging socially, Vygotsky (1978) proposed that human learning, the development of uniquely human higher cognitive functions, requires the appropriation of cultural tools through a process of mediation. This process is illustrated in Figure 1.1.

The simple brilliance of Figure 1.1 illustrates Vygotsky's assertion that higher cognitive functions are necessarily mediated, while lower, elementary functions, illustrated at the base of the triangle, are innate and shared with animals. This represented a clear departure from the Piagetian epistemic subject popular at the time of Vygotsky's writing. In Figure 1.1, elementary mental functions (those shared with animals) take place at the base of the triangle. That is, the subject acts directly on the object; however, higher cognitive functions, those functions unique to humans, must necessarily be mediated, as indicated in the triangle's apex. Wertsch (1985) points out that Vygotsky conceived of this as the difference between the 'natural' line of development and the 'social' or 'cultural' line of development that converts elementary forms into higher cognitive functions. Wertsch (1985, p. 25) outlines the four major criteria that distinguish elementary from higher cognitive functions:

1   The emergence of voluntary regulation, indicated in a shift from environmental to individual control.
2   The emergence of conscious realization of mental processes.
3   The social origin and nature of higher cognitive functions captured in Vygotsky's general genetic law, which states that all higher cognitive functions begin in external, social interaction, before turning inward.

> The very mechanism underlying higher mental functions is a copy from social interaction; all higher mental functions are internalized social relationships . . . Their composition, genetic structure, and means of action [forms of mediation] – in a word, their whole nature – is social. Even when

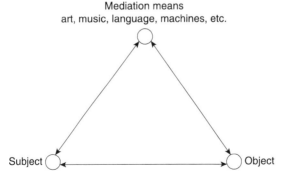

Figure 1.1 Vygotsky's human learning through mediation

we turn to mental [internal] processes, their nature remains quasi-social. In their own private sphere, human beings retain the functions of social interaction.

(p. 25)

4   The use of signs to mediate higher cognitive functions. Vygotsky distinguishes between object-oriented external technical tools and subject-oriented internal, psychological tools (or signs).

> [A technical tool] . . . serves as a conductor of humans' influence on the object of their activity. It is directed toward the external world; it must stimulate some changes in the object; it is a means of humans' external activity, directed toward the subjugation of nature.
> (Vygotsky, quoted in Wertsch, 1981)

A psychological tool, or sign, however:

> changes nothing in the object of a psychological operation. A sign is a means for psychologically influencing behaviour – either the behavior of another or one's own behaviour; it is a means of internal activity, directed toward the mastery of humans themselves. A sign is inwardly directed.
> (Vygotsky, quoted in Wertsch, 1981)

Languages, maps, mnemonic techniques are some examples Vygotsky gives of psychological tools. Kozulin (2003, p. 16) defines psychological tools as:

> those symbolic artifacts – signs, symbols, texts, formulae, graphic organizers – that when internalized help individuals master their own natural psychological functions of perception, memory, attention, and so on (see Kozulin, 1998). Each culture has its own set of psychological tools and situations in which these tools are appropriated.

What is of interest in the Kozulin quote is the focus on how culture plays a central role in the acquisition of psychological tools. This is of interest, especially, in South Africa that is a multicultural society. We may well expect to see performance differences on tasks, depending on the nature of the psychological tools actors bring to bear on the task. It is important therefore to keep in mind that psychological tools are social in origin and are not innate. For Miller (2011):

> the mediating role of signs is directed at mental activity, or what he [Vygotsky] called higher mental functions, the point being that these mental functions are "higher" precisely because of the mediation of signs. The notion of an agent lugging a cultural toolkit around . . . manages to miss entirely Vygotsky's core idea that the mediational means or psychological tools are part of the constitution of the agent, of the development of the agent's higher mental

functions, and not a constituent part of the agent's actions "-with-" which, or by means of which, an action is accomplished . . . In Vygotsky's conception . . . mediational means are not things an agent acts with or uses to accomplish an action like a carpenter acting with a hammer, or a vaulter with a pole, or a researcher with graph paper. Mediation in Vygotsky's terms is what determines the form of the action and not what constitutes the action. In this sense, it refers to higher mental processes that precede and shape the action, processes that enable the carpenter to reach out for the hammer to achieve a certain goal rather than the act of hammering-with-the-hammer.

(pp. 314–315)

Implicit and explicit mediation

Explicit mediation is the intentional use of objects, people or signs by an individual that "overtly and intentionally introduces a 'stimulus means' into an ongoing stream of activity" (Wertsch, 2007, p. 180) that is obvious and non-transitory. Implicit mediation, on the other hand, is less obvious but involves signs, especially language and communication. Whether mediation operates through direct intervention or through language and signs, individual transformation, by necessity, includes both explicit (tools and signs operating on other minds) and implicit (internal tools and signs actions) operating modes of mediation. But Vygotsky also used the term mediation in another way related to reflective and non-reflective mediation. Reflective mediation is about thinking about the tool/sign while undertaking an activity, and during non-reflective activity the subject/actor is concentrated on the particulars of a task without thought of the tool/sign.

Mediation can be viewed from different perspectives, but always includes either a material tool or a cognitive sign; may also be explicit or implicit; and may include reflection or not. In addition, mediation is hierarchical, and "not only refers to the nature of what goes on between people . . . but also to the process of co-creation between the social world and the internal world of ideas, feelings, and personal development" (Edwards, 2008, p. 174). Finally, for Vygotsky (1978), the primary form of mediation is semiotic; it is primarily through language that the social becomes personal. Hasan (2002) posits that there are a number of implications that arise as a result of linking higher mental functions to semiotic mediation. First, the origins of consciousness lie in the social interpersonal interactions, and second, the enabling nature of higher mental functions contributes to the evolution of humanity and allows us to sidestep the dualism contained in the nature/nurture debates by emphasizing that mind is in fact social.

Mediation with educational technology

The intentional use of explicit and implicit mediation in learning design could offer us a mechanism to ensure that we more carefully marry social-cultural theory to practice. Wertsch (2007) spoke of the intentional insertion of a tool, or sign, into an ongoing stream of activity (explicit) and also the intentional inclusion of opportunities for dialogue (dialogical activity). In the following authentic task, the different forms of mediation (**explicit** versus *implicit*, and <u>tool</u> versus <u>sign</u>)[1] are highlighted:

> Your Head of Department (HOD) has just had one of those cathartic moments: game-based learning is the way to go! While this may be an interesting development, the HOD has asked you, as one of the productive researchers in your department, to undertake a small research project to evaluate how games, one of the most complex technologies available to teachers, could be used in teaching and learning. To help you, the HOD has provided you with a number of papers and a review instrument that you could use to evaluate the teaching designs and outcomes detailed in each paper. The HOD has requested that your evaluations should be presented as a mind map to the members of your department.

> 1   Activity 1: With a <u>*colleague*</u>, **read the paper abstracts** to gain a general understanding of the ideas, research methodology, results and findings. <u>*You and your partner*</u> need to complete the online review for each paper using the <u>**review instrument**</u> that is available in the resources section.
> 2   Activity 2: Use this **data** (Google spreadsheet) collected during the first activity to <u>***visually analyse the data with your colleague***</u> and individually <u>***create a mind map***</u> using **FreeMind** for the HOD. Export your mind map as a PDF file and post it to the forum for <u>*group discussion*</u>.

The pedagogical design described above includes people working together to first understand the pedagogical design in a number of game-based research papers using a review instrument. Then, using the data from the use of the review instrument, they create a visual representation of the pedagogical analyses of the papers. The intentional use of a review instrument to help the participants to better understand the pedagogical practices described in the research papers is an example of explicit mediation. Similarly, graphical representation of the data in Excel and subsequent use of a mind mapping tool are other examples of explicit mediation – the intentional use of tools to support the development and representation of ideas. The inclusion of conversations between participants is implicit mediation, included to support interpersonal co-construction of knowledge. Inclusion of explicit and implicit mediation into learning design, therefore, stimulates higher-order functions that aim to lead to individual and, ultimately, social transformation.

Mediation and learning

Conceptualizing learning as mediated by a culturally more competent 'Other' implies a pedagogy that is overtly structured. The presence of a culturally more competent Other opens up a unique learning/teaching space that Vygotsky called the Zone of Proximal Development (ZPD). This unique learning/teaching space creates a bridge between what the student knows and what she needs to learn. The discussion of mediation within the ZPD is suggestive of how students learn in a lecture hall and indicates that pedagogy must be explicit and structured to facilitate students' access to novel knowledge. The question becomes: what is it that students learn through mediation in a lecturing/tutorial context? That is, what is the object of pedagogy in the academy? It is disingenuous to suggest that students necessarily learn what lecturers intend them to learn. However, it is necessary to have some theoretical mechanism for understanding what lecturers/tutors intend students to learn, even if in the end, students fail to acquire the requisite knowledge. Vygotsky's (1986) work provides such a mechanism for understanding the object of an academic activity. He distinguishes between scientific concepts that are *necessarily* taught, and everyday concepts that a child is able to learn from practical empirical experience. Scientific concepts are meaningful, and their meaning is not idiosyncratic and personal but, rather, social and general. Vygotsky's distinction between the 'sense' and 'meaning' of a word brings out the complex task of acquiring scientific concepts:

> A word's sense is the aggregate of all the psychological facts that arise in our consciousness as a result of the word. Sense is a dynamic, fluid, and complex formation that has several zones that vary in their stability. Meaning is only one of these zones of sense that the word acquires in the context of speech. It is the most stable, unified and precise of these zones. In different contexts, a word's sense changes. In contrast, meaning is a comparatively fixed and stable point, one that remains constant with all the changes of the word's sense that are associated with its use in various contexts.
>
> (Vygotsky, 1987, pp. 275–276)

What Vygotsky's work gives us, then, is a basis for understanding teaching/learning as socially and culturally situated. Mind, then, becomes conceptualized as emerging socially. Following Vygotsky's early death, his theory was developed further most notably (in psychology) by A.N. Leontiev.

Second generation AT: Leontiev to Engeström

While Vygotsky's learning theory points the way towards an understanding of learning as distributed, rather than located solely in the individual, it does not develop an analytical framework capable of situating learning within a wider context, accounting for the collective and dynamic nature of activities (Engeström, 1987; Wells, 1999). The distinction between individual action and collective activity implied, but not articulated in Vygotsky's theory, was elaborated by A.N. Leontiev whose famous example of the "primeval collective hunt" clarified the distinction between individual action and collective activity (1981, pp. 210–213) and placed the division of labour firmly within his definition of

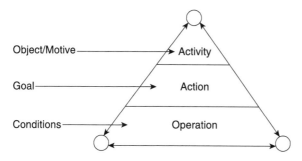

Figure 1.2 Leontiev's three-level model of activity

activity. Leontiev's hierarchical model of functioning conceives of activity as driven by the object, while individual actions are directed at goals, see Figure 1.2 (Engeström, 1987; Leontiev, 1981). Fossilized actions become operations.

Leontiev's (1981) focus on division of labour as a central historical process in the development of higher cognitive functions and the hierarchical structure of activity that it implies, adds to Vygotsky's initial model of human action by illustrating how individual actions are goal-oriented while collective activity is object oriented. Leontiev's three-level model of activity represented in Figure 1.2 distinguishes between individual goal-directed actions and operations and collective object-oriented activity. Activity is driven by an object-oriented motive, which is social; actions are conscious and are directed at goals and at the final, lowest level of the model, automatic operations are called into play by the tools and conditions of the action being carried out. The concept of 'motive' is central to Leontiev's theorizing of human activity and has been taken up in recent years by scholars such as Hedegaard (2002) and forms the basis for developmental teaching, which draws on the work of Davydov (1998).

Leontiev's elucidation of division of labour as historically implicated in the development of higher cognitive functions, together with his development of the notion of 'motive' develops Vygotsky's original thesis by illustrating the hierarchical structure of activity. However, while accounting for hierarchical levels of human functioning, Leontiev's theory does not go far enough to situate human functioning in context, illustrating how individual actions are transformed into shared, *collective* objects through interactions with community members or indeed *how* the division of labour impacts on individual actions in a collective activity. This is where Engeström's (1987) conceptualization of an activity system (see Figure 1.3) as the basic unit of analysis serves as a useful *tool* for situating pedagogy in context.

Figure 1.3 illustrates the basic unit of analysis (an activity system) proposed by Engeström's Activity Theory model (1987, p. 78). Figure 1.3 represents a development of Vygotsky's original triadic view of human activity by adding a more nuanced focus on the social context in which development occurs.

What we can see from Figure 1.3 is that the *subject* acts on the *object* in order to transform it using *mediating artefacts* in order to arrive at specific *outcomes*. In turn,

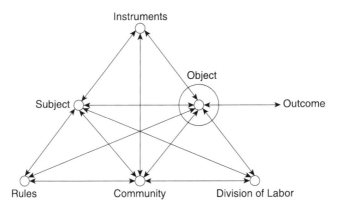

Figure 1.3 Engeström's conceptualization of an activity system

Source: Engeström (1987, p. 78)

the rules of the system mediate between the subject and his/her community, and the division of labour mediates between his/her community and the object (Daniels, 2001; Engeström, 1987; 1991). In this expanded version of Leontiev's (1981) work, the individual action represented at the pinnacle of the triangle is situated within a context in which power relations and rules impact on the subject's actions (Wells, 1999).

The notion of an activity system, then, illustrates how one might understand Leontiev's (1981) suggestion that actions can only be understood against the background of an activity; here we have a theoretical idea of what that 'activity' incorporates. Arising from Engeström's doctoral work (1987), this contemporary and popular version of CHAT is premised on the notion of learning as "expansive". The two-way arrows in Figure 1.3 indicate the dynamic nature of the nodes of the triangle. This is the very basic unit of analysis. Engeström has gone on to develop this model further, into third-generation activity theory represented by Figure 1.4. In this version of systems thinking, two activity systems (at the minimum) interact with a shared object.

Engeström (1987; 2005) uses an activity system as the basic unit of analysis for developing his expansive learning theory, which incorporates the methodology of Developmental Work Research (DWR) and subsequently the development of the Change Laboratory methodology for studying novel learning in a workplace setting. This methodological aspect of Engeström's work does not inform this chapter. Rather, this chapter seeks to elaborate Engeström's systems thinking in relation to pedagogy and the cases reported draw narrowly on second-generation activity theory except for Wood et al.'s Chapter 3 which utilizes third-generation systems thinking. It must be noted, therefore, that the development of Engeström's work in this chapter is the author's own and cannot be identified with his current project. Readers interested in Engeström's (2005) current project are referred to The Centre for Research on Activity, Development and Learning (CRADLE) at

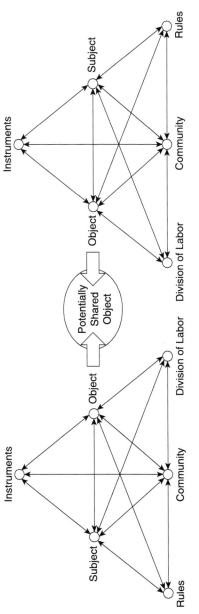

Figure 1.4 Third-generation activity theory

the University of Helsinki and to Daniels' (2001) and Daniels and Leadbetter's (2005) development work research. For this chapter, Engeström's systemic model enables one to view pedagogy along the following dimensions:

1   *Subject:* For our purposes, the lecturer/tutor is the subject of the pedagogical activity. His/her epistemic assumptions about how students learn will impact on his/her use of tools in order to teach.
2   *Mediating artefact:* In a simplistic formulation, one might view mediating artefacts as the resources the lecturer mobilizes in order to act on her/his object. In the cases informing this Part of the book, tools can be both material (such as a blog) and ideal (such as a concept).
3   *Object:* There is much debate in AT circles about what the object of an activity is and how one might study it, as it arises during the actual activity. Space constraints militate against an in-depth discussion of these debates in the current chapter and readers are referred to Hardman (2007b) for a discussion of this. In order to avoid conceptual slippage, in the current chapter the object of a pedagogical activity is understood as "the 'raw material' or '"problem" space' at which the activity is directed and which is moulded and transformed into outcomes with the help of physical and symbolic, external and internal mediating instruments, including both tools and signs" (Engeström, 1987, p. 79).
4   *Rules:* These are the norms or conventions and social interactions that animate the subject's actions in the activity.
5   *Community:* The lecturer is a member of a community who participates in acting on the shared object. There is a division of labour within the community, with responsibilities, tasks and power continuously being negotiated (Cole & Engeström, 1993).
6   *Division of labour:* This is both vertical and horizontal and refers to the negotiation of responsibilities, tasks and power relations within a classroom as well as across the school. In the current chapter, the division of labour is conceptualized as playing itself out in the roles that participants occupy in the lesson. So for example, generally, the lecturer's role is to teach and the students' role is to learn.

Emerging technology and transformative pedagogy

Engeström's second- and third-generation activity theory provides the theoretical and analytical foundation for the work presented in this book, which is concerned with understanding how emerging technology potentially can transform pedagogy in higher education. CHAT, in Engeström's articulation of it, enables one to study how the introduction of a novel tool (emerging technology) can alter an activity system. As Daniels notes '[t]he introduction of new tools into human activity does more than improve a specific form of functioning – it transforms it' (2010, p. 29). In addition to this, CHAT provides a basis for understanding pedagogy as multi-voiced and embedded in power relations (Paavola et al., 2004). Given that the object of transformative pedagogy is to develop students who are able "to perceive social, political, and economic contradictions, and to take action against the oppressive elements of reality" (Brown, 2004, p. 77), CHAT's capacity to surface contradictions enables one to study change in context by elaborating the essentially Hegelian notion of 'contradiction' or double bind – that dynamic site of change where dissonance forces transformation (either progressively or regressively).

Contradictions exist within and between activity systems and happen at various levels of the activity system. At level 1, the primary contradiction lies within each component of the activity. So, for example, a lecturer's object might be to develop critical thinking in his/her students. However, the need to cover an established body of knowledge could lead to a contradiction between curriculum coverage and the development of critical thinking; time constraints narrow the lecturer's object from depth knowledge to potentially superficial acquisition of content. Secondary contradictions arise between the constituents of the central activity, such as, for example, between tool and object. At the tertiary contradiction level, a contradiction exists between the object/motive of the dominant form of the central activity and the object/motive of a culturally more advanced form of the central activity. Finally, quaternary contradictions arise between the central activity and its neighbouring activities. Surfacing contradictions enables one to see where transformation in the system or between systems is likely to occur.

Conclusion

This chapter outlines the broad theoretical field in which the book situates itself, namely Cultural-Historical Activity Theory. The theory, underpinned by the dialectical logic of Vygotsky's work, helps one to situate individual action in the social context in which actions form part of larger activities. Engeström's early work, in particular, enables the case study authors to understand learning with technology as a mediated activity that potentially leads to transformation in the education system, in this instance, higher educational settings. Chapters 2 and 4 in Part I mobilize Engestrom's second-generation activity systems triangle as a heuristic device to investigate students' learning through practice in the professional training field of Architecture and mediation in an online course, respectively. Chapter 3 utilizes third-generation activity theory to analyze an educational intervention in Australia. In Part IV, Chapter 13 animates the theory discussed here in a number of case studies that illustrate how one can use CHAT to study teaching/learning with novel technology.

Note

1   Think of explicit mediation as "dropping" a tool into an activity and thus requires some **weight**; as implicit mediation is about language and we often use *italics* to quote someone; and as the use of signs requires higher order functions such mediation is <u>underlined twice</u> while material tools require a <u>single underline</u>.

References

Brown, K. (2004). Leadership for social justice and equity: Weaving a transformative framework and pedagogy. *Educational Administration Quarterly*, *40*, 77–108.

Cole, M., & Engeström, Y. (1993). A cultural-historical approach to distributed cognition. In G. Saloman (Ed), *Distributed cognition: psychological and educational considerations* (pp. 3–17). Cambridge: Cambridge University Press.

Daniels, H. (2001). *Vygotsky and pedagogy*. London: RoutledgeFalmer.

Daniels, H., & Leadbetter, J. (2005). Learning in and for interschool working to promote creativity. Paper presented at the 1st International ISCAR conference, September, 20–25, Seville, Spain.

Davydov, V. V. (1998). What is real learning activity? In M. Hedegaard & J Lompscher (Eds.), *Learning activity and development* (pp. 211–243). Aarhus: Aarhus University Press.

Edwards, M. G. (2008). "Every today was a tomorrow": An integral method for indexing the social mediation of preferred futures. *Futures*, *40*(2), 173–189.

Engeström, Y. (1987). *Learning by expanding: An activity-theoretical approach to developmental research*. Helsinki: Orienta-Konsultit.

Engeström, Y. (1991). Non scolae sed vitae discimus: Toward overcoming the encapsulation of school learning. *Learning and Instruction*, *1*, 243–59.

Engeström, Y. (2005). *Developmental work research: Expanding activity theory in practice*. Berlin: Lehmans Media.

Evans, S. (2013). SA ranks its maths and science second last in the world. *Mail and Guardian*. 17 April: 7.

Hardman, J. (2007a). Towards a methodology for using Activity Theory to explicate the pedagogical object in a primary school mathematics classroom. *Critical Social Studies*, *9*(1), 53–69.

Hardman, J. (2007b). Making sense of the meaning maker: Tracking the object of activity in a computer-based mathematics lesson using activity theory. *International Journal of Education and Development Using ICT*, *3*(4).

Hardman, J., & Ng'ambi, D. (2003). A questioning environment for scaffolding learners' questioning engagement with academic text: A university case study. *South African Journal of Higher Education*, *17*(2), 139–146.

Hasan, R. (2002). Semiotic mediation and mental development in pluralistic societies: Some implications for tomorrow's schooling. In G. Wells & G. Claxton (Eds.), *Learning for life in the 21st century: Sociocultural perspectives on the future of education* (pp. 112–126). Oxford: Blackwell.

Hedegaard, M. (2002). *Learning and development: A cultural-historical study*. Aarhus: Aarhus University Press.

Howie, S. (2001). *Mathematics and science performance in grade 8 in South Africa, 1998/1999*. Pretoria: Human Sciences Research Council.

Kozulin, A. (1998). *Psychological tools: A sociocultural approach to education*. Cambridge, MA: Harvard University Press.

Kozulin, A. (2003). Psychological tools and mediated learning. In A. Kozulin, B. Gindis, V. S. Ageyev & S. M. Miller (Eds.), *Vygotsky's educational theory in cultural context* (pp. 15–38). Cambridge: Cambridge University Press.

Leontiev, A. N. (1981). The problem of activity in psychology. In J. V. Wertsch (Ed.), *The concept of activity in Soviet psychology* (pp. 37–71). Armonk, NY: M. E. Sharpe.

Miller, R. (2011). *Vygotsky in perspective*. Cambridge: Cambridge University Press.

Vygotsky, L. S. (1978). *Mind in society: The development of higher psychological processes*. M. Cole, V. John-Steiner, S. Scribner, & S. Souerman (Eds. and Trans.). Cambridge, MA: Harvard University Press.

Vygotsky, L. S. (1986). *Thought and language*. E. Hanfmann & G. Vakar (Eds. and Trans.). Cambridge, MA: MIT Press.

Vygotsky, L. S. (1987). *The collected works of L.S. Vygotsky*, Vol. 1: *Problems of general psychology*. R.W. Rieber and A. S. Carton (Eds.), N. Minick (Trans.). New York: Plenum Press.

Wells, G. (1999). *Dialogic inquiry. Towards a socio-cultural practice and theory of education*. Cambridge: Cambridge University Press.

Wertsch, J. V. (1981). *The concept of activity in Soviet psychology*. Armonk, NY: M. E. Sharpe.

Wertsch, J. V. (1985). *Vygotsky and the social formation of mind*. Cambridge, MA: Harvard University Press.

Wertsch, J. V. (2007). Mediation. In H. Daniels, M. Cole, & J.V. Wertsch (Eds.), *The Cambridge companion to Vygotsky* (pp. 178–192). New York: Cambridge University Press.

2 Learning in sites of practice through a CHAT lens

James Garraway and Jolanda Morkel

Introduction

In this small-scale research project we were interested in university students' learning through practice in the outside world in the professional training field of Architecture. Students were interviewed during and immediately after their practical experiences at two different off-campus sites of learning: the architectural office and a community service project. In the office, students would spend 10 months working as junior interns, and in the two-week community project students were engaged in building an improvement in a primary school space. Students' reported experiences were then analyzed and interpreted through an activity theory lens and different affordances and motivations for learning were identified. We found that both sites provided students with opportunities to participate in authentic work practices, but that community service was strongly motivating as it afforded more opportunity to contribute to changing the lives of others.

Periods of learning through practice have long been common in career-focused education. This is so that students may become aware of how knowledge is used in particular organizational set-ups (Billet, 2009). Billet further stresses the particular importance of students' exposure to problems for which there are no easy solutions, as this necessitates that they engage in often-collaborative efforts of meaning and decision-making.

A communities-of-practice approach to learning in organizations suggests that work communities are typified by particular shared meanings, knowledge repertoires and typical ways of doing things that may be different from other such communities (Wenger, 1998). Learning through work is thus a process of adopting these particularities through participation and "situated learning", initially as a peripheral participant towards a progressive synthesizing of one's own identity and that of the community. However, exactly how learning occurs in such communities, or what conditions best enable or constrain it, are not always sufficiently theorized (Billet, 1994).

For practice to enable learning, it needs to offer affordances for significant learning within that field (Billet, 2009) but this alone is not enough. Students also need to be motivated themselves to learn through the exercise of agency. In this chapter, agency refers to individuals and groups being able to find meaning and to practise intentionality, i.e. to follow their own purposes, in the work they do (Billet, 2009; Eraut, 2010). One suggestion put forward is that the theme of contribution and change to the lives of others through conducting work may provide these affordances and motivations. In so doing, the chapter draws on Activity Theory's approaches to systems change and learning (see Hardman & Amory, Chapter 1, in this volume) and Stetsenko's (2008; 2010) transformative activist stance on learning. From this position Stetsenko argues that learning which is embedded in practices that change and possibly improve the lives of others makes such learning deeply meaningful for those engaged in it; such forms of learning are thus potentially powerful. The field of Architecture, too, has a vision of addressing people's needs and improving the quality of lived environments. Socially responsible learning is thus not only potentially meaningful and powerful, but also commensurate with the professional practices in the field of Architecture.

In the Architectural Technology Diploma, students study subjects (e.g. structures, history, drawing and computer assisted drawing (CAD), for example) in class for application in supervised studio practice. Sandwiched between two years of university study, students also do a ten-month practicum in the office of a registered architectural professional. Employers here act as mentors and have a responsibility to induct students into typical professional practices as students learn through working with the regular office staff. In addition, students are required to complete a range of specific tasks that are signed off in a logbook by the employer. Even though the student is at work, there is also a level of monitoring from the academic staff through office visits, occasional on-campus workshops and, more recently, online engagement through information and communication technology and social media. The purpose statement which structures approaches to teaching and learning at sites of learning on and off campus in the Diploma programme is as follows:

> A person achieving this qualification will be a competent Architectural Technologist who can conduct relevant routine technical research and under supervision perform architectural services in construction, detailing and administration in the public and private, formal and informal sectors in the built environment.

In keeping with this outcome, students are mostly involved in drawing and detailing of building designs under the instruction of a more senior colleague, in order to meet local council requirements. However, in the past two decades we have seen a considerable expansion in the role of architects. Whether referred to as "humanitarian architecture, design as activism, public interest design, community-based design or service learning", these new roles are redefining the identity of the architect and testing the limits of contemporary architectural practice (UKAERG, 2013, p. 6).

The American Institute of Architecture Students identified the need for change in academic programmes to "produce healthier, more optimistic, and more engaging architecture school graduates" (AIAS, 2002, p. 5). They suggest that proactive change is needed to address the changes in the world and practice, and a form of education is needed which not only teaches methods but also has a strong orientation to the needs of community. Furthermore, change is needed to prepare students to practise architecture in which they will play a leading role in developing adequate built environments for people, which necessarily involves engagement with social and cultural factors in the built environment (AIAS, 2002).

These needs are being addressed by the recent emergence (only in the last two decades) of design-build, service learning or live projects at only a few architecture schools globally. Live projects and design-build service learning projects present a negotiated, collaborative mode of learning which leads naturally to an experience that can become transformative, and in a manner which demands that students exercise their own judgement (Voulgarelis, 2012). Furthermore, community projects that are situated in real contexts and which are negotiated and collaborative, present opportunities for individual and social transformation where students are introduced to the lived worlds of their user communities (Morrow & Brown, 2012).

In response to this need for change in education, as well as doing practice work in the office, students work on a community service project which is related to their architectural studies. This occurs towards the end of the year, during two weeks of the sandwich office practice period, Both community service learning and work experience in university courses serve to connect learning inside the university to outside society; service learning can thus be seen as a special form of work experience (Stanton et al., 1999; Furco, 1996). However, unlike work experience in general, service learning focuses on the development of both the student and the client; students contribute to the well-being of others rather than just learning for themselves (Stanton et al., 1999).

Students, with their lecturers, are involved in the design of an improvement in a primary school space in a semi-rural farming community. This improvement is one which has arisen from both observation of the school and its surroundings and discussion with the teachers, in response to the school approaching the University for assistance. The intervention takes the form of a high-roofed outdoor classroom/play space structure and garden attached to the side of the school. The task of the students over the two weeks is to collectively build the classroom and landscape the surroundings (approximately 30 students are involved here). Students are further assisted and guided by professional architects and lecturers, and may have to work with materials' suppliers as well. In working on the project, students draw on knowledge and tools learnt at university and sometimes the office. There is constant interaction between teachers, children and students (Figure 2.1).

In order to better understand learning at the different sites of practice at the office and in the community, we pose three distinct but related pedagogies.

Three pedagogies for learning

Sfard (1998) suggests that at least two pedagogies operate in the schooling system. The first, acquisition, is primarily concerned with the learner learning given facts

Figure 2.1 Students being thanked by learners, in the outdoor classroom

Source: Photographer, Shaun Uys, Cape Peninsula University of Technology

and concepts that are relatively fixed. In this pedagogy, the learner has little control over what is learnt. This would refer to many a typical classroom or lecture theatre's teaching and learning practices. Second, Sfard was also interested in more active forms of learning and engagement in which knowledge is learnt through dialogue and co-construction of meaning, what she refers to as learning through participation. However, there is also more facilitated induction through interaction with more knowledgeable others (teachers) so that students learn the language and culture of particular fields, and may, through successive interactions, even become recognized as expert/proficient in that field. In this second pedagogy of learning, Sfard is clearly mobilizing the concepts of situated learning in communities of practice and peripheral participation in such communities to promote more active forms of classroom learning. Collis and Moonen (2001), however, regard participation alone as insufficient to optimize learning, particularly when students are engaged with more flexible and digital forms of learning in higher education. These forms often involve students in acting collectively to develop new ideas and to solve problems. They suggest, in addition to participation, a third pedagogy of contribution, in which students are not just actively engaging and constructing knowledge within the confines of the accepted knowledge of the community, but also contributing learning materials and ideas to the system. Collis and Moonen further acknowledge that learning through participation and contribution are particularly relevant to student engagement in more practice-based activities.

This position is further supported in higher education and work-studies by the practice learning theorist, Eraut (2004).

Stetsenko (2008, 2010), drawing on the work of Vygotsky and Dewey, is also interested in students' learning and development through participation in and contribution to communities of practice. But this is insufficient unless students are also able to exert some form of agency, some possibility of changing the world they are interacting with rather than just being active participants within it. Other activity theorists researching work and learning are also interested in agency and change. For example, Blackler (2009) describes how both individuals and organizations change and learn through their interactions in work practices. This may occur because students bring fresh perspectives on knowledge and ways of operating to workplaces that, over time, may have become set in their ways (Tuomi-Grohn & Engeström, 2003; Le Maistre & Pare, 2004). Konkola et al. (2007), for example, describe how health students doing their practicums were able to mobilize university learning to bring into effect new protocols for stroke patients' rehabilitation in health centres; students thus acted to change the previously fixed system of operations.

Stetsenko (2008) argues further that change (transformation) is not neutral in activity theory terms, but that it is also fundamentally activist in nature. Activism, drawing on the Marxist roots of activity theory, refers to transforming the world to improve the human condition and through this particular interaction actors come to realize their own humanity. Furthermore, as discussed by Hardman and Amory (Chapter 1, in this edited collection), activity is always purposeful for the individual subject and this purposefulness/ motive drives them to engage in the system. Where, as Stetsenko suggests, the purpose of activity within an activist transformatory framework is one of social uplift or social justice, then this too becomes the main driving force for engagement in the activity.

Student learning experiences in the office and community service project

In the office, students draw on their training in drawing and detailing following current regulatory frameworks both in the classroom and in studio work. In practice, they are often required to learn new computer-assisted drawing programmes or other ways of operating in that particular company; students thus often draw on the experiences of other more senior employers, and their work is subject to critique from them. In a sense, students are thus part of the community of practice of the workplace, as the following quotes from student interviews illustrate:

> They show us the work they have done, how and why they did it so it is quite cool . . . you can ask around and they will tell you about new technologies . . . there is always someone you can ask . . . even in small companies where they are quite busy.

And, in addition:

> It is the people that you are employed for that can fill those gaps and it also has to come from you to go that extra half mile.

However, students are still learners rather than full members of the workplace community. This in turn may be difficult for students as they attempt to seek help in their work. Students are thus often both part of the community but also partly outside of it, what Lave and Wenger (1991) refer to as "peripheral participants":

> In the office you are an employee first [then] a student. You don't want to nag so you go and struggle with something . . . and they have got deadlines and everything and people won't give you that consideration.

Furthermore, students tend be given quite specific tasks to do in the office which may be repetitive as well as segmented, such that students cannot always see the whole work project in the same way that the architect can:

> The architect does the designs, then work is passed down to us . . . . In the office you often only work on one thing, like ceilings.

In addition, students do not usually deal with outside clients or suppliers. Taken together, these factors can be said to demonstrate students' incomplete membership of the work community.

Of particular interest to us as researchers were students' perceptions of the differences between working on the project and office work. One important observation in the community service project was that students felt a connection, or a bond to the teachers and children they were working for; students refer to 'responsibility', both to the clients but also to one another:

> I think the responsibility part . . . here, you really get people out of their comfort zone, the work ethic is tested a lot, and we have found value in each other. I think the responsibility of the workplace is a lot watered down to what we have experiencing here because in the workplace you are still regarded as a student . . . in the office you just draw, you do not put life into your drawings. Here you make that special bond . . . there is somebody at the end of the drawing.

There is a sense of immediate purpose to what they are doing and a sense of partly being able to control the direction of their work in the community project, rather than being continually directed by others in the office. Students also perceive themselves as having knowledge and expertise to carry out the work of building the school; something, which is less prevalent or even absent in office work.

[In the office] you just form part of the business you are going to do what they want you to do. Like now, we have our knowledge and we can take initiative, we can try to work it out and do it ourselves, it is our responsibility.

At work we get paid 1/5 the salary, we are like a cheap commodity but here we have got this amazing skill that is somehow being squandered and you get to help these people who have nothing.

There are obvious differences between the two sites of practice but what was particularly interesting to us were the different cultures and social arrangements, or, in Activity Theory terms, the rules and divisions of labour in the two systems. As is shown in Figure 2.2, office rules are those of instruction rather than self-initialization, whereas those in the community project lean more towards a sense of responsibility and accountability. In divisions, office work is similarly clearly defined and itemized for the 'junior' student, whereas in community work the student operates in a more integrated and relatively knowledgeable role.

Analyzing the data through an Activity Theory lens

As was suggested by Hardman and Amory in Chapter 1 (in this volume), the object is something of a prospect which the activity is directed towards which is subsequently reshaped through interaction with the elements of the activity system. With reference to Figure 2.2, in the office system, students are part of the office community, learning from and with their more senior colleagues. In terms of divisions, students occupy a relatively low status as apprentices and their focus is often on the completion of a particular task rather than engagement in a whole project. The rules of the office are focused on getting jobs done effectively and efficiently and students are instructed in what to do rather than initializing work themselves. It can then be suggested that these divisions and rules are well designed to 'shape' the object into something that is quite close to the official purpose of the programme outlined at the beginning of the chapter. In other words students learn to become competent in architectural services under the supervision of more expert others. For students in the community service project, the sociocultural conditions are quite different. Students occupy a more 'expert' or leading role in conjunction with their fellow experts (divisions), and are more able to initialize their work as problems arise (rules and norms). Furthermore, there is a strong culture of care and consideration for those they are working for (norms). Again, it can be suggested that these conditions serve to act on the raw material/object such that it is potentially changed into a learning experience (outcome) of contributing to and transforming others' lives. Being able to experience contribution and transformation in the work that they do can, furthermore, provide students with a strong motive to engage in architectural practice as best they possibly can, thus providing for a potentially powerful site for learning.

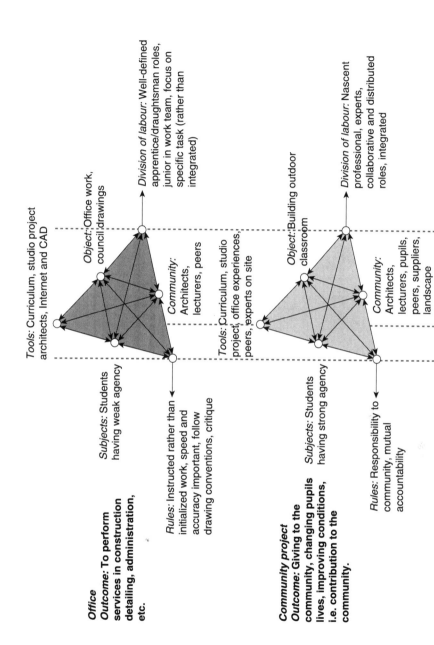

Office
Outcome: To perform services in construction detailing, administration, etc.

Tools: Curriculum, studio project architects, Internet and CAD

Object: Office work, council drawings

Community: Architects, lecturers, peers

Subjects: Students having weak agency

Rules: Instructed rather than initialized work, speed and accuracy important, follow drawing conventions, critique

Division of labour: Well-defined apprentice/draughtsman roles, junior in work team, focus on specific task (rather than integrated)

Community project
Outcome: Giving to the community, changing pupils lives, improving conditions, i.e. contribution to the community.

Tools: Curriculum, studio project, office experiences, peers, experts on site

Object: Building outdoor classroom

Community: Architects, lecturers, pupils, peers, suppliers, landscape

Subjects: Students having strong agency

Rules: Responsibility to community, mutual accountability

Division of labour: Nascent professional, experts, collaborative and distributed roles, integrated

Figure 2.2 Comparing the activity systems of the community service project and the workplace

Learning through transformation

Our study involved an analysis of learning through practice in the Architectural office and in a service-learning project. Through interviewing students and, in particular, using an Activity Theory methodology, we were able to better understand student experiences in practice, and the affordances offered for learning in community service projects. As was pointed out by Hardman and Amory in Chapter 1, learning, when viewed through an Activity Theory lens, is culturally situated, complex and often imbued with issues of power and control, and this can be seen to be the case at both sites of learning. The office environment involves participation in the office community as an apprentice, under the wing of a mentor, but also working cooperatively with team members. The benefits that accrue would be those of becoming individually more skilled as well as contributing to the more immediate work the company needs to do (for example, through preparing council drawings). In the community service project, on the other hand, the student is collaboratively working in a committed way to transform the lives of others. As Stetsenko (2008, p. 488) suggests: "Collaborative, purposeful transformation of the world is the core of human nature and the principled grounding for learning and development."

Such a stance on learning involves working on different objects with different ensuing outcomes. These outcomes are in turn more in line with the changing focus of architectural education discussed earlier towards "the role and responsibility of their profession as something intrinsically tied to human existence and lived experience" (Salingaros & Masden, 2008, p. 132).

It is hoped that conclusions drawn can aid in the improvement of practice-based learning, including learning through community service in Architecture and other career focused fields in the future. One immediate observation would be that highly technical purpose statements without reference to more contributory and agentic influences on learning may no longer suffice to direct the sort of engaged and committed learning required in career-focused (professional) education.

Furthermore, we would like to believe that a greater focus on and understanding of the learning potential of community project work contributes to the aims of this book, to expose readers to more transformative higher education pedagogical practices.

References

AIAS (American Institute of Architecture Students) Studio Culture Task Force (2002). *The redesign of studio culture*. Washington, DC: AIAS.

Billet, S. (1994). Situated learning in the workplace: Having another look at apprenticeship. *Industrial and Commercial Training*, *26*(11), 9–16.

Billet, S. (2009). Realising the educational worth of integrating work experiences in higher education. *Studies in Higher Education*, *3*(7), 827–843.

Blackler, F. (2009). Cultural-historical activity theory and organization studies. In A. Sannino, H. Daniels, & K. Gutierrez (Eds.), *Learning and expanding with activity theory*. Cambridge: Cambridge University Press.

Boyer, E., & Mitgang, L. (1996). *Building community: A new future for architectural education and practice*. Princeton, NJ: Carnegie Foundation for the Advancement of Teaching.

Collis, B., & Moonen, J. (2001). *Flexible learning in a digital world*. London: Kogan Page.

Eraut, M. (2004). The transfer of knowledge between settings. In H. Rainbird, A. Fuller, & A. Munro (Eds.), *Workplace learning in context* (pp. 201–221). London: Routledge.

Eraut, M. (2010). The balance between communities and personal agency. Paper presented at the conference Enabling a More Complete Education: Encouraging, Recognizing and Valuing a Life-Wide Learning in Higher Education, University of Surrey, Guildford, 13–14 April.

Furco, A. (1996). Service learning: A balanced approach to experiential learning. In *Expanding boundaries: Service and learning*. Washington, DC: Corporation for National Service.

Konkola, R., Tuomi-Gröhn, T., Lambert, P., & Ludvigsen N. (2007). Promoting learning and transfer between school and workplace. *Journal of Education and Work, 20*(3), 211–228.

Lave, J., & Wenger, E. (1991). *Situated learning: Legitimate peripheral participation*. Cambridge: Cambridge University Press.

Le Maistre, C., & Paré, A. (2004). Learning in two communities: The challenge for universities and workplaces. *Journal of Workplace Learning, 16*(1/2), 44–52.

Morrow, R., & Brown, J. B. (2012). Live projects as critical pedagogies. In M. Dodd, F. Harrison, & E. Charlesworth (Eds.), *Live projects: Designing with people* (pp. 140–152). Melbourne: RMIT Training Pty Ltd.

Salingaros, N. A., & Masden, K. G. (2008). Intelligence-based design: a sustainable foundation for worldwide architectural education. *Archnet-IJAR International Journal of Architectural Research, 2*(1), 129–188.

Sfard, A. (1998). On two metaphors for learning and the dangers of choosing just one. *Educational Researcher, 27*, 4–13.

Stanton, T., Giles, D., & Cruz, N. (1999). *Service learning: A movement's pioneers reflect on its origins, practice and future*. San Francisco: Jossey-Bass.

Stetsenko, A. (2008). From relational ontology to transformative activist stance. *Cultural Studies of Science Education, 3*, 471–491.

Stetsenko, A. (2010). Teaching–learning and development as activist projects of historical becoming: Expanding Vygotsky's approach to pedagogy. *Pedagogies: An International Journal, 5*(1), 1–16.

Tuomi-Gröhn, T., & Engeström, Y. (2003). Conceptualising transfer: From standard notions to developmental perspectives. In T. Tuomi-Gröhn & Y. Engeström (Eds.), *Between school and work: New perspectives on transfer and boundary-crossing* (pp. 121–140). Oxford: Elsevier Science.

UKAERG (UK Architectural Education Review Group) (2013). *Pathways and gateways: The structure and regulation of architectural education*. Preliminary Report, April. London: UKAERG.

Voulgarelis, H. (2012). Investigating design-build as an alternative model for architectural education. Paper presented at ACSA International Conference CHANGE, Architecture, Barcelona, Spain.

Webster, H. (2004). Facilitating critically reflective learning: Excavating the role of the design tutor in architectural education. *Art, Design & Communication in Higher Education, 2*(3), 101–111.

Wenger, E. (1998). *Communities of practice: Learning, meaning and identity*. Cambridge: Cambridge University Press.

3 The Anangu Tertiary Education Program in remote northwest South Australia

A CHAT perspective

Denise Wood, Deirdre Tedmanson, Bruce Underwood, Makinti Minutjukur and Katrina Tjitayi

Introduction

The need to improve the education outcomes of remote Indigenous learners in Australia and to improve the participation of Indigenous students in post-compulsory education has been the focus of considerable research over the past two decades (McLoughlin, 2000; Price & Hughes, 2009). Recent reports suggest that some progress has been made in improving Indigenous student access to, participation and retention in education (Price & Hughes, 2009; Ottmann & White, 2010; Asmar, Page, & Radloff, 2011). However, "the continuing under-representation of Indigenous people in higher education and the low rates of success, retention and completion for Indigenous students" (DEEWR, 2009, cited in Price & Hughes, 2009; James & Devlin, 2006, p. 2) remain areas of major concern. *The More Aboriginal and Torres Strait Islander Teachers Initiative*, which is a project focusing on improving the retention, success, and graduation rates of Aboriginal and Torres Strait Islander teacher education students (Patton et al., 2012, p. 7), has identified several strategies likely to improve the achievement of these outcomes. These include "supporting Indigenous students through enrolment; providing smooth transition into university life; supporting students culturally, social, academically and with financial assistance when required"; as well as "flexibility in course progression" and the provision of "professional development and awareness-raising of non-Indigenous staff and faculty" (p. 7).

The Aboriginal and Torres Strait Islander Higher Education Advisory Council (ATSIHEAC), which provides advice to the Australian Government on enhancing outcomes for Aboriginal and Torres Strait Islander people in higher education and research, has emphasized the leadership role that Australian universities must play in ensuring that Indigenous Australians have equality of access to higher educational opportunities. James and Devlin (2006) also note the interrelationship between education and the need for social, cultural, and economic development of Indigenous communities. Yet the discussions about appropriate strategies for achievement of these aspirational goals need to be understood within the broader cultural historical context with a legacy of Australia's colonial past and the ensuing struggles of Indigenous people to assume self-management and control over their own affairs (McDonald, 1993, cited in McLoughlin, 2000). In her " A letter to Australians", Makinti Minutjukur (2006) echoes these concerns, asserting that "our people and our communities are being systematically disempowered" and "held back by a lack of thoughtful, respectful and culturally aware consultation and planning between us Anangu, and governments and their agents on whom, unavoidably, we depend".

This discussion highlights the complexity of issues impacting on educational outcomes in remote Indigenous communities, and this chapter attempts to unpack these complexities through the lens of third-generation Cultural-Historical Activity Theory (CHAT) (Engeström, 2001). Such an analysis recognizes that Indigenous students and teachers' mediated activities are complex and situated within a context in which relations and rules impact on their actions (Wells, 1999).

The Anangu Tertiary Education Program (AnTEP) was established by the University of South Australia (UniSA) – formerly the South Australian College of Advanced Education – in several Anangu communities located across the Anangu Pitjantjatjara Yankunytjatjara (APY) Lands in remote northwest South Australia (see Figure 3.1) 30 years ago.

The aim of the program is to enable Anangu people to undertake tertiary studies, particularly teacher education, without leaving their homelands. In this way the program seeks to address issues of "cultural isolation, lack of appropriate support, homesickness and other factors", which have led to students returning to their homelands prior to completing their course (Report of the Select Committee on Pitjantjatjara Land Rights, 2004).

The following analysis draws on the reflections of the Program Director and members of the Anangu community who were consulted about this chapter, based on a published report (Osborne & Underwood, 2010), using CHAT as a framework for understanding the complexity of teaching and learning in remote Indigenous communities.

Context of the case study

AnTEP is a collaborative program involving UniSA, Department for Education and Child Development (DECD – through the Aboriginal Lands District) and the Pitjantjatjara Yankunytjatjara Education Committee (PYEC). PYEC has operational control of education in the APY Lands and the Anangu Schools are operated by DECD. School-based Anangu tertiary tutors are employed by DECD under the direction of PYEC to support AnTEP students undertaking their studies. The teacher training program is offered in three stages: Stage 1: the Advanced Certificate in Education (Anangu Education); Stage 2: the Diploma in Education (Anangu Education); Stage 3: the Bachelor of Teaching (Anangu Education). To date, 87 students have completed the Advanced Certificate in Education qualifying them as Aboriginal Education Workers (AEWs), eligible for employment in the local schools; 62 have completed the Diploma in Education, qualifying them for senior AEW roles in the schools; and 28 have completed the

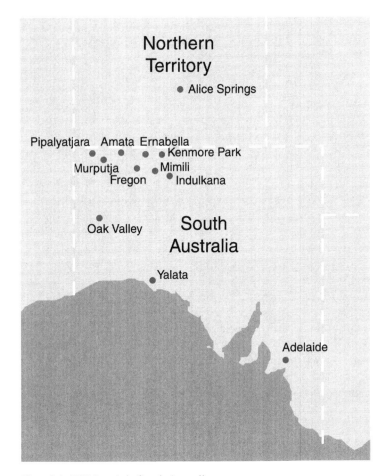

Figure 3.1 APY Lands in South Australia

Bachelor of Teaching, which qualifies graduates to be employed as teachers in the schools. Students may exit with the Advanced Certificate after completion of Stage 1 (one year) of the programs.

Consistent with pedagogies aimed at improving Indigenous learning outcomes by connecting students, community and the curriculum (Rennie, 2013), the AnTEP program is based on principles that teaching and learning:

- should be compatible with the defence, maintenance and growth of Anangu students' cultural identity;
- must be contextualized, culturally appropriate and related to the workplace;
- should be based on Anangu students' perspectives, expertise, interests and needs;
- should proceed from practice to theory involving Anangu students in purposeful learning activities;

- are part of a negotiated process in the design of learning programs, assessment and evaluation activities;
- model sound primary teaching methodology which students can adopt as teachers in their own right;
- entail the use of culturally appropriate pedagogies, curriculum and resources;
- involve the continual exploration of teaching methods and curriculum which are successful with Anangu students.

Despite these aims, as the following analysis illustrates, the complexity of the cultural historical context in which AnTEP operates poses several challenges for UniSA lecturers/tutors, AnTEP students and their communities, demanding a more nuanced understanding to be able to identify opportunities for more transformative pedagogical approaches in such remote communities. CHAT provides an appropriate theoretical framework for undertaking such an analysis and for identifying opportunities for what Engeström (2001) refers to as expansive learning.

Cultural-History Activity Theory (CHAT)

As Hardman and Amory explain in Chapter 1, CHAT focuses on the activity as the primary unit of analysis in any activity system; acknowledging that activities need to be analyzed within the context in which those activities take place (Jonassen & Rohrer-Murphy, 1999). CHAT recognizes that learning is a collectively shared process with significant cultural and historical dimensions (Vygotsky, 1978). The approach draws on Vygotsky's (1978) concept of the Zone of Proximal Development, which is the distance between what an individual can achieve on their own and what they can accomplish when guided by more capable peers or adults (for example, their peers, tertiary tutors, lecturers) through social inter-actions that take place in a historical and cultural context. Building on Vygotsky's (1978) approach, Leontiev's (1978) second-generation interpretation of an activity system recognizes that an activity system is composed of a subject, object, mediated actions, and operations. A subject is a person or a group engaged in an activity, in this example, the subjects within the activity system are the AnTEP students. An object is what drives or motivates the activity, in this case, the object is for students to complete a tertiary qualification in teacher education. The mediated activities involve the use of both cognitive and material tools (including traditional tools and information and communication technologies) to assist students in their studies, and the operations are the specific set of activities undertaken by students to achieve the learning outcomes of the program within the courses they study.

Engeström's (2001) third-generation CHAT interpretation argues that activity systems also include a community with multiple points of view, traditions and interests, noting that members of a community play different roles (the division of labour) within an activity system. Engeström's (2001) approach recognizes the multiple perspectives and networks of interacting activity systems, arguing that the interactions of two or more activity systems will reveal contradictions in the objects of each system. Expansive learning, he argues, occurs when the objects of activity systems are shared, or jointly constructed. Engeström (2001) identifies five principles characterizing a CHAT analysis of activity systems:

1   The tool-mediated and object-oriented activity system is the prime unit of analysis.
2   An activity system is a community of multiple points of view, traditions and interests, and members of the community play different roles (the division of labour) within the activity system.
3   Activity systems need to be understood and analyzed against their own history.
4   Activity systems are subject to contradictions arising from structural tensions within and between activity systems, and these contradictions are opportunities for change and development.
5   Expansive transformation can be achieved when the object and motive of the activity are reconceptualized in response to such contradictions.

The interactions of at least three activity systems (the AnTEP program; the Anangu school in which the AnTEP student may be employed as an AEW; and the Anangu community in which the AnTEP student lives) are evident in the following CHAT analysis of the AnTEP program.

CHAT analysis of AnTEP

A CHAT analysis of the AnTEP program's activity system identifies that the AnTEP students' and lecturers/tutors' mediated activities are complex and situated within a context in which culture, history, relations and rules impact on their actions (Wells, 1999) and outcomes across different activity systems. The components of the AnTEP activity system are as follows.

Subject

The AnTEP students are the subjects in this activity system, many of whom fulfil multiple roles as UniSA students enrolled in the AnTEP program, AEWs are employed to work in APY Lands schools, and also as members of their own Anangu family community.

Object

The Program Director and a co-author of this chapter describe the object for AnTEP students as complex and multi-layered, and at times contradictory with the object of the lecturer/tutor. For example, the object may be what students would like to complete for their studies, which may differ from what the AnTEP lecturer/tutor would like them to complete, what the teacher with whom they work may wish them to complete to enable them to teach a planned lesson, and these objects may conflict with the priorities of their community. An expansive learning approach involves a process of negotiating the object of the AnTEP activity system to achieve a shared/co-constructed object across the activity systems. For example, the AnTEP lecturer/tutor could design an assessment task that will require each student to demonstrate the learning outcomes of the course he/she is studying through the development of a lesson plan for the APY Lands school in which he/she is employed. In this scenario, the objects of each of the systems would be complementary, thereby supporting a more expansive learning approach.

Tools

AnTEP students use a variety of tools depending on the course assessment task, their local situation and their personal preferences. For example, the assessment task may well be a written report on local contact history, but students may choose how to present the task using a variety of tools from pen and paper, poster and pens, or paint, or they may choose to use ICTs such as PowerPoint to present their assignment. However, students are limited in their choice of tools either by the knowledge/capabilities of their AnTEP lecturer/tutor and/or by limited access to ICTs in some communities.

As noted in Chapter 1, tools are both material and cognitive; language is a particularly important cognitive tool in the Anangu context. However, the language of instruction in the AnTEP program is English and this presents problems for most AnTEP students who speak English as a second, third or even fourth foreign language. Research has shown that children learn best in their first language (Waller, 2012), particularly in the early years of school, until they get stronger in their second language. However, as Waller (2012) argues, non-Indigenous teachers in remote communities face the considerable challenge of not speaking the language of their students. Students are encouraged to use their own language, especially in the Cultural Studies and Community and Environment Studies strands, and when Anangu elders are invited to participate in the presentation of courses. However, the challenge for AnTEP students is that they are training to become teachers of a foreign language in a foreign language. This presents enormous difficulties for both AnTEP lecturers and students as they come to terms with both assessment tasks in courses of study and with their current roles as AEWs and their future roles as teachers.

Community

AnTEP students are members of an Anangu community, which brings with it a range of cultural and social responsibilities that can affect their studies and create conflicts in priorities. As co-author Underwood notes, some of the major factors influencing Anangu students include:

- comparatively low levels of English language, literacy and oral skills for most students;

- AnTEP students are undertaking a program based on Western academic systems of teaching and learning, which are not a close match with those of students' experiences;
- there is no strong tradition of formal academic education in most remote communities;
- students are under-prepared, given their limited access to secondary education with education at primary level often interrupted;
- there is a high incidence of ill-health among students and their communities.

Division of labour

AnTEP lecturers/tutors are cultural and academic brokers working with AnTEP students to bridge a number of divides between the western-based education program in which Anangu students are enrolled and the world of Anangu. There are many challenges that arise for both Anangu lecturers/ tutors and students when Anangu knowledge, culture and power are not reflected in their program of studies. The challenges for students are complicated further by their employment as AEWs in Anangu schools. As a result, the labour tasks are not always easily identified by the students who are both AnTEP students reliant on the broker role of lecturers/tutors to bridge the divide and employees working in Anangu schools with associated responsibilities to the teachers who have their own expectations of the students' performance and contributions to the school.

Rules

Similarly, AnTEP students are subject to varying and at times contradictory rules across the various activity systems within which they operate. As UniSA students, they need to observe the policies and procedures of a western-based tertiary university system; as AEWs, they are governed by the rules of DECD and the school in which they are employed; and as members of their Anangu community they have cultural and social responsibilities, which may conflict with the priorities associated with their roles as students and employees.

CHAT analysis of the complexity of the context in which AnTEP students are operating is depicted in Figures 3.2 and 3.3. Figure 3.4 highlights the apparent contradictions between the three activity systems and identifies opportunities for expansive learning (Engeström, 2001).

There is of course a third activity system evident; that of the Anangu community in which the AnTEP students live. An expansive system that embraces Indigenous culture within the AnTEP program and the APY Lands schools would incorporate this third system with yet another set of shared and co-constructed objects into the CHAT diagram. Such a system, as Funnell (2013) notes, creates a space where new pedagogical possibilities can be pursued by applying AEWs' cultural understanding and awareness to guide teachers in ensuring their teaching in the school embraces the wider community, while also identifying barriers and facilitators to the

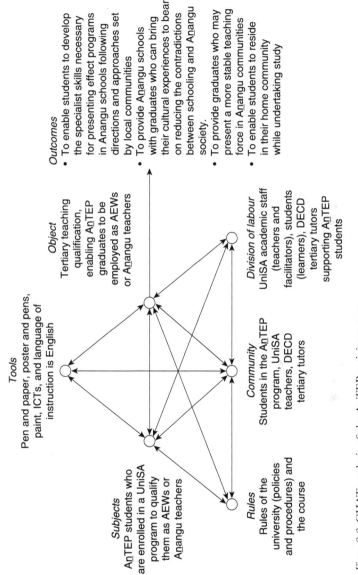

Tools
Pen and paper, poster and pens, paint, ICTs, and language of instruction is English

Object
Tertiary teaching qualification, enabling AnTEP graduates to be employed as AEWs or Anangu teachers

Outcomes
- To enable students to develop the specialist skills necessary for presenting effect programs in Anangu schools following directions and approaches set by local communities
- To provide Anangu schools with graduates who can bring their cultural experiences to bear on reducing the contradictions between schooling and Anangu society.
- To provide graduates who may present a more stable teaching force in Anangu communities
- To enable students to reside in their home community while undertaking study

Subjects
AnTEP students who are enrolled in a UniSA program to qualify them as AEWs or Anangu teachers

Community
Students in the AnTEP program, UniSA teachers, DECD tertiary tutors

Rules
Rules of the university (policies and procedures) and the course

Division of labour
UniSA academic staff (teachers and facilitators), students (learners), DECD tertiary tutors supporting AnTEP students

Figure 3.2 CHAT analysis of the AnTEP activity system

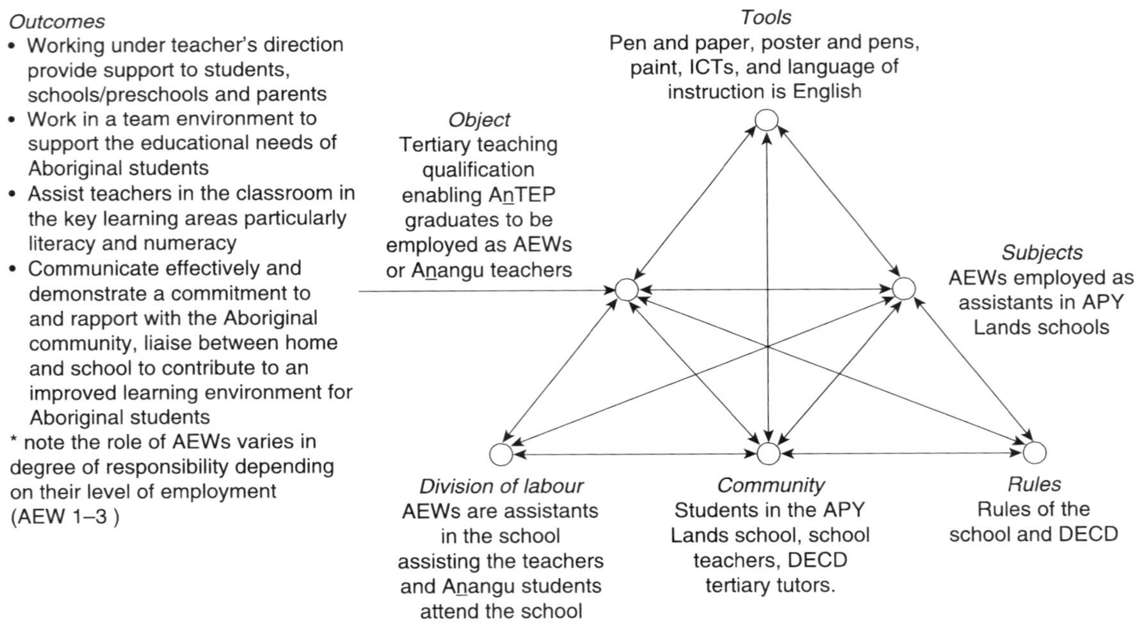

Tools
Pen and paper, poster and pens, paint, ICTs, and language of instruction is English

Subjects
AEWs employed as assistants in APY Lands schools

Rules
Rules of the school and DECD

Community
Students in the APY Lands school, school teachers, DECD tertiary tutors.

Object
Tertiary teaching qualification enabling AnTEP graduates to be employed as AEWs or Anangu teachers

Division of labour
AEWs are assistants in the school assisting the teachers and Anangu students attend the school

Outcomes
- Working under teacher's direction provide support to students, schools/preschools and parents
- Work in a team environment to support the educational needs of Aboriginal students
- Assist teachers in the classroom in the key learning areas particularly literacy and numeracy
- Communicate effectively and demonstrate a commitment to and rapport with the Aboriginal community, liaise between home and school to contribute to an improved learning environment for Aboriginal students
* note the role of AEWs varies in degree of responsibility depending on their level of employment (AEW 1–3)

Figure 3.3 CHAT analysis of the Anangu schools activity system

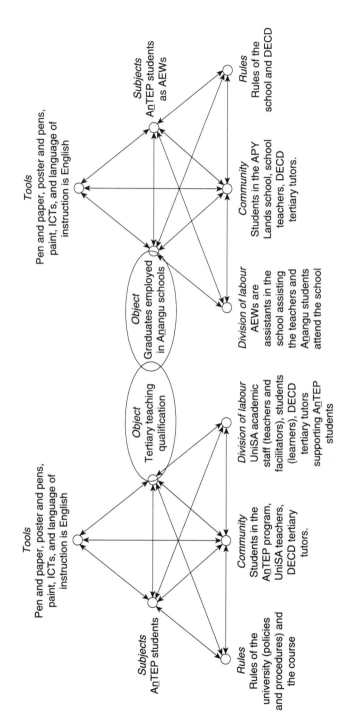

Figure 3.4 CHAT analysis of the two activity systems

Tools
Pen and paper, poster and pens,
paint, ICTs, and language of
instruction is English

Subjects
AnTEP students
as AEWs

Rules
Rules of the
school and DECD

Community
Students in the APY
Lands school, school
teachers, DECD
tertiary tutors.

Object
Graduates employed
in Anangu schools

Division of labour
AEWs are
assistants in the
school assisting
the teachers and
Anangu students
attend the school

Tools
Pen and paper, poster and pens,
paint, ICTs, and language of
instruction is English

Object
Tertiary teaching
qualification

Division of labour
UniSA academic
staff (teachers and
facilitators), students
(learners), DECD
tertiary tutors
supporting AnTEP
students

Community
Students in the
AnTEP program,
UniSA teachers,
DECD tertiary
tutors.

Subjects
AnTEP students

Rules
Rules of the
university (policies
and procedures) and
the course

embedding of Indigenous and specifically A<u>n</u>angu knowledges and contextual relevance in the curriculum.

Discussion

As the foregoing CHAT analysis identifies, there are many benefits of a program of this kind, as well as considerable challenges, not the least being the impact of Indigenous social obligations whereby social and cultural relationships are often prioritized over employment and education commitments (Jordan, 2011).

A<u>n</u>TEP students are embedded within their own communities and on the periphery of the school in which they work. The social world in which they move is complex and involves many challenges, including the feeling of being left out by the language and the system of education carried out in the school in their community. The use of online technology for supporting flexible teaching and learning is also significantly limited due to issues of isolation, poor telecommunications and low levels of computer literacy (Dyson, 2004; Young et al., 2005).

Engeström's (2001) concept of expansive learning recognizes that the multivoice aspect and historicity of activity systems inevitably lead to contradictions within and between activity systems. By analyzing the A<u>n</u>TEP program through the lens of Cultural Historical Activity Theory, the complexity of the activity system becomes readily apparent.

CHAT analysis highlights the many considerations that need to be taken into account when designing learning activities that seek to overcome such barriers. The analysis acknowledges the need to connect students, the school in which they are employed, their community and the curriculum to open up possibilities for expansive learning. The analysis also identifies a need to identify strategies for addressing the students' limited access to digital technologies, recognizing the potential of ICTs as cognitive tools to "help scaffold and stimulate thinking and knowledge creation across a range of school-based contexts" (Pea, 1987, cited in Elliott, 2009, p. 2).

CHAT exposes contradictions in the objects of different activity systems and, as noted in previous sections of this chapter, points to strategies for designing expansive learning approaches through the design and development of shared/co-constructed objects across activity systems. Osborne (2013), a former principal of Ernabella A<u>n</u>angu School, proposes an even more progressive expansive learning approach, suggesting that "the development of language, local history materials and resources . . . move beyond student benefit alone and new non-Indigenous staff [are] required to engage in community-driven learning in local language, histories and cultural engagement" (p. 179). Such an approach would involve exposing contradictions and identifying opportunities for shared/co-constructed objects across the three activity systems: the A<u>n</u>TEP program; the A<u>n</u>angu school in which the A<u>n</u>TEP student is employed; and the A<u>n</u>angu community in which the A<u>n</u>TEP student lives. Drawing on Osborne's (2013) alternative transformative pedagogy, an expansive learning approach "could shift the sense of Aboriginal identity, values and cultural norms in schools, from one that is distanced to one that is centred as essential knowledge for professional engagement in remote Aboriginal schools and communities" (p. 179).

Conclusion

Analysis of the AnTEP program through the lens of third-generation Cultural Historical Activity Theory highlights the complexity of the activity systems within which the AnTEP students are required to operate to achieve the learning objectives of the AnTEP program.

CHAT analysis provides a means by which it is possible to identify the multiple perspectives of Anangu students who interact as members of their local community, members of the UniSA AnTEP learning community and as Anangu Education Workers employed in Department for Education and Child Development schools. The challenges facing students undertaking a western-based academic curriculum, which are identified in this analysis, highlight the benefits of CHAT as an analytical tool for examining contradictions between these three activity systems (the AnTEP program; the Anangu school; and the Anangu community). Exposing these challenges and the contradictions of the motives of students and their respective stakeholder groups provides an opportunity for refashioning the curriculum to be more responsive to the student experiences in the remote context by opening up expansive learning opportunities through the effective use of emerging technologies as cultural tools.

The alternative expansive learning approach advocated by Osborne (2013) embraces language and the traditions of their culture in ways that can enable the AnTEP students to co-construct their knowledge with their communities and the schools in which they are employed. Such an approach is consistent with that advocated by Kerwin and Van Issum (2013) who argue that successful models of Indigenous education demonstrate a strong relationship with communities as being a prerequisite to better schooling outcomes.

Note

1   Anangu is the Pitjantjatjara language word for 'people' from the Anangu Pitjantjatjara Yankunytjatjara Lands of South Australia.

References

Aboriginal and Torres Strait Islander Higher Education Advisory Council (n.d).Retrieved from: http://education.gov.au/aboriginal-and-torres-strait-islander-higher-education-advisory-council (accessed 26 December 2013).

Asmar, C., Page, S., & Radloff, A. (2011). *Dispelling myths: Indigenous students' engagement with university.* Retrieved from: http://research.acer.edu.au/ausse/2/ (accessed 26 April 2013).

Dyson, L. E. (2004). Cultural issues in the adoption of information and communication technologies by Indigenous Australians. In *Proceedings of Cultural Attitudes towards Communication and Technology*, 58–71.

Elliott, A. (2009). Empowering Indigenous learners in remote Australian communities. In *Proceedings of the Prato CIRN Community Informatics Conference*, 1–20.

Engeström, Y. (2001). Expansive learning at work: Toward an activity theoretical reconceptualization. *Journal of Education and Work*, *14*(1), 133–156.

Funnell, R. (2013). Indigenous education workers: A special case of educational assistant. In R. Jorgensen, P. Sullivan, & P. Grootenboer (Eds.), *Pedagogies to enhance learning for Indigenous students: Evidence-based practice* (pp. 45–66). Singapore: Springer Science + Business Media.

James, R., & Devlin, M. (2006). *Improving Indigenous outcomes and enhancing Indigenous culture and knowledge in Australian higher education*. Canberra: Indigenous Higher Education Advisory Council.

Jonassen, D., & Rohrer-Murphy, L. (1999). Activity theory as a framework for designing constructivist learning environments. *Educational Technology Research and Development*, *47*(1), 61–79.

Jordan, K. (2011). *Work, welfare and CDEP on the Anangu Pitjantjatjara Yankunytjatjara Lands: First stage assessment*. Canberra: Centre for Aboriginal Economic Policy Research, ANU.

Kerwin, D., & Van Issum, H. (2013). An Aboriginal perspective on education: policy and practice. In R. Jorgensen, P. Sullivan, & P. Grootenboer (Eds.), *Pedagogies to enhance learning for Indigenous students: Evidence-based practice* (pp. 1–20). Singapore: Springer Science + Business Media.

Leontiev, A. N. (1978). *Activity, consciousness, and personality*. Englewood Cliffs, NJ: Prentice-Hall.

McLoughlin, C. (2000). Cultural maintenance, ownership, and multiple perspectives: Features of Web-based delivery to promote equity. *Journal of Educational Media*, *25*(3), 229–241.

Minutjukur, M. (2006). A letter to Australians. *Indigenous Politics*, *1*, 13 Sept. 2006. Retrieved from: http://newmatilda.com (accessed 26 April 2013).

Osborne, S. (2013). Learning versus education: Rethinking learning in Anangu schools. *The Australian Journal of Indigenous Education*, *42* (Special Issue 02), 171–181. doi: doi:10.1017/jie.2013.24.

Osborne, S., & Underwood, B. (2010). AnTEP Review (Anangu conversations): Community consultations (September–December 2010). Retrieved from: http://w3.unisa.edu.au/antep/review/AnTEP%20Review-Dec%202010-final-2.pdf (accessed 26 April 2013).

Ottmann, J., & White, N. (2010). Notes from the editors: Special edition. *Ngoonjook: A Journal of Australian Indigenous Issues*, *34*, 5–12.

Patton, W., Lee Hong, A., Lampert, J., Burnett, B., & Anderson, J. (2012). *Report into the retention and graduation of Aboriginal and Torres Strait Islander Students enrolled in initial teacher education*. Adelaide: More Aboriginal and Torres Strait Islander Teachers Initiative, University of South Australia.

Price, K., & Hughes, P. (2009). *What works. The work program. Improving outcomes for indigenous students: stepping up. What works in pre-service teacher education*. National Curriculum Services and the Australian Curriculum Studies Association.

Rennie, J. (2013). Connecting children, community and curriculum. In R. Jorgensen, P. Sullivan, & P. Grootenboer (Eds.) *Pedagogies to enhance learning for Indigenous students: Evidence-based practice* (pp. 154–174). Singapore: Springer Science + Business Media.

Report of the Select Committee on Pitjantjatjara Land Rights (2004). Adelaide: SA Parliament, Third Session, Fifteenth Parliament, pp. 47–49.

Vygotsky, L. S. (1978). *Mind in society*. M. Cole, V. John-Steiner, S. Scribner, & E. Souberman (Eds.). Cambridge, MA: Harvard University Press.

Waller, L. (2012). All talk, no action. *Australian Educator, 75*, 24–27.

Wells, G. (1999). *Dialogic inquiry: Towards a sociocultural practice and theory of education.* Cambridge: Cambridge University Press.

Young, M., Robertson, P., Sawyer, G., & Guenther, J. (2005). *Desert disconnections: e-learning and remote Indigenous peoples.* Report funded by Australian National Training Authority. Brisbane: Australia Flexible Learning Network.

4 Mediating learning in a blended postgraduate course

Dick Ng'ambi and Cheryl Brown

Introduction

One of the challenges of teaching a cross-continental blended postgraduate course is how to design learning activities for students with varied levels of preparedness for postgraduate studies. Thus, the potential to engage individual learners in their Zone of Proximal Development (ZPD) (see Hardman and Amory in Chapter 1) provides a way to bridge the gap between learners' actual knowledge (what they currently know) and learners' potential knowledge (what they have yet to learn). This bridge can be constructed through engagement with what Vygotsky called a more knowledgeable other (MKO) or as Hardman and Amory term it a "culturally more competent" other. This refers to someone with a better understanding or a higher ability level than the learner, with respect to a particular task, process, or concept. The MKO may be a teacher, an expert or even a peer.

In this chapter we look at how an authentic task (as outlined by Herrington in Chapter 5) can be designed to work within students' ZPD using collaborative cloud-based technologies to mediate their engagement with a MKO and thus increase their learning potential.

Description of a blended course

The module reported in this chapter is one of the four modules of a blended postgraduate programme in Information and Communication Technology (ICT) in Education at the University of Cape Town, South Africa.

The programme comprises two parts: coursework involving four modules and a minor dissertation. Students who pass the coursework with 60 per cent or more can undertake the dissertation and continue to a Master's degree. All four modules have three components; an online pre-contact task, a week face-to-face sessions and an independent project written as an academic paper. The structure of the programme is as follows: The first module, "ICTs in Education: Issues & Debates" introduces students to technology-enhanced learning and the issues that arise when technology is used to mediate learning. The second module (on which this chapter is based) "Educational ICT in developing contexts", focuses on the use of ubiquitous technologies in resource-constrained environments. The third module, "Learning, cognition and technology", introduces students to Vygotskian notion of Cultural and Historical Activity Theory (CHAT). The final module, "Online learning design", focuses on the principles and process of design of online learning interventions.

The activity system

The module "Educational ICT in developing contexts" situates the context in which the activity system is located (see Figure 4.1).

- *Subject*: The students on the course are from higher education institutions across six countries: South Africa, Namibia, Zambia, Zimbabwe, Uganda, and Nigeria. These students are full-time professionals with either a supporting role in integrating technology-enhanced learning at their institutions or are educators. Some come from a technology-based disciplinary background, others an educational background.
- *Object*: Given the focus of the module on ICT in developing contexts, one of the topics covered was philanthropy. The motivation to include this topic in the module arose from the general lack of skills at most institutions in developing contexts, to write funding proposals for ICT interventions. Thus, the goal is to design learning tasks in which students work collaboratively to respond to a call for funding, write a proposal for an ICT intervention for a hypothetical institution and present it to an authentic funder.
- *Outcome*: The significance of this module lies in its focus on the context of the learners and is premised on in-depth reflection on own context. The outcome this module seeks to realize is students' ability to critically investigate the

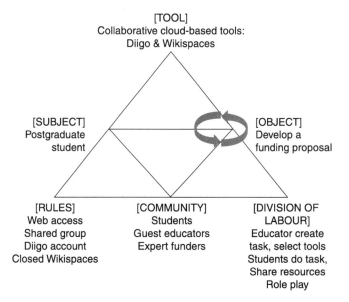

Figure 4.1 An activity system of a postgraduate module

interface between contextual educational needs, infrastructural constraints, affordances of emerging technologies and their impact on educational outcomes.

- *Tools*: Emerging technologies, whether socially focused or collaborative, are symbolic of the presence of a knowledgeable other. Even when a person engages with a technology as an individual the trace of a larger community is evident. Emerging technologies, particularly Web 2.0 technologies, have the potential to enable collaboration and co-learning depending on the purpose of use (Samuel et al., 2013). The tools chosen to mediate the subjects' realization of the object were a cloud-based social bookmarking tool, Diigo and a cloud-based collaborative writing tool, Wikispaces

- *Community*: With the advent of emerging technologies, the concept of a most knowledgeable other has evolved. Students can draw on a wider community of most knowledgeable others with the help of connected networks. In this course this includes not only the teacher and peers but also visiting lecturers and experts.

The rules in which the subject operates are the general university and course policy and processes. The division of labour is mixed between learner, peer, teacher and expert.

Mediating learning

To the extent that students enrol in the programme looking for answers to their own contextual challenges, authentic learning underpins the pedagogical design. It is imperative that students reflect on their own contexts in order to identify challenges needing to be addressed. In order to accommodate this expectation, the module is structured such that students are continuously challenged to question everything they learn through the lens of their own context.

Kaptelinin and Nardi (2009) outline three ways that emerging technologies can serve as a mediating tool in an activity system: (1) mediating the relationship between the subject and the object; (2) mediating the relationship between the subject and the community; and (3) mediating the relationship between the community and the object. In this system, all three of these apply as technology (in this case specifically cloud-based collaboration tools) mediated the students' and communities' engagement with the object as well as with each other. The use of emerging technologies transformed the object of the activity (i.e. developing a funding proposal).

Affordance analysis of tools

While tools provide a subject with possibilities to manipulate and hence transform different objects, the extent to which an object is manipulated is limited by what a tool is designed to do (Verenikina, 2010). It is therefore important to understand the affordances of tools, and appropriately match them with the object of the activity system. For example, Rambe and Ng'ambi (2012) use an Instant Messaging tool, to show how context, control, communication and the affordances of the tool enable the creation of an activity system that exploits participatory engagement to achieve the following outcomes: (1) administrative scaffolding; helping a student to manage his/her own learning in a connected environment; (2) instructional scaffolding; helping students to learn in a network; (3) social scaffolding: helping students to promote human relationships and work together; and (4) technical scaffolding: ensuring students' comfort and ease in using the system.

It needs to be emphasized that the use of emerging technologies to mediate learning presupposes that its affordances are aligned with the design of the task, are socio-culturally relevant, and the subject would focus on the object of the activity with technology being invisible.

Drawing on Bower's (2008) affordance analysis we propose systematically answering four questions in order to determine the most appropriate tools to mediate learning in an activity system:

Question 1: What is the purpose of the learning activity?

This question is premised on Hung, Lee and Lim's recommendation that any participation in a phenomenon, especially for a long time, should provide users/participants "with opportunities to create an explicit artifact and knowledge about something" (2012, p. 1076). For example, crowd learning which is a process of learning from the expertise and opinions of others, shared through online social spaces, websites, and activities (Sharples et al., 2013).

Question 2: What is the most appropriate learning task learners will do to achieve the purpose stated in question 1?

Although one of the authentic learning elements is to have an ill-defined task (see Herrington, Chapter 5), van Loon, Ros and Martens (2012) caution that the lack of structure in digital learning tasks tends to increase the risk of information overload and may cause students to lose sight of the objectives of the task. It is therefore important to ensure a good balance between ill-defined task and increased learner autonomy. According to van Loon et al., complementing learner autonomy with structure increases motivation and learning performance of students in the process of digital learning.

Question 3: Which tool has affordances that match the requirements of the task?

Hung et al. (2012) provide an example of how to match affordances of a tool with the requirements of the task, the online worlds may be appropriate if the task requires construction of communities that may have a physical localities or face-to-face interactions. Conversely, social media may be ideal for tasks involving community-collectives that include members from different localities who need to collaborate to achieve a common goal.

> Question 4: Is the task clearly outlined, tools to be used explained and rules of engagement stated?

The use of case problems has the affordance of being authentic and multi-disciplinary (Dabbagh & Dass, 2013). In their comparative study of 51 case problems, Dabbagh and Dass identified six emergent themes that characterize any constructivist-based pedagogical case problem. These are problem complexity, nature of topic, problem task or challenge, problem solving activities, type of effort and type of output.

The use of these questions to outline a task ensures clarity and, when coupled with a description of the rules of engagement it aids students' awareness of the bigger picture that underpins the learning task.

Designing a learning task

The task was a blend of pedagogical strategies that included an individual component, a group activity, role play and expert feedback and a written output. The individual component was undertaken when students were in their respective countries whereas the group activity that included the writing of a funding proposal and role-play took place during the face-to-face block session. In order to equip students with the skills to understand their contextual educational challenges across a diverse range of contexts, it was important to design a task that was grounded on knowledge that would be relevant to students' respective contexts. The assumption was that students were familiar and comfortable with their local discourse around ICTs and were able to make some sense of this as starting point.

Activity 1: Social bookmarking

Despite students' likely awareness of their own institutional contexts, the first part of the task required students to gather evidence on the discourse of ICT in their respective countries. Our thesis was that by focusing students' attention to local discourses of ICTs, we provided a language of description they (students) could draw on when exposed to the global discourse of ICTs in developing contexts. To this end, students identified, collected, described, commented on artifacts (text, video, audio, visual) that made reference to ICTs and e-learning (i.e. government policies, ministers speeches, e-learning papers, etc.) within their context.

A single course user and password were created on a social bookmarking tool, Diigo (www.diigo.com/) and students were asked to bookmark links to the resources they had found. The use of a single account was to enable the creation of a course repository which was to be useful during the proposal writing phase during face-to-face sessions. There was a match between the requirements of the task and the affordances of the tool (Diigo) which included:

- allowing users to collaboratively collect resources found on the web and store results in the cloud;
- that it works on both desktop, and mobile devices, hence enabling anyone with a mobile phone to engage. This was particularly important given that mobile phones were ubiquitous in developing contexts.
- can bookmark any online resource;
- can tag a resource;
- can highlight and add comments on a resource.

Students engaged with the resources, used tags to categorize according to the level at which resources were positioned and the ICT focus of the resources. More specifically, the task required students to add tags to a resource in Diigo, i.e. the country the resource originated from, the type of resource and whether it was a resource belonging to the macro/meso/micro level (these levels of classification was elaborated in a separate document sent to students).

The students identified different types of resources:

- *socio-economic*: for example, a White Paper on e-learning; Minister of Education speech; newspaper articles, etc.
- *organizational*: for example, Vice-Chancellor's speech; annual reports; institutional newsletter; mission statements; policy; procedures; strategic plans; staff promotion and recognition; distinguished teachers' award criteria; budget (if possible), etc.
- *pedagogical*: for example, teaching and learning policy; assessment policy; teaching & learning annual reports; review reports, etc.
- *technological*: for example, infrastructure provision to staff and students; ICT policy; Learning Management System (LMS); procedures and rules in teaching labs; bookings, etc.

At the start of this activity, each student focused on their own context and what resulted was a shared resource of artifacts on ICT discourse from students' home countries.

Activity 2: Case problem based on hypothetical institutions

In the second part of the task, the convenor created two hypothetical institutions, the University of Bia and the University of Gola, both located in

---

This is a fictitious university and does not represent any existing directly (students received a detailed handout).
  Please would you analyse their report to do the following?:

1. Identify and analyse the challenges facing or opportunities open to this institution
    1.1. At the level of the socio-cultural context
        1.1.1. identify the key social/economic/political discourses of ICTs
        1.1.2. identify the key institutional/organisational discourses of ICTs
    1.2. Describe what synergies or contradictions are inherent within the socio cultural context.
    1.3. Examine the challenges or opportunities faced by the institution according to the given key factors

---

Figure 4.2 Extract from the task

resource-constrained contexts. The details about these institutions were used to formulate the constraints of two case studies. This was useful to ensure students detached from their own institutions and yet enabled us to provide an institutional context that was as close to reality as possible. Figure 4.2 depicts an extract from the task.

The class was divided into four groups: Groups 1 and 3 were assigned the University of Gola, and Groups 2 and 4 were assigned the University of Bia. The objective of this task was to provide students with a space to engage with internal self-conversations, adjusting one's thinking with the thoughts and actions of other group members and allowing these mushed ideas to inform an action (i.e. relational agency).

The aim was to draw on the collective power of the class (i.e. the 'most knowledgeable others') and also on the artifacts on discourses of ICT that were collectively gathered in the Diigo. Students were expected to provide evidence (from the resources individually collected but collaboratively collated in Diigo) to support their responses to Figure 4.2. The response to this task was posted on Wikispaces.

This cloud-based collaborative writing tool (http://www.wikispaces.com/) was used to collaboratively to develop work on the hypothetical task. Where Diigo enabled the group to bookmark and tag together, Wikispaces enabled the following:

*   asynchronous collaboration;
*   public interface;
*   versioning capabilities to record the evolution of the site and its content;
*   opportunity to examine the various individual contributions of a group task.

In their groups, students drew on the resources captured in Diigo to provide the evidence of the local context in order to better situate the problem which the funding proposal had to address and frame an appropriate learning intervention.

The affordances of the wiki to maintain a history of a document revisions and ability to revert to previous versions, empowered students to confidently attempt the task without worrying about losing the current version.

Activity 3: Writing an authentic funding proposal

In aiming to achieve the goal of helping students understand the relationship between education, development and technology, we engaged them in a hypothetical philanthropic project, namely preparation of a proposal for funding. The third part of the task involved writing this proposal. We created a fictitious company, Technology Enhanced Learning, and adapted an expired call for funding proposal from Shuttleworth Foundation,[1] requesting that the groups respond based on the scenario from the fictitious universities of Bia and Gola. This meant that students were working on an authentic call though it had expired. This process was scaffolded through clearly outlined instructions (see Figure 4.3).

In four groups of between 3 and 4 people, students had to prepare a funding proposal according to guidelines provided and present these to the class with a 'jury' of funders listening to and assessing the proposals.

Activity 4: Role-play proposal presentation

The fourth phase of the activity was proposal presentation. This phase involved role-playing. In the role-play, each group had an opportunity to play the role of a funder, to interrogate the proposal through asking questions, and eventually make a decision whether they would fund a proposal or not, and if not, why not. The University of Gola groups were assessed by their University of Bia counterparts and vice versa. In attendance at these proposal presentations was an expert from the Shuttleworth Foundation, whose responsibility was to give expert feedback at the end of the session.

The culmination of this activity was for students to post a blog entry on their reflections on the proposal writing process with particular reference to what they had learnt.

---

2. Identify necessary or recommended investigation or research that needs to take place in this institution in order to address a problem

  2.1. Identify the key internal, short-term decision-making types of investigation to be under taken at this institution

  2.2. Identify the key scholarly research to be under taken at this institution/organisation

  2.3. Explain how the investigation / research relates to the socio cultural context as described earlier and how this will influence the micro level of use of ICTs on the ground.

Figure 4.3 Extract from a pre-funding proposal group task

In summary, though the students were familiar with their own context, in Activity 1, students searched for artifacts on local and global discourses on ICT. The focus of the activity was bookmarking resources and less about the content of the resource. This suggests that Activity 1 was a reflective mediation as students were preoccupied with affordances of Diigo in the process of accomplishing the task. In Activity 2, the hypothetical institutions case problem, shifted the focus from the tool to responding to the task (see Figure 4.2), hence a non-reflective mediation. Activity 3 on writing an authentic funding proposal in response to an authentic call for funding was an example of an authentic learning task. The use of Wikispaces allowed group members to collaborate in the writing of the proposal. The use of a discussion tool in the Wikispaces enabled reflective engagement. The hypothetical case problem provided a realistic context in which the proposal was written. In Activity 4, groups took turns to role-play funder and were required to motivate their decisions. As an authentic expert from the Foundation that originated the call for funding, gave feedback, exemplifies a typical authentic learning task.

The learning activity shows how learners were initially engaged as individuals, then as a class, then in groups, were provided with expert feedback and finally reflective individually on the process.

Reflections

As Rambe and Ng'ambi (2011) suggest, expansive learning processes are evidenced through a change in social practices such as establishing new connections within an activity system. The process of finding and establishing these new connections between ideas or concepts with support from other sources (i.e. most knowledgeable other) is therefore instrumental in fostering an expansive activity system. Put simply, it can be argued that as students reflect on their own practice, and assess their pedagogical knowledge through engagement with MKO, there is potential for a change to their own education practice. According to Verenikina (2010), when people engage in processes of social construction of knowledge, they acquire the methods of collaborative performance and use them in their independent performance later. It can be inferred from Verenikina's work that, like other social practices, education practices tend to be easily reproduced, because learning is also acquired through the process of modelling either purposefully or unintentionally.

Although the learning activities were interrelated, students were introduced to the task in stages so that they could make their own connections between ideas and concepts. As each step as it unfolded, students began to see the linkages and could look back at how these developed in their final reflections.

> The lab sessions were practical and I was able to learn how to use Wikispaces to categorize my artifacts. By the end of this day, I had begun to understand why I had collected my artifacts through the group activity designed to help us understand the discourse by letting us do a hands on approach to analysis doing the group activity.
>
> (S4)

One of the unintended consequences of the teaching this module, is the modelling of teaching with technologies. Although this is described as unintended, it is consistent with what Edwards (2007) described as the subject being changed by the object, thereby impacting on future actions:

> The saying that we teach the way we are/were taught is very true. After working on Wikispaces and creating my own mobile site, I am more confident to introduce and expose my own students to such technology, these tools encourage student creativity and the sharing of knowledge.
>
> (S1)

It can be inferred from the above statement that students exhibited capacity to align internal thoughts and make adjustments during the mediation process which in this case involved making a decision to change how they taught.

This demonstrates the potential for expansive learning, as it involves, as Rambe and Ng'ambi (2011) note, student engagement in a transformative learning processes that trigger changes in their ways of reasoning.

This has ramifications for technology-enhanced learning as the more educators acquire pedagogical knowledge; they change how they teach, hence disrupting traditional methods of teaching and disrupting an activity system. To the extent that the disruption is not the goal of the activity system but an unintended outcome it is therefore a contradiction. Another contradiction is that despite the number of institutions' staff development initiatives, there is no corresponding impact on teaching and learning practices (Sharpe, Beetham, & De Freitas, 2010; Price & Kirkwood, 2014). As Bertolo (2008) advocates, educators cannot be expected to provide students with an individualized learning experience when they themselves have never experienced one. This is particularly relevant in the postgraduate programme where participants are educators at their respective institutions. It can be inferred from this that mediating learning in this context may involve two levels: individual knowledge acquisition and the social practice level.

For others, it was the affordance of the tool, in particular, Wikispaces, to trace revisions that fostered the relational agency. The opportunity to become a co-producer of knowledge was also noted: "I enjoyed the opportunity of tracking every revision that is made to the Wikispace, also there is no frustration of losing your work by deleting unless by the creator of the space" (S7).

The learning activities were designed so that an individual learner needed to revisit their own assumptions, listen/read about thoughts of others, watch their actions, make interpretations and take action in response to those interpretations. Some were able to make explicit this internal adjustment of thought:

> I also learned about funding proposal writing, what the funders look for and how to write the proposal. The group task was quite enlightening especially when we did the presentations and we were required to critique each other over the proposal also helped to give a better understanding of the exercise.
>
> (S6)

The above statement is significant in that it reflects on the experience of writing a funding proposal in response to an authentic call, and obtaining feedback from an expert who authored the call, and evaluated the 'official' proposals. Although the student proposals were presented in a role-play with the expert observer, to the extent that learning is reported to have happened, it confirms that the learning activities mediated learning in a blended postgraduate program.

The external examiner, who assessed the module, remarked on the assessment as "extremely well written" and said "students [were] encouraged to work at the interface or overlap between socio-cultural perspectives and educational perspectives". To the extent that the examiner who reviewed the module found it to have been designed at an intersection of socio-cultural and educational perspectives, in this module, learning is a process of participating in cultural practices and shared learning activities. In order for this participation to be meaningful, an authentic learning pedagogy, if properly done, has the potential to achieve a transformative transactional relationship of the subject and the object. The feedback from students, reported in this section, show that this goal was achieved to some degree.

Sfard's (1998) use of metaphors to distinguish between two types of learning—an acquisition metaphor and a participatory metaphor—provides another point of comparison. The acquisition metaphor involves video lectures, recommended readings and staged assessment, and is currently the most dominant approach in higher education (Sharples et al., 2013). According to Oshima, Oshima, and Matsuzawa (2012), in an acquisition metaphor, knowledge is viewed as a property or capacity of an individual's mind. In a participatory metaphor (the metaphor on which this task design is based), learning is a process of participating in cultural practices and shared learning activities. It is in the context of this participatory metaphor that the use of emerging technologies has had a strong influence. The design of an activity system modelled on this participatory metaphor, required careful thought about the interrelationships between subject, mediating tool, context, control and communication.

Teaching in the ZPD implies co-construction of knowledge between the teacher and the learner (and, in our system, peers and experts) and the subsequent transformation of actual to potential knowledge through collaboration and co-learning with most knowledgeable others (Verenikina, 2008).

Conclusion

This chapter has reported on the role of emerging technologies in mediating learning in a postgraduate program. It has exemplified the need to ensure that the tool chosen to mediate learning is appropriate and has demonstrated how the use of an affordance analysis approach has the potential to address this challenge. The chapter has also shown how using technology can be used as a tool for collaboration with a 'most knowledgeable other' to enable meaningful learning within a learner's ZPD, and provides scope for expansive learning to occur. It has also been demonstrated that emerging technologies can create environments which enable mediation between the subject and the object; subject and the community; the community and the object. While the activity systems theory provides a framework with which to visualize these interactions, the context, reason to engage, rules of engagement, and access to the tools need also to form part of an authentic task design. During these interactions, the subject, object and community are transformed. Thus, this chapter has provided a way of using emerging technologies to design authentic learning tasks that mediate learning within a learner's ZPD through a most knowledgeable other in a postgraduate course at a higher education institution.

Note

1 See www.shuttleworthfoundation.org/.

References

Bertolo, E. (2008). Web 2.0: Unlearned lessons from previous virtual learning environments. *Bioscience Education*, 11. Retrieved from: http://journals.heacademy.ac.uk/doi/pdf/10.3108/beej.11.7

Bower, M. (2008). Affordance analysis: Matching learning tasks with learning technologies. *Educational Media International*, *45*(1), 3–15.

Burnapp, D. (2011). Developments in information and communications technology (ICT) and the growth of E-learning. In D. Burnapp et al. (Eds.), *The strategic implications of different forms of international collaboration in Higher Education*. Northampton: The University of Northampton. Retrieved from: http://nectar.northampton.ac.uk/3700/36/Burnapp20113700g.pdf.

Dabbagh, N., & Dass, S. (2013). Case problems for problem-based pedagogical approaches: A comparative analysis. *Computers & Education*, *64*, 161–174. Retrieved from: www.sciencedirect.com/science/article/pii/S0360131512002291.

Edwards, A. (2007). Relational agency in professional practice: A CHAT analysis. Retrieved from: www.chat.kansai-u.ac.jp/english/publications/actio/pdf/1_Edwards.pdf.

Graham, C. K., Cagiltay, J., Craner, B. L., & Duffy, T. M. (2000). *Teaching in a web-based distance environment: An evaluation summary based on four courses*. (CRLT Technical Report No.13-00). Bloomington, IN: WW Wright Education.

Herrington, J., Reeves, T. C., & Oliver, R. (2010). *A guide to authentic e-learning*. New York: Routledge.

Hung, D., Lee, S-S., & Lim, K. Y. T. (2012). Authenticity in learning for the twenty-first century: Bridging the formal and the informal. *Education Technology Research and Development*, *60*, 1071–1091. DOI 10.1007/s11423-012-9272-3.

Kaptelinin, V., & Nardi, A. B. (2009). *Acting with technology: Activity theory and interaction design*. Cambridge, MA: MIT Press.

Khoza, S. B. (2011). Who promotes web-based teaching and learning in higher education? *Progressio*, *33*, 155–170.

Oshima, J., Oshima, R., & Matsuzawa, Y. (2012). Knowledge Building Discourse Explorer: A social network analysis application for knowledge building discourse. *Education Technology Research and Development*, *60*, 903–921. DOI 10.1007/s11423-012-9265-2.

Price, L., & Kirkwood, A. T. (2014). Using technology for teaching and learning in higher education: A critical review of the role of evidence in informing practice. *Higher Education Research & Development 33*(3), 549–564. DOI 10.1080/07294360.2013.841643.

Rambe, P., & Ng'ambi, D. (2011). Towards an information sharing pedagogy: A case of using Facebook in a large first year class. *Informing Science: The International Journal of an Emerging Transdiscipline, 14.*

Rambe, P., & Ng'ambi, D. (2012). Using Ubiquitous Technologies to cognitively scaffold academically underprepared learners: Student contextualized learning in mobile learning environments. In *IADIS International Conference on Internet Technologies & Society (ITS 2012)*. Eds. P. Kommers, T. Issa & P. Isaías. Perth, Australia, 28–30 November.

Sfard, A. (1998). On two metaphors for learning and the dangers of choosing just one. *Educational Researcher, 27*(2), 4–13. Retrieved from: http://people.ucsc.edu/~gwells/Files/Courses_Folder/ED%20261%20Papers/Sfard_ER1998.pdf.

Sharpe, R., Beetham, H., & de Freitas, S. (Eds.). (2010). *Rethinking learning for a digital age: How learners are shaping their own experiences*. London: Routledge.

Sharples, M., McAndrew, P., Weller, M., Ferguson, R., FitzGerald, E., Hirst, T., & Gaved, M. (2013). *Innovating pedagogy 2013: Open University Innovation Report 2*. Milton Keynes: The Open University.

van Loon, A-M., Ros, A., & Martens, R. (2012). Motivated learning with digital learning tasks: What about autonomy and structure? *Education Technology Research and Development, 60*, 1015–1032. DOI 10.1007/s11423-012-9267-0.

Verenikina, I. (2008). Scaffolding and learning: its role in nurturing new learners. Retrieved from: http://tinyurl.com/odyb3db.

Verenikina, I. (2010). Vygotsky in twenty-first-century research. In *Proceedings of World Conference on Educational Multimedia, Hypermedia and Telecommunications 2010* (pp. 16–25). Chesapeake, VA: AACE. Retrieved from: www.editlib.org/p/34614 (accessed February 17, 2014).

Part II

Authentic learning

5 Introduction to authentic learning

Jan Herrington

Introduction

Learning in formal contexts rarely encompasses the context and supports that are provided in solving real-world problems. In everyday life, people solve problems and learn new and better ways to do things by assessing a problem and then using their existing knowledge together with the context, resources and means available to them. They do not always do this in a logical, sequential manner, sometimes simply trying one solution based on the best evidence available, then another, until a successful outcome is achieved. Authentic learning is based on such an approach. Through observing problem solving in the real world, and situating learning in the context of its future use, authentic learning emerged as a viable model for facilitating learning.

Authentic learning is best described as a pedagogical model. It is not a learning theory in its own right. Rather, it is an approach that can be adopted by teachers to design effective and engaging learning environments for their students to enable them to learn. Unlike other instructional design approaches such as the systems approach (cf. Gagné, Briggs, & Wager, 1992, pp. 403–404), or the generic ADDIE approach (Branch, 2009), authentic learning does not seek to teach concepts and skills in a formal setting. Instead, it focuses on aligning the conditions and enablers for learning, where the task governs the activities that students perform, the teacher's role is a supportive one, and the outcome is a genuine and worthwhile product. It is the students who decide upon the most effective pathways to learning, as they engage collaboratively in the creation of genuine, worthwhile and meaningful artefacts.

The framework of authentic learning has grown out of a body of work conducted largely since the late 1980s, where educators began considering the model of learning exemplified in apprenticeships, and tried to distil the effective elements of the master/apprentice into a new model of cognitive apprenticeships. Brown, Collins and Duguid (1989) were among the first researchers to use the ideas to produce a proposal for a model of instruction that had implications for all sectors of education: the theory of *situated cognition*, or *situated learning*. They called for a model of instruction to operationalise these theories for the classroom, a call which has resulted in the pedagogical model of authentic learning. A framework of authentic learning was developed, applied first to multimedia learning environments (Herrington & Oliver, 2000) and then more generically to learning and e-learning environments in higher education (Herrington & Herrington, 2006; Herrington, Reeves, & Oliver, 2010). This framework can be used to guide the design of innovative authentic learning by considering the nine key elements of its design.

Elements of authentic learning and authentic tasks

The following are the elements of authentic learning and authentic tasks:

1   *An authentic context that reflects the way the knowledge will be used in real life*: In designing technology-based learning environments, the context needs to be all-embracing, to provide the purpose and motivation for learning, and to provide a sustained and complex learning environment that can be explored at length (e.g., Brown et al., 1989; Reeves & Reeves, 1997).

2   *Authentic tasks*: The learning environment needs to provide ill-defined tasks that have real-world relevance, and that present a single complex task to be completed over a sustained period of time, rather than a series of shorter disconnected activities (Bransford, Vye, Kinzer, & Risko, 1990; Brown et al., 1989; Lebow & Wager, 1994). Subsequent research on characteristics of authentic learning tasks (Herrington, Reeves, Oliver, & Woo, 2004) proposed further refinement of the nature of such tasks, specifically that they are: ill-defined, requiring students to define the tasks and sub-tasks needed to complete the activity; investigated by students over a sustained period of time; can be integrated and applied across different subject areas and lead beyond domain-specific outcomes; seamlessly integrated with assessment; create accomplished products valuable in their own right; and allow competing solutions and diversity of outcome.

3   *Access to expert performances and the modelling of processes*: In order to provide expert performances, the learning environment needs to provide access to expert thinking and the modelling of processes, access to learners in various levels of expertise, and access to the social periphery or the observation of real-life episodes (Brown et al., 1989; Collins, Brown, & Newman, 1989; Lave & Wenger, 1991). The facility of the Internet to create global communities of learners, who can interact readily via social networking, enables countless opportunities for the sharing of narratives and stories.

4   *Multiple roles and perspectives*: In order for students to be able to investigate the learning environment from more than a single perspective, it is important to enable and encourage students to explore different perspectives on the topics from various points of view (e.g., Collins et al., 1989; Spiro, Feltovich, Jacobson, & Coulson, 1991).

5   *Collaborative construction of knowledge*: The opportunity for users to collaborate is an important design element, particularly for students who may be learning at a distance. Collaboration can be encouraged through appropriate tasks and communication technology (e.g., Brown et al., 1989; Collins et al., 1989).

6 *Reflection*: In order to provide opportunities for students to reflect on their learning, the learning environment needs to provide an authentic context and task, as described earlier, to enable meaningful reflection. It also needs to provide non-linear organisation to enable students to readily return to any element of the site if desired, and the opportunity for learners to compare themselves with experts and other learners in varying stages of accomplishment (e.g., Boud, Keogh, & Walker, 1985; Kemmis, 1985; Schön, 1987).

7 *Articulation*: In order to produce a learning environment capable of providing opportunities for articulation, the tasks need to incorporate inherent—as opposed to constructed—opportunities to articulate, collaborative groups to enable articulation, and the public presentation of argument to enable defence of the position (e.g., Collins et al., 1989; Edelson, Pea, & Gomez, 1996; Lave & Wenger, 1991).

8 *Coaching and scaffolding*: In order to accommodate a coaching and scaffolding role principally by the teacher (but also by other students), the learning environment needs to provide collaborative learning, where more able partners can assist with scaffolding and coaching, as well as the means for the teacher to support learning via appropriate communication technologies (e.g., Collins et al., 1989; Greenfield, 1984).

9 *Authentic assessment*: To provide integrated and authentic assessment of student learning, the learning environment needs to provide the opportunity for students to be effective performers with acquired knowledge, and to craft polished performances or products in collaboration with others. It also requires assessment to be seamlessly integrated with the activity, and to provide appropriate criteria for scoring varied products (e.g., Reeves & Okey, 1996; Wiggins, 1993; cf. Herrington, Reeves, & Oliver, 2014, pp. 403–404).

The elements of this framework are best considered as *guidelines* for design rather than a checklist of components to be ticked off as accomplished. It is better to think of each element as one extreme of a continuum (such as authentic vs academic, collaborative vs individual, authentic assessment vs norm-referenced testing), giving an overall trend of the learning environment's authenticity.

Issues in designing and implementing authentic learning designs

One of the most difficult challenges of designing an authentic learning environment is to be able to imagine and then design an authentic context and task. Ideally, a whole semester of work should contribute to the investigation of a single significant problem. For example, student can engage in complex and multi-faceted explorations of content areas, as they are assigned to roles such as: an historian researching the life of a real soldier in World War I (Morrissey, 2006); a member of a space agency planning a mission to Mars (Reeves, Laffey, & Marlino, 1997); a professional lawyer working in a firm in a small town (Barton, McKellar, & Maharg, 2007); an accomplished researcher employed to investigate the closure of a school in a rural community (Angus & Gray, 2002); a group mapping media and communication industry establishments in a large city (Collis, Foth, & Schroeter, 2009); an editor of an online journal on North American fiction and film (Fitzsimmons, 2006); an expert consultant employed to investigate imbalance in ecosystem (Brickell & Herrington, 2006); or a practising doctor conducting cervical screening tests (Keppell et al., 2003). Designing such tasks requires creativity and deep reflection on where and how the knowledge in the subject matter of the curriculum would be implemented to solve real problems.

Implicit in the design of authentic environments is the importance of crafting complex tasks that enable multiple and diverse outcomes. Such tasks cannot be completed with a simple Google search where students use the Web to *search* rather than *research* (Brabazon, 2007). Students are encouraged to create meaningful products that take much time and effort in collaboration with others, that are refined and polished until they are worthy of public presentation and publication.

When designing authentic tasks, it is easy to misconstrue the approach, and to conclude that it is enough to simply have a semblance of reality, or to include multiple realistic examples, so that students might be informed of how the knowledge of skills might be used in real situation. This approach is of course helpful, but it would not be considered authentic in the manner described here.

Another misconception about authentic tasks include word problems, frequently used in mathematics and the sciences such as: If three-quarters of a pizza is shared among four people, how much does each person get? Students often perceive these problems as artificial and not really worth solving. Bottge and Hasselbring (1993) were scathing of these types of problems noting that they typically "include key words such as *in all* or *how many more* that can trigger a specific number operation— unlike real problems that offer no such clues; and there is usually only a single correct answer, which takes only a few minutes to solve" (p. 36).

Similarly, most computer games fail the authenticity test on a number of counts. Games have the capacity to reflect real-world contexts and endeavours, using realistic 3D images that enable users to readily engage within their worlds. However, most immersive and real-world type games are designed for recreational purposes and learning becomes incidental to their purpose. While tacit learning may indeed occur, the failure to engage players in genuine productivity is the key weakness in computer games when measured against authentic learning criteria.

Over-simplification of complex knowledge and skills is another mistake often made in the design of authentic learning. In some cases, educators have access to detailed web-based resources such as simulated workplaces, which have great potential to be used effectively for learning. Such complex environment requires complex responses, but some teachers simplify and break down the issues for students by providing short answer questions and prompts for what to look out for. Spiro et al. criticised such oversimplification, claiming:

> [It] makes it easier for teachers to teach, for students to take notes and prepare for their tests, for test-givers to construct and grade tests, and for authors to write texts. The result is a massive 'conspiracy of convenience'.
>
> (1987, p. 180)

Conclusion

Authentic learning is appealing as a pedagogical approach because it situates knowledge in realistic contexts, and it challenges students with realistic tasks, requiring them to think and problem-solve as they might in the real situation. It requires the creation of meaningful products that are worthy of the investment of time and effort that students put into them, and they can be shared and published to contribute to knowledge.

Designing and developing authentic learning are often challenging for teachers in higher education, who need to commit philosophically and practically to the approach. The importance of professional learning and collaborative effort cannot be over-estimated in this regard. This volume provides further chapters and case examples where teachers have accepted the challenge of introducing authentic learning, and their practical and theoretical insights are described in more detail, including stories of how students move from learning *about* a profession, to becoming actively engaged and reflective practitioners.

References

Angus, M., & Gray, J. (2002). *Description of a situated learning approach in a research methods postgraduate subject.* Retrieved from: http://www.learningdesigns.uow.edu.au/exemplars/info/LD13/.

Barton, K., McKellar, P., & Maharg, P. (2007). Authentic fictions: Simulation, professionalism and legal learning. *Clinical Law Review, 14,* 143–193.

Bottge, B. A., & Hasselbring, T. S. (1993). Taking word problems off the page. *Educational Leadership, 50*(7), 36–38.

Boud, D., Keogh, R., & Walker, D. (1985). Promoting reflection in learning: A model. In D. Boud, R. Keogh, & D. Walker (Eds.), *Reflection: Turning experience into learning* (pp. 18–40). London: Kogan Page.

Brabazon, T. (2007). *The University of Google: Education in the [post] information age.* Hampshire: Ashgate.

Branch, R. M. (2009). *Instructional design: The ADDIE approach.* New York: Springer.

Bransford, J. D., Vye, N., Kinzer, C., & Risko, V. (1990). Teaching thinking and content knowledge: Toward an integrated approach. In B. F. Jones & L. Idol (Eds.), *Dimensions of thinking and cognitive instruction* (pp. 381–413). Hillsdale, NJ: Lawrence Erlbaum.

Brickell, G., & Herrington, J. (2006). Scaffolding learners in authentic problem-based e-learning environments: The Geography Challenge. *Australasian Journal of Educational Technology, 22*(4), 531–547. Retrieved from: http://www.ascilite.org.au/ajet/ajet522/brickell.html.

Brown, J. S., Collins, A., & Duguid, P. (1989). Situated cognition and the culture of learning. *Educational Researcher, 18*(1), 32–42.

Collins, A., Brown, J. S., & Newman, S. E. (1989). Cognitive apprenticeship: Teaching the crafts of reading, writing, and mathematics. In L. B. Resnick (Ed.), *Knowing, learning and instruction: Essays in honour of Robert Glaser* (pp. 453–494). Hillsdale, NJ: LEA.

Collis, C., Foth, M., & Schroeter, R. (2009). The Brisbane media map: Participatory design and authentic learning to link students and industry. *Learning Inquiry, 3*(3), 143–155.

Edelson, D. C., Pea, R. D., & Gomez, L. (1996). Constructivism in the collaboratory. In B. G. Wilson (Ed.), *Constructivist learning environments: Case studies in instructional design* (pp. 151–164). Englewood Cliffs, NJ: Educational Technology Publications.

Fitzsimmons, J. (2006). Speaking snake: Authentic learning and the study of literature. In A. Herrington & J. Herrington (Eds.), *Authentic learning environments in higher education* (pp. 162–171). Hershey, PA: Information Science Publishing.

Gagné, R. M., Briggs, L. J., & Wager, W. W. (1992). *Principles of instructional design* (4th ed.). Orlando, FL: Harcourt, Brace, Jovanovich.

Greenfield, P. M. (1984). A theory of the teacher in the learning activities of everyday life. In B. Rogoff & J. Lave (Eds.), *Everyday cognition: Its development in social context* (pp. 117–138). Cambridge, MA: Harvard University Press.

Herrington, A., & Herrington, J. (Eds.). (2006). *Authentic learning environments in higher education*. Hershey, PA: Information Science Publishing.

Herrington, J., & Oliver, R. (2000). An instructional design framework for authentic learning environments. *Educational Technology Research and Development, 48*(3), 23–48.

Herrington, J., Reeves, T. C., & Oliver, R. (2010). *A guide to authentic e-learning*. New York: Routledge.

Herrington, J., Reeves, T. C., & Oliver, R. (2014). Authentic learning environments. In J. M. Spector, M. D. Merrill, J. Elen, & M. J. Bishop (Eds.), *Handbook of research on educational communications and technology* (4th ed., pp. 401–412). New York: Springer.

Herrington, J., Reeves, T. C., Oliver, R., & Woo, Y. (2004). Designing authentic activities in web-based courses. *Journal of Computing in Higher Education, 16*(1), 3–29.

Kemmis, S. (1985). Action research and the politics of reflection. In D. Boud, R. Keogh, & D. Walker (Eds.), *Reflection: Turning experience into learning* (pp. 139–163). London: Kogan Page.

Keppell, M., Gunn, J., Hegarty, K., Madden, V., O'Connor, V., Kerse, N. et al. (2003). Using authentic patient interactions to teach cervical screening to medical students. In D. Lassner & C. McNaught (Eds.), *World Conference on Educational Multimedia, Hypermedia and Telecommunications 2003* (pp. 1439–1446). Norfolk, VA: AACE.

Lave, J., & Wenger, E. (1991). *Situated learning: Legitimate peripheral participation*. Cambridge: Cambridge University Press.

Lebow, D., & Wager, W. W. (1994). Authentic activity as a model for appropriate learning activity: Implications for emerging instructional technologies. *Canadian Journal of Educational Communication, 23*(3), 231–144.

Morrissey, P. (2006). Not just a name on the wall. Retrieved from: www.notjustanameonawall. com/.

Reeves, T. C., Laffey, J. M., & Marlino, M. R. (1997). Using technology as cognitive tools: Research and praxis. In R. Kevill, R. Oliver, & R. Phillips (Eds.), *What works and why: Proceedings of the 14th Annual Conference of the Australian Society for Computers in Learning in Tertiary Education* (pp. 269–275). Perth, WA: Curtin University.

Reeves, T. C., & Okey, J. R. (1996). Alternative assessment for constructivist learning environments. In B. G. Wilson (Ed.), *Constructivist learning environments: Case studies in instructional design* (pp. 191–202). Englewood Cliffs, NJ: Educational Technology Publications.

Reeves, T. C., & Reeves, P. M. (1997). Effective dimensions of interactive learning on the World Wide Web. In B. H. Khan (Ed.), *Web-based instruction* (pp. 59–66). Englewood Cliffs, NJ: Educational Technology Publications.

Schön, D. (1987). *Educating the reflective practitioner: Toward a new design for teaching and learning in the professions*. San Francisco: Jossey-Bass.

Spiro, R. J., Feltovich, P. J., Jacobson, M. J., & Coulson, R. L. (1991). Cognitive flexibility, constructivism, and hypertext: Random access instruction for advanced knowledge acquisition in ill-structured domains. *Educational Technology, 31*(5), 24–33.

Spiro, R. J., Vispoel, W. P., Schmitz, J. G., Samarapungavan, A., & Boeger, A. E. (1987). Knowledge acquisition for application: Cognitive flexibility and transfer in complex content domains. In B. K. Britton, & S. M. Glynn (Eds.), *Executive control processes in reading* (Vol. 31, pp. 177–199). Hillsdale, NJ: Lawrence Erlbaum Associates.

Wiggins, G. (1993). *Assessing student performance: Exploring the purpose and limits of testing.* San Francisco: Jossey-Bass.

6 Learning to conduct research by doing

A case study in a postgraduate health education program

Brenda Leibowitz, Walter Liebrich, Ilse Meyer, Chivaugn Gordon, and Carina de Kock

Introduction

With the advent of mass participation in higher education and the internationalization of post-graduate studies, there are a number of challenges for students participating in master's and doctoral programs in the social sciences. These might include some or all of the following: distance from the institution where the program is taught, leading to isolation from peers and a community of practice; having to make the transition from one academic level to another, possibly at an institution where the academic demands are greater than at the previous institution; having to make the transition from one discipline to another, for example from the health sciences to health science education (Koen & Bester, 2009) or from the health sciences to higher education in general (Adendorff, 2011); having to manage the load of professional and family commitments in additional to study commitments (Pugsley, Brigley, Allery, & MacDonald, 2008; McCormack, 2009); and having to study in a language other than one's own.

The idea of having to design, implement and report upon a research project is particularly daunting for students, especially when one is crossing domains, for example, from quantitative to qualitative research, or from an experimental design, to an interpretive approach. There could be an expectation that coursework master's and doctoral programs would ameliorate these challenges, where they do exist. Despite the support of these taught programs, however, students continue to require substantial scaffolding and guidance. One response to these challenges is teaching via an authentic learning approach, in which students work with knowledge in order to produce artefacts that can be used in non-classroom settings, for real purposes and real audiences, with a strong reliance on experiential and collaborative learning. Chapter 5 of this volume by Jan Herrington provides a more extended definition of authentic learning, and its roots in situated learning and the apprenticeship model. One reason why authentic learning is particularly suitable for teaching research methods is that in addition to a conceptual dimension, research in the social sciences has a strong practice-based dimension. Like literacy practices (Barton & Hamilton, 2000), research as practice is embedded in the social, is mediated by text, and is purposeful.

In this chapter we explore how a postgraduate module on research in health science education based on an authentic learning approach can be of benefit to both the lecturer and the students. In doing so, we will show how within this approach, issues of role and identity can be complex, requiring careful attention and planning.

The study on which this chapter is based was conducted as a module entitled "Education Research for Change". This is a 10-credit module that forms part of an MPhil on Health Sciences Education at the University of Stellenbosch, South Africa. The module sits alongside an additional and more formal academic research module, in which students are given tuition on quantitative and qualitative research methods, in preparation for their 60-credit major research assignment the following year. The module is conceived as a form of apprenticeship, where students are coached or scaffolded (Collins, Brown, & Holum, 1991) into the role of educator-researchers by being given structured opportunities to participate in a team research project as well as to undertake a very basic research project of their own. By "learning from experience", and reflecting on this learning, health science students would be "thinking about learning" (Boud, 1993, p. 39) – an essential requirement of a program on health science education. They would also gradually be inducted into the role, identity, and practices of being a researcher. The chapter begins by describing the pedagogic design of the module, elaborating on the research design components where necessary.

Module design

The module is nested within an MPhil program which has one contact week a year, and assignments and discussions conducted for the rest of the year via a Learning Management System, Blackboard. The compulsory module, "Educational Research for Change", is offered in the first year of the degree. It is introduced to students over seven hours during the contact week at the beginning of the academic year. Students submit assignments and participate in tutorials during the contact week and during the allocated time for the module, later in the same year. During the contact session, students are orientated to the module and are invited to participate in research on the module. They are also provided with a research proposal written by the lecturer, explaining its implications for students. The proposal, which has been reviewed and approved by the faculty's ethics committee, contains the basic design of a study, in which the students are both subjects and co-researchers, and if they wish, they can participate in the analysis and writing up of the research, together with the lecturer, in the form of a publishable article.

The students sign the ethical consent forms, then conduct the first data-gathering activity: drawing a map of themselves as students on the module, using smiling and unsmiling faces, labels and arrows to show the various anticipated positive and negative influences that can bear on their study. This is an adaptation of the use of Participatory Learning and Action (PLA) techniques, which are suitable for participatory research and for eliciting information quickly, and for providing the basis for group discussion (Bozalek & Biersteker, 2010; Grant & Hurd, 2010).

After discussing their drawings in groups of three, students are provided with brief training on how to conduct one-on-one interviews about their prior learning and their expectations of the module, with a pre-determined semi-structured questionnaire designed by the lecturer. They divide into pairs and interview each other. They then debrief on this experience, and are given guidance on data coding and report writing. For the first assignment in the module, students post a short report and transcript of the interview each conducted on the discussion forum so that they have access to all the transcripts and reports. The short reports are assessed by the lecturer, and feedback is sent to each student privately. During the allotted time for the module later in the year, the students post a draft codebook based on their analyses of the interview transcripts, with definitions and examples of each code on the discussion forum. They discuss their codes with each other. This gives them the opportunity to reconsider how they will code all the data in their final reports. The lecturer assesses the codebooks and each student receives his or her own marked codebook privately. As the final part of the first assignment, each student writes a report based on all the drawings and the interviews, which is posted into the assignments section of Blackboard. An important component of these reports is the recommendations for how the lecturers could re-structure the program, to take into account students' experiences. These are also assessed and returned to the students.

To facilitate their transition into the discipline of health science education, students take an assignment they wrote in another module ("Contextualizing Health Science Education") to the University's Writing Centre for discussion. They are required to discuss the assignment with a peer in the class and write a short report detailing what they learnt from the various forms of feedback they experienced giving and receiving (see Leibowitz, 2013, for more information about this aspect of the module). This assignment is designed to foster the students' metacognitive awareness of their writing approaches, their ability to be reflective as a writer, and to share critiques and reflections with others.

In preparation for the third assignment, students are required to share with one other student in the module and with the lecturer, ideas they have about conducting a very basic data gathering activity, and are given feedback via email. Subsequent to this they gather the data and write it up as a report, which is then assessed, and feedback is given via the Blackboard system. Students are required to append to the final research report a few paragraphs reflecting on their experience on the module and on what they have learnt. The assignments, the timing and weighting of the score against the total for the module are summarized in Table 6.1.

Analyzing the data

After the module was concluded, four students elected to collaborate with the lecturer to analyze the data and write this chapter. Several others indicated that

Table 6.1 Summary of data collection, discussion and assessment activities for ERC module

Activity	Timing	Weighting
Draw PLA map	Contact session	–
Conduct interview about prior learning and expectations	Contact session	–
Assignment 1A: Report on interview	February	10
Assignment 1B: Code interview transcripts and PLA drawings	August	10
Discuss codes online	August	–
Assignment 1C: Final report on all interview transcripts and drawings	August	30
Assignment 2: Report on (peer and Writing Centre) feedback to essay on contextualizing health science education	April	10
Discussion with peer and lecturer on plans for research piece (two communications)	September	–
Assignment 3: Final assignment on data collected in own teaching setting and final paragraph reflecting on the module	September	40

they would have liked to contribute, but were feeling too pressured by the combination of work, studies and other commitments, to do so.

As the authors of this chapter, the four students (Walter, Ilse, Chivaugn and Carina) and the lecturer (Brenda) agreed that each of us would write a substantial reflective piece on our experience and observations of the module. We engaged in several meetings to discuss all of the data that had been collected during the course of the module and to plan the analysis of this data. Each person in the team nominated what role they would play in the preparation of the article. One of the writing team generated an analysis of the reflective pieces generated by the five authors on the basis of the nine elements of authentic learning developed by Herrington, Reeves and Oliver (2010). We each commented on this analysis on the basis of our readings of all the data, our experiences of the module and on the basis of our engagement with the literature. This analysis is reflected in the section entitled "Participants' experiences of the module": All the extracts cited in the findings are derived from the assignments or reflective pieces of the five authors. Hence there is no use of pseudonyms, as is traditionally the case in qualitative research.

For this chapter, we use the evaluative lens for authentic learning developed by Herrington et al. (2010) to reflect on the module and the potential of authentic learning to advance students' learning about research in health science education. The findings are discussed in more detail below.

Findings

Students in the study

There were nine students in the module group, of whom one lived outside of South Africa, with the rest working and studying in the town where the university is located. This was the smallest, most local and homogeneous of the cohorts on the program, which at the time of writing this chapter, was in its seventh year. Only two students worked at the University itself. All were working full-time and studying part-time. The student group included medical doctors, medical scientists, and trainers of physiotherapists and nurses. According to the initial interviews and the PLA drawings, challenges that this cohort faced were similar to those that gave rise to the research proposal in the first place: the students were under pressure as they were studying and working at the same time, most as parents, having to shoulder familial responsibilities. Most students in the module reported encouragement from their workplace and families and a determination to succeed, but reported experiencing anxiety about having to conduct educational research for the first time. None had undertaken significant qualitative research before. These challenges are typical for working postgraduate students crossing disciplinary, professional or paradigmatic boundaries, as discussed in the introduction to this chapter, and for academics crossing disciplinary, professional or paradigmatic boundaries, especially into the discipline of education (Adendorff, 2011).

Sample research output

The assignments in the form of reports on all the interviews (Assignment 1C) were of a high quality, with an average overall score of 73 per cent. Students were able to present the data analysis in a polished and accurate manner and to suggest implications and recommendations arising from the data. The following is an excerpt from a concluding summary from one of the reports. The significance of the data is expressed particularly well:

> A set of interviews conducted during the contact week of the MPhil in Health Science Education 2012 was analyzed using an inductive approach. The main findings were as follows: Course participants were mostly white females of variable age. Allied health care workers were strongly represented. While all students had at least some educational experience, actual educational training was mostly limited or absent. Most had no real experience with research to date. The main motivation to enrol in the course appeared to be a desire to improve teaching skills. Participants were concerned about everything being new as well as time constraints. All the students needed support from the social and work environment, which was of more general nature. They specifically needed support from the course itself in the fields of information technology and research. They had difficulties realizing their own strengths, in particular how these strengths could be shared as a group. Some of these

aspects will have to be confirmed within a bigger study cohort. Some future aspects of investigation were suggested.

(Walter)

Aspects of the data were shared with the program committee during the year and were used as part of a presentation the lecturer made to an institutional strategic planning meeting for Deans and senior managers.

Participants' experiences of the module

For this section, we have selected comments from the reflective reports of the authors (students and lecturer). We are aware that, because the students self-selected to participate in the authoring of the chapter, these comments might provide a more "rosy" picture of the experience than might otherwise have been the case. However, we cross-checked these comments against all other sources of data, and found these comments to be a fair representation of the experiences, as these have been expressed in assignments and on-line communication by the whole class. In the sections below, students' experiences have been analyzed and aligned with Herrington et al.'s (2010) nine elements of authentic learning:

> Statement 1: Provide authentic contexts that reflect the way the knowledge will be used in real life.

The roles of the lecturer and students on the module were influenced by the fact that the students were all participating in a research project that resulted in an authentic outcome and product. Ilse felt that this encouraged students to "trust" the lecturer. Participation in authentic learning contexts that reflect the way knowledge will be useful in real life was experienced most intensely by those who agreed to be part of the writing team, "As I have said, the opportunity to be included as an author in this article is invigorating" (Chivaugn).

Learners were motivated because of personal involvement, especially in the final projects in which they were to collect data on their own teaching and learning contexts, and make a genuine contribution to knowledge through the writing of an article.

> The results of the project were very illuminating, and I even had the sense that it had the potential to be formalized into a proper, ethics-approved study. The student comments had real implications for the curriculum of their foundational years – they spoke of deficiencies in their earlier courses, which would clearly be a sensitive topic to broach with the relevant convenors. This highlighted the potential for far reaching consequences of research – and this was just one small project!
>
> (Chivaugn)

Statement 2: Provide authentic activities.

Despite the fact that the lecturer thought the tasks associated with conducting and coding interviews were relatively straightforward, authentic activities that were open to multiple interpretations (Herrington et al., 2010), some students perceived the tasks as challenging, which in the case of Ilse, led to deeper cognitive engagement:

> This was a new and daunting experience for each one of us . . . We were responsible for recording our own interviews and analyzing the actual data. We were inundated with a variety of interpretations and this required a higher cognitive process while coding the data. I really grappled with the data for days as I reasoned with it from different perspectives. I was motivated to work towards a deeper level of this thinking process, as I felt personally involved as a participant of the research.
>
> (Ilse)

The authentic activities allowed for an experiential learning approach, which was appreciated:

> In this module we were allowed to get our fingers dirty and learn by doing. In this sense it was one of the few 'practical' experiences within a rather theoretical course overall. The fact that we were given the opportunity to write up a paper with the lecturer provided a particularly strong motivation for me.
>
> (Walter)

Statement 3: Provide access to expert performances and the modelling of processes.

Expert performance and modelling occurred principally through the lecturer's sharing of the research design and research techniques, such as interviewing, in the contact week. Students did not comment on this aspect of the module at all, at any stage. If anyone commented on it, it was the lecturer, who thought she was modelling aspects of expertise by sharing the research proposal with the students, and her own approach to teaching with the students: "Because learning to do research by doing it, is how I learnt to do it, so I feel I can share some of that enthusiasm with the students" (Brenda).

Statement 4: Provide multiple roles and perspectives.

All the students had different ways of recording and analyzing the data, which illustrates the importance of having more than one researcher on a project. There was opportunity for trial and error:

> One key learning point here was that the nine of us had different ways of interpreting the data, which highlighted the qualitative conundrum, and the importance of having more than one researcher work on coding in a given study, in order to improve validity.
>
> (Chivaugn)

Opportunity to experiment and to learn from one another requires an element of trust on the part of the lecturer. Among the students there is a reservoir of prior knowledge and skills for them to draw upon and share with each other. Furthermore, students require enough skill, confidence and preparedness to be able to learn from one another. This raises essential questions about the fairness of an approach based on collaboration in contexts of educational inequality, which persist even at postgraduate level in relatively high status settings such as health science education.

Statement 5: Support collaborative construction of knowledge.

All the participants enjoyed the collaborative learning approach. Social and communicative skills were honed, "By participating, we as a group developed a caring relationship and interdependence among ourselves" (Ilse). However, for the lecturer this presented some challenges, as she became concerned about how relations of power and inequality would influence the interaction:

> I want people to learn as much as possible, so they should learn from each other, but at the same time they must be assessed on their individual contributions . . . These tensions might compromise either the assessment, or the collaborative learning elements
>
> (Brenda)

Walter stressed the fact that authentic learning is not exactly like "real life". In contrast to the lecturer's misgivings, he felt it to be a safe learning environment as it "lacks actual threats and competitiveness".

Statement 6: Promote reflection to enable abstractions to be formed.

The opportunity to reflect was confirmed by respondents. Terms such as "learn deep", and "read between the lines" were used to describe the experience. According to Chivaugn, "The final module activity was to reflect on the module exercises. It was during this exercise that I was able to uncover the subtleties mentioned above. As such, the reflection was indispensable."

Statement 7: Promote articulation to enable tacit knowledge to be made explicit.

Students engaged with each other in dialogue, for example on how to code or how to plan for their data gathering activities:

> When engaging in conversation on the discussion board of Blackboard, it was important to consider the structuring of my language and sentences in order to communicate in a constructive way with my peers. I learned from my peers by interacting with them through dialogue.
>
> (Ilse)

Statement 8: Provide coaching and scaffolding by the teacher at critical times.

The lecturer was seen as a coach, someone who could be approached for support:

> It was comforting to know I could contact the module coordinator for help, if needed, to fill the missing gaps which I still required to complete the assignments.
>
> (Ilse)

However, she was not always seen as providing enough input:

> One area in which I fell down was in the understanding of certain key concepts and terms pertinent to qualitative research. This may be my own fault in that I may not have read enough, but again, I do feel that we needed a bit more input with regards to the theory, such that the theoretical frameworks underpinning our study could have been better understood.
>
> (Chivaugn)

A question which arises at this point is: is this lack of theoretical depth a key challenge of experiential or authentic learning opportunities, where "doing" might be promoted at the expense of theory?

Carina, on the other hand, found the input on research methods to be less effective, and that feedback on assignments and the opportunity to practise were for her important catalysts for learning:

> This MPhil and module on research, gave a lot of background and theory, but still it didn't quite 'click'. . . . My biggest learning curve was the feedback I got from my assignments – maybe one should grasp the concepts and principles before attempting an assignment, but I had no idea where to start in any case. So for me – trial and error worked best.

Statement 9: Provide for authentic assessment of learning within the tasks.

Learners appreciated that the assignments were completed as cumulative units as well. They valued the feedback, as noted by Carina above. There was also the sense of the students as agents of their own learning, learning alongside each other, and for purposes with which they could identify—identification with the purpose being a crucial component of the act of writing (Clark & Ivanič, 1997).

> By the time of the final assignment, a mini-research project, the overall sense for me as a student was then to use this as a real opportunity to explore various ideas and approaches rather than 'getting it right' in order to secure a good mark . . . It afforded me to try out various approaches and find out which of these work for me and which don't.
>
> (Walter)

Some challenges

In reflecting on the roles the students were expected to play as researchers, Walter articulated that too many of the students were more concerned with their roles as students, than as partners or apprentices, alluding to a sense of lack of clarity with regard to role during the experience. He felt that the learners defined themselves by their fears, concerns and lack of understanding, even though they gained confidence with time and felt that concerns were addressed.

The lecturer recorded multiple challenges to role definition and challenges posed by the complexity of the module design for her: "A challenge that I face, is that I was primarily interested in giving the best experience to the participants . . . The problem is that there are multiple aims" (Brenda).

A final challenge with regard to the design, including the lack of strong structure and muliplicity of perspectives, is that how students responded to it depended a lot on their learning preferences and personalities, for example, their levels of confidence and sense of autonomy.

Conclusion

On the basis of this study, it would seem that authentic learning design is able to promote a strong motivational impetus and multiple opportunities for depth of engagement, collaboration and learning. Authentic learning dovetails well with experiential learning approaches. A strong element of this authentic learning opportunity, which had the potential to advance student engagement, was the offer for students to collaborate in a meaningful way such as through the writing of a paper with the lecturer. On the basis of our reflections on this module, we would encourage teachers of post-graduate modules on research methods, especially those which require students to cross geographical or disciplinary boundaries, to consider the use of authentic learning approaches in order to induct students into these research practices.

This study is based on one module in a specific educational setting. Further research on the use of authentic learning to induct students into educational research could benefit from similar investigations. Fruitful avenues to deepen this research could explore the role that issues such as prior learning and varied student identities play in the induction process, and how these may complicate or enhance the learning process.

References

Adendorff, H. (2011). Strangers in a strange land: On becoming scholars of teaching. *London Review of Education, 9*(3), 305–315.

Barton, D., & Hamilton, M. (2000). Literacy practices. In D. Barton, M. Hamilton, & R. Ivanič (Eds.), *Situated literacies: Reading and writing in context* (pp. 7–15). London: Routledge.

Boud, D. (1993). Experience as the base of learning. *Higher Education Research and Development, 12*(1), 33–44.

Bozalek, V., & Biersteker, L. (2010). Exploring power and privilege using participatory learning in action techniques. *Social Work Education, 29*(5), 551–572 .

Clark, R., & Ivanič, R. (1997). *The politics of writing*. London: Routledge.

Collins, A., Brown, J., & Holum, A. (1991). Cognitive apprenticeship: Making thinking visible. *The American Educator*. Available at: www.academia.edu/281205/Cognitive_Apprenticeship_Making_Thinking_Visible (accessed 1 November 2012).

Grant, S., & Hurd, F. (2010). Incorporating critical pedagogy into the scholarship of teaching and learning: making the journey alongside our students. *International Journal for the Scholarship of Teaching and Learning, 4*, 2. Available at: www.georgiasouthern.edu/ijsotl.

Herrington, J., Reeves, T. C., & Oliver, R. (2010). *A guide to authentic e-learning*. New York: Routledge.

Koen, M., & Bester, M. (2009). Two master's students' perspectives on higher education studies. In E. Bitzer (Ed.), *Higher education in South Africa: A scholarly look behind the scenes* (pp. 283–303). Stellenbosch: Sun Media.

Leibowitz, B. (2013). Attention to student writing in postgraduate health science education: Whose task is it – or *how*? *Journal of Academic Writing*, *3*(1), 30–41. Retrieved from: http://e-learning.coventry.ac.uk/ojs/index.php/joaw/index (accessed 14 October 2013).

McCormack, C. (2009). Postgraduate research students' experience: It's all about balancing living. In M. Tight, K. Mok, J. Huisman, & C. Morphew (Eds.), *The Routledge international handbook of higher education* (pp. 18–194). New York: Routledge.

Pugsley, L., Brigley, S., Allery, L., & MacDonald, J. (2008). Making a difference: Researching master's and doctoral research programs in medical education. *Medical Education*, *42*, 157–163.

7 Authentic learning in an undergraduate research methodologies course

Tamara Shefer and Lindsay Clowes

The key characteristics of authentic learning are that students are engaged in and learning through exploration and inquiry that is closely connected to the world outside the classroom, where learning is focused on matters that interest the learners themselves. Learning takes place through authentic activities drawing on prior knowledge. It is student-driven, emphasizes collaboration and peer learning and is complemented by coaching, mentorship and guidance from teachers and other experts beyond the classroom. Learning is usually interdisciplinary and draws students into making increasingly more complex connections leading to the development of higher-order thinking skills, such as analyzing, synthesizing, designing, manipulating, and evaluating information (Herrington, Reeves, & Oliver, 2010). This chapter explores the extent to and ways in which a third-year module on research methodologies offered in the Women's and Gender Studies Department (WGS) at the University of the Western Cape (UWC), a South African higher education institution, provides a space for authentic learning.

The pedagogical approach underpinning all courses in WGS is strongly shaped by a feminist focus on power, inequality, hierarchy, and the ways in which these shape knowledge production both inside and outside the classroom (see Maher & Thompson Tetreault, 2001; Choules, 2007; Crick, 2009;). Our teaching thus aims to place students at the centre of their own learning, and in the case of the research methodologies module discussed here, this is achieved through doing socially relevant research. Directly focused on developing research skills through a participatory process, the module sees students escorted through the 'natural' stages of research from developing a proposal to producing a final research report. A central goal of the module is to equip students with core research skills required for postgraduate study and that are of value in any professional career. Additionally, we hope to facilitate an induction into a scholarly identity, an imperative for those continuing with postgraduate studies. A core module for the Social Work degree and for students aiming to major in Women's and Gender Studies, the semester-long course attracts well over 100 students each year who meet for three hours a week.

Authentic learning is a pedagogical approach that encourages students to explore, discuss, and meaningfully construct concepts and relationships in contexts that involve real-world problems and projects that are relevant to students themselves (Herrington & Herrington, 2006; Herrington & Kervin, 2007; Herrington, Reeves, & Oliver, 2010). It was developed as a pedagogical model by Herrington and Oliver (2000) to better prepare students for professional practice. To this end, Herrington et al. (2010, p. 18) identify nine elements, which they argue characterize authentic learning designs.

In the discussion that follows, we consider whether and how the teaching and learning taking place in this course meet each of these nine components. The chapter ends with an assessment of the extent to which we have created an authentic teaching and learning environment, one in which students are able to imagine themselves as producers of knowledge, and reflects on the challenges and value of authentic learning in this module and in higher education more generally.

Authentic context

A key feature of authentic learning is authentic context. This refers to how the teaching and learning reflect and model material practice in the complex world outside the classroom (Herrington et al., 2010). As an expression of an existing research partnership with a local research institute based jointly in the Medical Research Unit (MRC) and UNISA (University of South Africa) that focuses on violence and health promotion, we suggest that the module provides an authentic context: Students are positioned as 'real' researchers in a collaborative study that produces original and publishable research that ultimately contributes to knowledge. Five co-authored papers, one of them co-authored by students themselves (see Ngabaza et al., 2013) emerging out of data collected by students in this module have already been published. Such achievements are foregrounded in the presentation of the course and contribute to the development of an authentic context: students clearly understand and value the knowledge that their work extends beyond degree purposes:[1]

> Also knowing that our result will be used for something more and not just after all hard work (as in many courses) only be read by teachers then put away is very fun.
>
> (Katarina)

Authentic tasks

Herrington (2005, p. 5) argues that students should be required to engage in "authentic tasks", that is, tasks comprising "ill-defined activities that have real world relevance" that are completed over a period of time.

In this module, the key assessment task is to produce, over the course of the entire semester, a research report that goes for external examination. Because the module is aimed at undergraduate students positioned as "junior researchers" (Herrington et al., 2010, p. 21) and who have limited research experience, the report is broken down into 'natural' steps. As outlined below, this involves establishing what is already known and how one intends to add to that knowledge, by developing a proposal, by gathering and analyzing data and by writing up a final report; by reflecting, in other words, real-world practice rather than tasks leading to the "enculturation into practices of universities and classrooms" (Herrington, 2005, p. 5).

The course begins with an introduction to the broad research field from one of our nationally known research collaborators. The ensuing discussion is used to generate a research question that emerges out of experiences with which students identify. In 2012, for example, while the broad topic focused on gender inequalities in heterosexual relationships, the final research question developed in class focused on how young men and women understood their rights and responsibilities in romantic love. One of the writing coaches reported:

> [The topic] captured the attention of many of the students . . . as it is very close to their lived experiences. Many who came to consult found it a challenge to write issues of romance that they experience in their day-to-day life particularly on campus.
>
> (Writing coach 1)

Once the research question has been developed, the course continues through a series of carefully scaffolded tasks that are the subject of participatory and collaborative sessions rather than formal lectures. The second class (covering what is formally known as a literature review) involves workshops to discuss the state of existing knowledge, with students offered training in research skills by a librarian. Students are then asked to find up to six texts that they consider relevant, and are encouraged to share these with co-learners. Once students have located what they consider to be relevant texts, they submit a short piece of writing evaluating their texts in the light of their research question. They are assisted by a writing coach (a postgraduate student) before submission, as well as with rewriting after obtaining written feedback. Over the course of the semester, students have multiple opportunities to develop, with the writing coach, this initial piece of writing. When they submit their final research report, for example, the literature review component will have been rewritten at least three times.

The workshop on existing knowledge is followed by another in which the methodology of the study is collaboratively developed in class within the stipulated framework of a feminist qualitative methodology involving individual indepth interviews. A second written task then is to produce (again assisted by the writing coach) a short piece on methodology and ethics. After feedback on their written work, students draw on the writing coach for help with the drafting of a research proposal that is again evaluated.

Subsequent classes provide a mix of formal and informal activities, but focus primarily on skills development through participatory student-centred activities such as developing an interview schedule and role-playing interviews before completing the task of conducting an interview. Transcribing of interviews and preliminary qualitative thematic analysis of data are the focus of another class and help prepare students for the analysis of their own data. Before they write this analysis, we invite a group of students to present their preliminary analyses to the class as a whole and to the outside experts collaborating with us. The sharing of insights and ideas that takes place during this class discussion is recorded and made available to students to further facilitate ways of thinking critically about their own data. Students are assisted in writing their analysis by the writing coach, are offered written feedback and the chance to rewrite their analysis of the final research report.

Evidence suggests that by the end of the course students reportedly under-stand, some for the first time, how the 'natural' components of research fitted together:

> [It] finally made sense why I had to do a critical literature review, why it was important for me to see the aims and objectives because at the end of the day, with the data analysis, . . . it was a conclusion of everything I had been going through. So, at the end of the day, I had to reflect. Did I meet the aims and objectives of my research? Did I understand the question and did I ask the proper questions? . . . that data analysis to me was the most important of them all coz everything came into a holistic kind of picture . . . then it really did make sense.
>
> (Neli)

Further, it is evident that students feel more confident about doing research and are beginning to imagine themselves as researchers in terms of thinking about postgraduate study: "I'm continuing it [my research] into my Master's thesis" (Katarina).

It is encouraging that of the 63 students who completed the online survey (OLS), 83 per cent believed they had a better understanding of research. They appear convinced that, as one student put it: "We really know what research is and you know which stage you can go, of which we have all the basics. It's OK, you can even start to do your own research" (OLS).

Access to expert thinking and modelling of processes

Herrington (2005, p. 5) insists it is important "to expose students to expert performance" in order to "give them a model of how a real practitioner behaves in a real situation". Ideally students should be exposed to a range of prac-titioners in addition to the lecturer, such as other more knowledgeable students, guest speakers, and perspectives offered by expert knowledge available on the internet. While the stereotypical lecture plays a role in sharing knowledge, "in itself it is insufficient to provide the elements of authentic learning" (Herrington et al., 2010, p. 25) for sharing expertise and modelling knowledge for real-life learning.

Expert performances are drawn into the module in a variety of ways. Well-known South African gender scholars attend the first class and the panel discussion class, and students value the intellectual engagement and sharing, including gains from co-learners:

> I think it was totally awesome . . . through the panel discussion I also drew out certain themes from interviews and also new things that I didn't think of, so it was very helpful.
>
> (Neli)

In addition, research skills are offered by librarians, alongside the modelling of more senior experiences of writing and research through the writing coach mentorship programme. The class on interviewing revolves around a critique of interviews role-played by staff members, while a small selection of first class final reports completed in preceding years are available in the Department's Resource Centre. In 2012, an online discussion forum that facilitated informal exchanges between students and staff outside the classroom was introduced. Evidence suggests that students found this forum useful in a variety of ways, particularly as a resource for peer support and sense of community:

> When I eventually visited the [discussion forum], I realized that I was not the only one who had problems in understanding some of the concepts in the course.
>
> (OLS)

> [B]y talking to people and also looking at the various comments from other students allowed me to see their concerns and how they are addressed.
>
> (OLS)

Provide multiple roles and perspectives

Authentic learning environments are those in which students encounter multiple and often competing and contradictory perspectives, environments in which debate and discussion are foregrounded (Herrington, 2005). Engaging with the same material at different times, in different ways, for different purposes helps students manage the complexity characterizing the real world and to develop critical thinking and cognitive skills.

An insistence on acknowledging and foregrounding a multiplicity of perspectives underpins all the teaching in the Women's and Gender Studies Department, and reflects the feminist theorizing lying at the heart of the departmental vision: we use classroom debate as a method of developing and deepening understanding of all components of the research process including the principles of conducting gendered and feminist research. In taking student meanings seriously, including their own subjective location as a researcher in relation to the topic and their participants, we are able to model the philosophy that all meaning is socially produced, subjective and contextual, and that no research is definitive and/or objective. Thus we begin the course by asking students in the class to share their own perspectives on the issue being researched before asking them to find out what other researchers think.

In generating debate, the validation of student perspectives helps students appreciate the multiple perspectives on the issue, and this is further reinforced through their reading of 'expert' literature. The final class presentations further reiterate the multiplicity of perspectives on the topic through highlighting individual and contrasting interpretations of both data and findings. In referring to the class in which students lead a discussion of their interviews, one student explained that:

> I think it was totally awesome, that is, the part where people starting talking about their experiences that they had and you find that there's interesting things because initially you think, initially, the question was how do young women and men understand their rights and responsibilities . . . you think, it's really nothing, then you understand that the meaning of love differs from person to person and maybe the kind of questions that you're asking, you've actually taken another question and added it on to the research question we already had.
>
> (Neli)

Support collaborative construction of knowledge

Herrington (2005, p. 6) insists that collaboration goes beyond cooperation to the extent that it involves "solving a problem or creating a product which could not have been completed independently" (Forman & Cazden, in Herrington et al., 2010, p. 28). While courses foregrounding more competitive ways of learning/assessment tend to encourage students to avoid creative (unorthodox or unconventional) solutions to complex problems, collaborative challenges facilitate sharing the risk of creative approaches, while simultaneously providing opportunities for students to engage with the different skills and kinds of expertise brought to the challenge by their collaborators. As suggested earlier, the emphasis on interactions with other students was valued, with students suggesting their work improved as a result:

> Well, I got a chance to interact with my peers and to get to learn new things from my Women's and Gender Studies peers.
>
> (OLS)

> The discussion forum helped me because it contributed ideas, people reply and you get to understand those areas that you did not understand before.
>
> (OLS)

Hearing other people's views helped me improve the ideas I already had in my essay.

(OLS)

The module sees students work in small groups or pairs with the writing coach, thus providing space for reassurance, collaborative working and problem solving and help in modelling appropriate responses to critical feedback. The online discussion forum demonstrates further the potential ways in which dialogue and collaboration are important for both shared problem solving and shared knowledge production.

Promote reflection to enable abstractions to be formed

Herrington et al. draw on the work of Knights (1985, in Herrington, 2005, p. 7) to suggest that, in an authentic learning environment, meaningful reflection requires the "aware intention" of another person, further underlining the roles of experts and collaborators. Reflection, in authentic learning environments, is understood as social and interdependent, with students working collaboratively in groups rather than individually. An authentic learning environment not only provides opportunities for students to reflect on their work while engaged with their tasks and after the tasks have been completed, it also facilitates the integration of these new understandings into their conceptual frameworks.

One element of reflection is rooted in the feminist qualitative research methodology applied in this module, which emphasizes the value and centrality of critical reflexivity in the research process. Students doing this module are required to reflect critically on the significance of the power relations in the interview process and to consider the investments and location of the researcher and the ways in which this has shaped their research (Ramazanoglu & Holland, 2002; Hesse-Biber, 2007). Students are also required to reflect on their work in this course through the non-linear structure of the course in which they have multiple opportunities to revisit each task after an expert has evaluated it. The entire course is focused on writing and research as a process involving multiple moments of feed-back, reflection on feedback and reworking in the light of inputs and support from others:

I'm thinking when I am sitting in class and I understand what this person is saying, but when I go back, there's other questions, that come up and I'm not sure how to write the things especially when it comes to structure and things like that so the coaches really helped.

(Mandisa)

This revisiting may also involve integrating new information or new ideas. Class discussion provided important spaces for students to share their own experiences of the interviews and to reflect on their initial analysis of their own interviews in the light of the findings of others:

You think and you rethink and you take advantage of the other things that they left and you can see this person is thinking love is, um, is water or something and someone is thinking loving is touching and feeling, and then you just say, ok, this was thinking love is water and according to Bhana, [an author], she was also thinking love is based on money, so it was so easy to me.

(Sindi)

Another example of how the reflective component of authentic learning operates in the module is through the ethics component where discussion in class reveals the four key components of ethical research: voluntary participation, confidentiality, anonymity, and the right to freely withdraw. Even though students promise anonymity or confidentiality in the consent document, many of them include the name of the participant in their transcript submission. It is only through the raising of this inconsistency in feedback and reflection on how such confidentiality is properly guaranteed that the student is able to make the link between theory and practice to adequately internalize ethical procedures.

Promote articulation to enable tacit knowledge to be made explicit

Authentic tasks create opportunities for students to "present and defend their arguments in appropriate forums" (Herrington, 2005, p. 7). As noted by Vygotsky (1978), intellectual growth takes place between people before it is internalized within the individual, and so it is important that students have opportunities to share their ideas and thoughts publically. Students have the chance to present ideas and defend arguments in the online discussion, group sessions with the writing coaches as well as class presentations and debate:

Hearing other people's views helped me improve the ideas I already had in my essay.

(OLS)

Wow, it was so interesting because you see how other people think on the perspective of love, like it was, ja [yes], I didn't know that that person can think that and then it was like a taboo when someone says something that you don't even agree on, and then you have to accept that, ok, that's how we discuss; it was very interesting to me because it was a variety of thoughts.

(Sindi)

Students are also invited to articulate their views in public fora such as the Medical Research Council Blog as well as participatory writing for publication as noted earlier.

Provide coaching and scaffolding

In an authentic learning environment the teacher's role is to provide coaching and scaffolding rather than the delivery of content: support and guidance are the teacher's primary roles. A more authentic environment provides space for coaching when it is needed as well as the scaffolding of support, "where the teacher and/or student peer mentors provide the skills, strategies and links that the students are unable to provide to complete the task" (Herrington et al., 2010, p. 35). This is particularly important given that this is an introductory course and was appreciated by students:

> I must say, as an exchange student from a university where we don't have access to either writing coaches or the possibility to rewrite assignments after being given comments, this course is amazing.
>
> (Katarina)

Over two-thirds (68 per cent) of those who participated in the online survey had found the services of the writing coach, in particular the assistance with structuring their writing, helpful:

> The writing coach helped me to organize my thinking and put my ideas on paper in a logical manner.
>
> (OLS)

> She explained the structure more in depth by using examples. That to me was useful.
>
> (OLS)

Others suggested that the writing coach helped clarify their understanding of what was required:

> They helped me to understand more what the different assignments are and as well in aiding me with questions of our research that I did not understand. I have a longer meeting tomorrow with them to go through the corrected assignments.
>
> (OLS)

The writing coach was further valued for reinforcing a range of learnings:

> She gave me a better understanding of research and to improve my writing skills and also to think more critically.
>
> (OLS)

> The writing coach helped me on how to substantiate my opinions and draw on authors' works. In this also is . . . editing and summarizing the authors' argument instead of using more quotations.
>
> (OLS)

Others still indicated that they had valued concrete feedback on their writing style as well as help in interpreting the comments made by markers:

> They explained in detail what was meant by the comments written in the previous assignments handed in.
>
> (OLS)

> The coach helped me by giving constructive feedback on my methodology assignment and that helped me to see where I lack.
>
> (OLS)

Writing coaches and a hands-on process of engaging small groups with how to rework and improve what they have already done thus complement classes, using demonstration, that is showing, rather than telling students how to do the next task. This process allows for a cycle of constant reflection, rewriting and refining of a "final" product that will eventually go for examination.

Provide for authentic assessment of learning within the tasks

The assessed task or "polished product" (Herrington, 2005, p. 9) is the final examinable report presented by students at the end of the course. As outlined above, this report is the product of carefully scaffolded, multiple, iterative processes of feedback from markers, writing coaches, peers and 'expert' visiting lecturers. Each part is evaluated at least once with some parts receiving detailed feedback up to four times. While, as Katarina observed, the "course is quite large, it feels like climbing a mountain at times", she also added "the layout of it is great. I get really nervous every time we are getting the assignments back but it feels better to know that I have more chances to do better." Overall, there was evidence that students had felt empowered through their learning and believed themselves to be better prepared for the next stage of their studies:

> I feel next year when I'm going to do my honours project, it's going to be, it's going to be much easier.
>
> (Zinzi)

> Ja, I have all the concepts and all the basics and the experience, we have also, we really know what is research and you know which stage you can go, of which we have all the basics, its ok you can even start to do your own research.
>
> (Sindi)

In addition, the texts emerging out of the data gathered by students, and published by staff and students, also serve to help 'authenticate' the learning, even for those who do not publish.

Conclusion

In conclusion, the case study described above reveals both the value and the challenges of an authentic learning classroom. One of our concerns, as also articulated by students in their evaluations is that students feel overwhelmed by the size of the task, especially since many have never engaged with a research project from beginning to end. On the other hand, as Edwards (2013) has observed, uncomfortable experiences are a necessary prelude to authentic learning. We are acutely aware of the fine line between creative discomfort and debilitating anxiety in learning and are alert to the importance of scaffolding and support at all stages in the module, which is also embedded in the principles of authentic learning. Further, it has become increasingly clear from students' feedback on the module that we need to extend the peer learning engagement within the course, for example, through peer review and use of resources for synchronous learning such as chat rooms (Nicol, Thomson, & Breslin, 2014).

Learning is always uneven and disorderly, and we cannot make any global claims for the successful impact of this module for all students who complete it. However, evidence above suggests that at least for some students the course provides a valuable authentic experience in engaging with research which is conducive to learning. The primary aim of the course is to facilitate the induction of students into the identity of 'researcher' by providing an experience of conducting a real-life research project in and outside the class on a topic of interest to the students. We suggest that on the basis of the above evidence, students' engagement in this entry-level research module constitutes an authentic learning experience that creates both a sense of research confidence and an inspiration to do research. Evidence above suggests that students feel more confident about doing research, feel more competent in the skills of research, and are beginning to imagine themselves as researchers and knowledge producers. Given the goals of higher education nationally and globally with respect to the development of critically engaged graduates who are confident, autonomous and appropriately equipped for the challenges of citizenship and meaningful employment in a rapidly changing world, we suggest that a course based on authentic learning principles as illustrated here, certainly has a role to play.

Perhaps evidence of gains made with respect to the development of independent critical thinking is best captured by this student's realization, in line with the core principles of authentic learning, that you cannot be taught how to be a scholar, but need to be actively engaged in your own learning:

> People, they expect to have or be given genius, instead of create genius, that's what I feel, like people were looking for genius to be taught instead of . . . producing your own genius.
>
> (Sindi)

Note

1   Quotes are drawn from interviews conducted in 2012 with students, a focus group with writing coaches, an oral recorded evaluation in the class, an anonymous online evaluation questionnaire (OLS) and the online discussion forum. Pseudonyms are used to ensure confidentiality.

References

Choules, K. (2007). Social change education: context matters. *Adult Education Quarterly, 57*(2), 159–176.

Crick, R. D. (2009). Inquiry based learning: Reconciling the personal with the public in a democratic and archaeological pedagogy. *The Curriculum Journal, 20*(1), 73–92.

Edwards, A. (2013). Designing tasks which engage learners with knowledge. Public lecture at the University of the Western Cape, 12 February.

Herrington, J. (2005). Authentic tasks in e-learning designs. *Studies in Learning, Evaluation, Innovation and Development, 2*(2), 1–8.

Herrington, A., & Herrington, J. (2006). What is an authentic learning environment? In A. Herrington & J. Herrington (Eds.), *Authentic learning environments in higher education* (pp. 1–13). Hershey, PA: Information Science Publishing.

Herrington, J., & Kervin, L. (2007). Authentic learning supported by technology: 10 suggestions and cases of integration in classrooms. *Educational Media International, 44*(3), 219–236.

Herrington, J., & Oliver, R. (2000). An instructional design framework for authentic learning environments. *Educational Technology Research and Development, 48*(3), 23–48.

Herrington, J., Reeves, T. C., & Oliver, R. (2005). *Authentic task design framework*. Retrieved from: www.authentictasks.uow.edu.au/framework.html.

Herrington, J., Reeves, T. C., & Oliver, R. (2010). *A guide to authentic e-learning*. New York: Routledge.

Hesse-Biber, S. (Ed.) (2007). *Handbook of feminist research: Theory and praxis*. Thousand Oaks, CA: Sage.

Maher, F., & Thompson Tetreault, M. K. (2001). *The feminist classroom: Dynamics of gender, race, and privilege*. New York: Basic Books.

Ngabaza, S., Daniels, D., Frank, O., & Maluleke, R. (2013). Contestations of the meanings of love and gender in a university students' discussion. *Agenda, 27*(2), 128–136.

Nicol, D., Thomson, A., & Breslin, C. (2014). Rethinking feedback practices in higher education: A peer review perspective. *Assessment and Evaluation in Higher Education, 39*(1), 102–122.

Ramazanoglu, C., & Holland, J. (Eds.). (2002). *Feminist methodology: Challenges and choices*. London: Sage.

Vygotsky, L. S. (1978). *Mind in society: The development of higher psychological processes*. Cambridge, MA: Harvard University Press.

8 Facilitating creative problem solving in the entrepreneurship curriculum through authentic learning activities

Noel Lindsay and Denise Wood

Introduction

Creativity and innovation are essential to the success of businesses in the networked information society of the twenty-first century (Florida, 2003; McWilliam, 2007; Wood et al., 2011). Our graduating students therefore need to be creative problem solvers and have the capacity to "persevere in the face of complexity and unresolvability" (McWilliam & Haukka, 2008, p. 660). The benefits of introducing creativity within the marketing curriculum have been widely reported in the literature (see, for example, Titus, 2000).

This chapter draws on the findings from the trial of such a creative problem-solving approach through authentic activities within a post-graduate course in entrepreneurship and innovation offered by the University of Adelaide in both Adelaide, South Australia, and Singapore. The authentic activities were designed to reflect the nature of the real-world entrepreneurial environment involving the development of new product ideas for a start-up business. Students were supported in the creative problem-solving aspects of these activities through the use of a CPS tool, *Ingenium*, which was developed through a national funded learning and teaching project supported by the Department of Education's Office for Learning and Teaching.[1] The example demonstrates an effective approach to embedding creativity within the entrepreneurship curriculum using an authentic learning approach.

Background

Graduates entering the twenty-first-century workforce need to be able to respond to complexity and uncertainty (Florida, 2003; Craft, 2006; McWilliam, 2007). Economic growth relies on the ability to attract a creative workforce capable of producing new ideas, business generation, and economic growth (Florida, 2003), and so creativity and innovation are important factors contributing to the success of businesses. The demands of our increasingly complex world and the challenge of responding to uncertainty require a different set of graduate attributes, including the ability to generate ideas and undertake creative work in digitally enhanced environments (Cunningham, 2006, cited in McWilliam, 2007) and use emerging technologies such as social media for customer relationship management (Wood et al., 2011). This represents a radical departure from the routine problem-solving tasks that have characterised the information age (Florida, 2003). However, evidence suggests that universities are failing to equip graduates with the creative skills they require to be effective in the twenty-first-century workplace (Craft, 2006). One way of addressing this gap between the demands of the workforce and the work readiness of our graduates may be to embed creative problem solving within authentic tasks designed to "reflect the way the knowledge will be useful in real life" (Brown, Collins, & Duguid, 1989, p. 2).

Creative problem solving involves three main components: (1) domain-relevant skills; (2) creativity-relevant processes; and (3) task motivation (Amabile, 1996). This model recognises that domain-relevant skills are required for learners to have access to the full range of response possibilities from which new responses are to be synthesised, and the information against which the new responses are to be judged (Csikszentmihalyi, 1999). Creativity-relevant processes determine the degree to which people's responses will surpass previous products or responses in the domain (Dewett, 2003), while task motivation refers to learners' attitudes and motivations for undertaking tasks as well as their understanding about why a task is being engaged (Amabile, 1996; Dewett, 2003). Creativity is more likely to be facilitated when tasks are intrinsically motivating (the experience of learning is its own reward) (Csikszentmihalyi, 1999) and authentic.

The principles of authentic learning derive from the theories of situated cognition (Brown, Collins, & Duguid, 1989) and cognitive apprenticeship (Collins, 1991). As Brown, Collins and Duguid (1989) argue, learning is a process of enculturation and students learn best through situated learning in which the activities are coherent, meaningful, and purposeful, and situated within the practices of the relevant professional culture. The pedagogical approach underpinning authentic learning is cognitive apprenticeship, which "supports learning in a domain by enabling students to acquire, develop, and use cognitive tools in authentic domain activity" (Brown, Collins, & Duguid, 1989, p. 9). Herrington, Reeves and Oliver's (2005, 2010) authentic learning framework provides a heuristic to guide academics in the design of learning activities based on these cognitive apprentice principles.

The following section describes a post-graduate entrepreneurship and innovation course, which incorporates creative problem-solving strategies embedded within authentic learning activities reflecting the characteristics of the authentic learning framework.

Context

Entrepreneurship & Innovation is a core course in the Master of Applied Innovation and Entrepreneurship program, offered by the University of Adelaide at both its Adelaide and Singapore campuses. For the purposes of this course, entrepreneurship can be thought of as the process of creating or seizing opportunities without regard to the resources they control (Stevenson & Jarillo, 1990). Innovation is defined as "the initiation, adaptation and implementation of an idea or proposal that will lead to a change within the organisation; and the installation of the adopted idea into a sustained identifiable pattern within the organisational behaviours" (Jarrar & Smith, 2013).

The course aims to facilitate the development of students' understanding of the nature of entrepreneurship and to further their understanding of the role of innovation as a key component in developing entrepreneurial strategies (Jarrar & Smith, 2013) to build sustainable, performance-oriented entrepreneurial businesses. More specifically, the course addresses the underlying characteristics of exceptional entrepreneurial opportunities, the importance of leadership in developing a cohesive entrepreneurial team, being resourceful, the importance of developing appropriate entrepreneurial strategies to grow the business, and the nature of entrepreneurial finance. Creative problem solving underpins all of these areas.

An action learning approach is adopted in the course whereby students 'learn through doing' by analysing relevant 'real-world' cases, engaging in interactive exercises that relate to lecture topics, and through role-plays that involve their assuming the identity of an entrepreneur/nascent entrepreneur or an investor/potential investor in an entrepreneurial business in a case situation. The aim of this approach is to encourage students to think about the types of decisions, strategies and issues that entrepreneurs and investors have to address in professional practice. On completion of the course, students should be able to do the following:

1   Critique a business plan associated with establishing a new venture.
2   Appreciate what characterises business opportunities.
3   Understand the importance of idea generation and creativity in developing new ventures.
4   Understand what is meant by entrepreneurship and innovation.
5   Describe the ways in which entrepreneurs manage risk, organise resources, and add value in the new venture creation process.

Design of the course

In designing the *Entrepreneurship & Innovation* course, the following authentic learning principles (Herrington, Reeves, & Oliver, 2005; 2010) were embraced. These are summarized in Table 8.1):

1   *Tasks have real-world relevance.* Students were exposed to relevant entrepreneur and investor tasks.
2   *Major tasks are ill-defined.* There were no pre-determined and/or defined outcomes for the major assessment tasks (interview with an entrepreneur, evaluation of a business plan and business opportunity and idea generation/creativity associated with developing additional business innovations that the

Table 8.1 Authentic learning principles applied to the design of an *Entrepreneurship &
Innovation* course

Principle	How addressed	Technologies used
1 Tasks have real-world relevance	Students exposed to relevant entrepreneur and investor tasks	Role-plays, individual and team interactions, use of Information and Communication Technologies (ICTs) including *Ingenium*
2 Major tasks are ill-defined	No pre-determined and/or defined outcomes for the major assessment tasks	Role-plays, individual and team interactions, use of ICTs including *Ingenium*
3 Complex tasks require completion over a period of time	Major assessment tasks occur over three days involving discussion among team members	Individual and team interactions, use of ICTs including *Ingenium*
4 Tasks provide an opportunity for students to examine situations from different perspectives	Students assume the role of both entrepreneur and entrepreneurial investor	Role-plays
5 Tasks provide the opportunity for students to collaborate	Course involves case study discussions and small group work	Role plays, team interactions, use of ICTs including *Ingenium*
6 Class situations provide an opportunity for students to reflect	Experiential exposure to real-world type tasks and practical nature of the course allow students to integrate and reflect upon how theory meshes with practice	Role-plays, team interactions
7 Tasks can be integrated and applied across different subject areas and beyond the immediate domain	Course founded upon a range of inter-disciplinary content topics. These are relevant for entrepreneurs	Individual interactions, use of ICTs including *Ingenium*
8 Tasks are integrated into assessment	Course assessment is experiential and is designed to be relevant for 'would-be' entrepreneurs/corporate entrepreneurs/social entrepreneurs. Course is developed around an entrepreneurial framework	Role-plays, individual and team interactions, use of ICTs including *Ingenium*

(Continued)

Table 8.1 (Continued)

Principle	How addressed	Technologies used
9 Tasks are valuable in their own right	Students leave the course with real-world tools relevant to work or personal situations	Role-plays, individual and team interactions, use of ICTs including *Ingenium*
10 Tasks provide for competing solutions and diversity of outcomes	Course tasks reflect real-world entrepreneurial situations where there are a range of potential outcomes	Role-plays, individual and team interactions, use of ICT including *Ingenium*

Source: Adapted from Herrington, Reeves, and Oliver (2005; 2010).

venture/entrepreneur could undertake). This is also reflected in the classroom teaching and learning environment where students are required to develop solutions to tasks that they believe are appropriate for "real-world" entrepreneurial situations.

3 *Complex tasks are provided to students.* Two of these involve completion over a period of time. The student interview with an entrepreneur (occurs over a few days) and the evaluation of a business plan and opportunity and the identification of additional innovations flowing from the existing venture occur over time (over three days with discussion among team members). This is a reflection of the real world of entrepreneurs and entrepreneurial investors.

4 *Tasks provide an opportunity for students to examine situations from different perspectives.* Students assume the role of both entrepreneur and entrepreneurial investor in the course so gaining an appreciation of each type of perspective.

5 *Tasks provide the opportunity for students to collaborate.* Class sessions involve case study discussions involving small group work and role-plays involve collaboration. The final assignment is a small group project requiring collaboration among team members.

6 *Class situations provide an opportunity for students to reflect.* Classroom role-plays and case studies provide the basis for students to consider various options available to entrepreneurs. The experiential exposure to real-world type tasks and the practical nature of the course allow students to integrate and reflect upon how the theory meshes with practice.

7 *Tasks can be integrated and applied across different subject areas and beyond the immediate domain.* The course draws upon a range of disciplinary content including financial management, marketing, leadership, and team building. Underlying the course are the fundamental principles of risk management and what involves being enterprising. These topics are important for many types of environments, including those that involve business and social entrepreneurs, corporate entrepreneurs, personal life situations, and work situations.

8 *Tasks are integrated into assessment.* The course assessment is experiential in nature and is designed to be relevant for 'would-be' entrepreneurs/corporate

entrepreneurs/social entrepreneurs. The course is developed around an entrepreneurial framework and this is used as the foundation of the course. All lectures and assessment are developed around this framework; thus, tasks are related and build upon each other.

9 *Tasks are valuable in their own right rather than as preparation for something else.* Students take away real-world tools at the end of the course that they can apply immediately in work or personal situations. For example, students are taught what investors look for in deciding whether to invest in a business or not. What is learned in the process can be applied immediately to work or personal investment situations.

10 *Tasks provide for competing solutions and diversity of outcomes.* The course tasks reflect real-world entrepreneurial situations where the problems are ill-defined and where the appropriateness of any outcome decision may not be known immediately, perhaps for three or more years, and where there may be more than one appropriate problem solution.

Assessment task

The overall assessment task involved students reviewing a business plan for a start-up entrepreneurial business venture and evaluating the business opportunity in terms of whether they would invest or not. Students also were required to critically examine the core product at the heart of the venture with a view to enhancing the product to facilitate growth in the business after the entrepreneurial start-up process had occurred. New ventures start with the identification of a business opportunity and then identifying particular products (or services) to take advantage of that opportunity. New ventures grow by engaging more with the existing customer base and selling more product to existing customers (market penetration), entering new markets (new market development), developing new products (new product development), and/or a combination of new market and new product development (diversification) (Ansoff, 1957; 1965). The specific task for the students was for them to first consider the existing product that the business was founded upon and then suggest how the business could be developed through enhancing this product to facilitate growth in the business. To achieve this outcome, students were provided with a creativity problem-solving (CPS) tool, *Ingenium*, which provided them with a framework to consider the nature of the problem and to facilitate the development of new product ideas for growing the business. The other strategies for venture growth identified by Ansoff (1957; 1965) were ignored in this exercise; the focus was only on product development.

Students were exposed to the *Ingenium* tool in lectures. They were directed to the *Ingenium* project website and they were instructed to review the tool in small groups in class. During this process, the lecturer interacted with the students. The tool includes a process for creatively solving problems, a mind mapping tool, and a case study that describes how the tool can be applied through the various stages of the creativity process.

At the end of the lecture, students were asked to reflect upon the *Ingenium* tool and apply this (in small groups) when completing the CPS course assessment task (described below). Students had three days to complete this task. An online support structure was provided for those students requiring assistance in using the tool. Students were required to submit the documentation they developed during the CPS process (mind maps, notes, etc.) so that an 'audit trail' could be established as to how their ideas metamorphosed from the original product to the new ones they identified. The following is the task as it was provided to the students:

> Develop five new ideas as to how you could build upon and expand the initial business idea into five other businesses. To do this, go to the *Ingenium* website http://www.creativity-project.net/ingentool.php and access the Mindmapping software http://www.creativity-project.net/mapping.php. Start with the existing business idea as your central idea and then develop a range of aspects associated with the theme. This will allow you to explore many facets of the topic that will reveal new insights and associations. Do some research on mindmaps and how they work. Next, go to the assumption page read the instructions and list 50 assumptions associated with the idea. Take 10 of these assumptions and challenge them as a means of provoking new possibilities. Develop five new business ideas from these (don't forget to develop a short write-up on each of your ideas). Submit your saved Mindmapping file as well as the assumptions you identified that were associated with the central idea, the 10 assumptions that you challenged, and the five new business ideas that you developed as a result of challenging the initial assumptions. Throughout this process, we encourage you to access the Facebook page *Unearthing Ideas online* https://www.facebook.com/unearthingideas and you will get support and feedback as you go through the process.

Each student group submitted at least five ideas for enhanced products that would provide the basis for helping the business grow. All were realistic and potentially feasible (though some were more achievable than others). The next phases would involve developing prototypes of the augmented products, undertaking preliminary costings including examining how the products would be manufactured, and then undertaking market research to determine if there was consumer interest. These steps, however, were over and above what was required for the course.

Evaluation

For the purposes of evaluating the impact of the CPS approach in the postgraduate *Entrepreneurship & Innovation* course, students completed an anonymous questionnaire evaluating both the lecturer and the course (including the assessment tasks). During this process, the lecturer left the classroom and an independent person administered an anonymous paper-based questionnaire to students incorporating a set of standard questions. There was also a space in the questionnaire for the student to provide open-ended comments about the lecturer and course. After completion of the questionnaire, the completed forms were collected by the independent person, and the lecturer then returned to the room. The student questionnaires were processed by an independent university unit and the lecturer received this feedback after the course concluded.

Findings and discussion

The CPS task was employed in a university postgraduate Master's course. The course was delivered in intensive mode with two intensive blocks of teaching spread approximately four weeks apart. Each intensive block involved two to three days of teaching. Interactions with the lecturer and other students occurred between the two intensives.

The course was delivered to two discrete student groups in two separate locations (Singapore and Adelaide) where the university has Campuses. There were 11 Singapore students and 40 Adelaide students. There were approximately 50 per cent of women in each class. The Singapore class was comprised of Singaporean citizens. The Adelaide class comprised a mixture of students from Australia, China, India, Holland, Sri Lanka, Pakistan, Vietnam, and Croatia. The same lecturer delivered both courses; the courses were identical in every possible way (content, assessment, learning objectives, etc). There are, of course, cultural differences between Singapore and Australia (Adelaide), though Singapore has a more Western-oriented Eastern culture than many other Asian countries.

Student feedback about the course and its CPS approach indicated that the students appreciated the 'real-life entrepreneur insights gained from the course and lecturer' and the ability to apply theory to practice. These insights are reflected in the following representative comments:

- I like the intensive delivery format—it improves the learning experience.
- I was able to obtain the foundation knowledge of entrepreneurship through the course.
- Real-life entrepreneur insights gained from the course and lecturer.
- Course was full of useful experiences and take-home messages.
- The topics are interesting . . . the case studies improve my critical thinking.
- Many real-life examples . . . appropriate discussion of the topics . . . integrated framework helps my remembering.
- I learned so much about entrepreneurial thinking from the course and assessment exercises and the lecturer.
- Theory was easy to apply.
- I learned about how to apply the topics to my field.

The study presented in this chapter presents an example of the way in which creative problem solving has been embedded within the entrepreneurship curriculum, the value of authentic learning activities in engaging students, and better preparing them for an increasingly complex world.

Recommendations for future use/advice for practitioners

Many people do not believe they are creative, yet creativity can be developed. In the course situations at hand, a number of the students were apprehensive about the assessment prior to the CPS exercise as they did not feel confident in developing enhanced potential products for the business (this was particularly the case in Singapore). Asked about their belief in themselves (to be able to generate creative solutions to a problem) *after* submitting the final assignment presented a much-changed evaluation of their abilities. Without exception, all students demonstrated an increased belief in their CPS abilities.

Thus, the *Ingenium* CPS tool provides a framework and process for facilitating creative problem solving in individual and group situations that is designed to provide a "road map" to support decision-makers confronted with situations that require creative solutions. It is easy to use and easily adapted to various situations. Although the *Ingenium* tool can be used in a classroom environment, it is relevant for facilitating creative problem solving solutions in practice . . . whether government- or industry-based (for profit or not-for-profit). The complex and dynamic environment that impinges upon our personal, work, and social lives presents us with a myriad of challenges, some of which require creative solutions. The *Ingenium* tool provides a support structure for those who want to develop their creative abilities and better understand how this can be done.

Creativity is relevant to everyone – not only artists, poets, writers, and those who work in the creative industries – and it is important in our different work, social, and personal situations. Teaching people how to be more creative should form an integral part of the education process – in schools, technical colleges, and universities. This is critical not only for our long-term survival but also for an augmented and improved personal and working life.

Note

1 The *Ingenium* tool described in this chapter arose from a Department of Education, Office for Learning and Teaching (formerly the Australian Learning and Teaching Council) funded project led by the University of South Australia. The project involved the design and development of a CPS framework and open source online CPS tool (*Ingenium*) to act as a scaffold for academics in the development and redevelopment of courses and a tool to guide students through the creative problem-solving process in their coursework. The project also developed guidelines for academics and students, case studies of the use of CPS in courses across a range of disciplinary fields, and a suite of resources available via the project site. The *Entrepreneurship & Innovation* course described in this chapter was one of these case studies. Further information about the project is available from the project site: http://www.creativity-project.net. The *Ingenium* tool used by the students in the *Entrepreneurship & Innovation* course can be accessed from: www.creativity-project.net/cpst/.

References

Amabile, T. M. (1996). *Creativity in context: Update to the social psychology of creativity*. Boulder, CO: Westview Press.

Ansoff, H. I. (1957). Strategies for diversification. *Harvard Business Review*, *35*(5), 113–124.

Ansoff, H. I. (1965). *Corporate strategy: An analytic approach to business policy for growth and expansion*. New York: McGraw-Hill.

Brown, J. S., Collins, A., & Duguid, P. (1989). Situated cognition and the culture of learning. *Educational Researcher*, *18*(1), 32–42.

Collins, A. (1991). Cognitive apprenticeship and instructional technology. In L. Idol & B. F. Jones (Eds.), *Educational values and cognitive instruction: Implications for reform* (pp. 121–138). Hillsdale, NJ: Erlbaum.

Craft, A. (2006). Creativity in schools. In N. Jackson, M. Oliver, M. Shaw, & J. Wisdom (Eds.), *Developing creativity in higher education: An imaginative curriculum* (pp. 19–28). London: Routledge.

Csikszentmihalyi, M. (1999). Implications of a systems perspective for the study of creativity. In R. Sternberg (Ed.), *Handbook of creativity*. Cambridge: Cambridge University Press.

Dewett, T. (2003). Understanding the relationship between information technology and creativity in organizations. *Creativity Research Journal*, *15*(2/3), 167.

Florida, R. (2003). *The rise of the creative class: and how it's transforming work, leisure, community and everyday life*. Victoria: Pluto Press.

Herrington, J., Reeves, T., & Oliver, R. (2005). *Authentic task design framework*. Retrieved from: www.authentictasks.uow.edu.au/framework.html.

Herrington, J., Reeves, T., & Oliver, R. (2010). *A guide to authentic e-learning*. New York: Routledge.

Jarrar, N. S., & Smith, M. (2013). Innovation in entrepreneurial organisations: A platform for contemporary management change and a value creator. *The British Accounting Review*, *46*(1), 60–76.

McWilliam, E. (2007). Is creativity teachable? Conceptualising the creativity/pedagogy relationship in higher education. In *Proceedings of 30th HERDSA Annual Conference: Enhancing Higher Education, Theory and Scholarship*, Adelaide.

McWilliam, E., & Haukka, S. (2008). Educating the creative workforce: New directions for twenty-first century schooling. *British Educational Research Journal*, *34*(5), 651–666.

Stevenson, H. H., & Jarillo, J. C. (1990). A paradigm of entrepreneurship: Entrepreneurial management. *Strategic Management Journal*, *11*, 17–27.

Titus, P. A. (2000). Marketing and the creative problem-solving process. *Journal of Marketing Education*, *22*(3), 225–235.

Wood, D., Lindsay, N., Gluth, S., Corso, R., & Bilsborow, C. (2011). Facilitating creative problem solving in the marketing curriculum in response to the demands of the networked information society. In *Proceedings of the 2011 AMS World Marketing Congress (WMC)*, Reims, France, July 19–July 23.

Part III

Emerging technologies

9 Introduction to emerging technologies

Dick Ng'ambi and Vivienne Bozalek

Part III of the book builds on the previous two Parts on Activity Theory and authentic learning, but the focus in this section is on foregrounding the potential use of emerging technologies (ETs) for transformative pedagogical practice in higher education. This introductory chapter seeks to provide a basic understanding of how ETs have been conceptualised and written about in higher education. The chapter elaborates on the characteristics of ETs and on their context-specific nature. The chapters that follow provide examples of the mediatory ways in which ETs contribute to transformative learning outcomes in different geographical higher education contexts; South Africa, New Zealand and Australia.

Introduction

While much debate in academic and lay circles have focused on what is meant by the concept 'emerging technologies' (see Gachago et al., 2013; Ng'ambi & Bozalek, 2013a, for a fuller discussion of these debates), there is a growing need to discover ways of using ETs to mediate transformative pedagogical practices. Thus, the aim of this chapter is to provide an understanding of how ETs have been conceptualised in literature, and provide an explanation of why we prefer to describe ETs in terms of their characteristics rather than relying on contested definitions. The chapters that follow this introductory session provide examples of how these transformatory learning outcomes can be achieved in South African, Australian and New Zealand contexts.

Conceptions and characteristics of ETs

The concept of emerging technologies or ETs, as we refer to them in this chapter, is contested and is understood in different, but often taken-for-granted ways in the higher education sector (Veletsianos, 2010). The Horizon Reports, which are produced each year by the New Media Consortium (NMC), mainly in the United States, the United Kingdom and Australian contexts, but more recently also in Latin America, provide an idea of which technologies are currently being used in various sectors such as higher education, and what will be used in future in these sectors. Although useful, these trends may not be similar in less-resourced environments and viewing ETs only from this perspective may therefore be limiting.

In the 2012 Horizon Report, there is an acknowledgement that there is a need to educate academics on uses of ET, and that the focus should be on innovative pedagogies rather than the technologies themselves (Johnson et al., 2012). The 2013 Horizon Report refers to ETs as "practices that are likely to enter mainstream use in their focus sectors within three adoption horizons over the next five years" (Johnson et al., 2013, p. 3). So according to the 2013 Horizon Report, ETs are not just about tools but also practices.

Most technologies used in education were not initially designed as educational tools but are appropriated to support teaching and learning. In the NMC report of 2014, Johnson, Adams Becker, Estrada and Freeman (2014) categorise technologies used in higher education into the following:

- *Consumer technologies*: initially designed for recreational and professional purposes and only appropriated for educational use.
- *Digital strategies*: these are not technologies but are ways of using devices and software to enrich teaching and learning, whether inside or outside of the classroom
- *Internet technologies*: these include techniques and infrastructure that enable interaction with the network more transparent and easier to use.
- *Learning technologies*: These are tools and resources developed expressly for the education sector, as well as pathways of development that may include tools adapted from other purposes that are matched with strategies to make them useful for learning
- *Social media technologies*: These are subsumed under the consumer technology category, but have become ever-present and widely used in every part of society
- *Enabling technologies*: These are those technologies that, like location awareness, have the potential to transform what we expect of our devices and tools.

We infer from these classifications that there are many technologies used in education, and none of the technologies are in themselves capable of bringing about transformative pedagogical practices.

Technologies on the Southern Horizon

As we have indicated above, each year Horizon Reports have been consistent in predicting the possible technologies and timelines for adoption in higher education (see, for example, Johnson & Adams 2011; Johnson et al., 2012; Johnson et al., 2013; Johnson et al., 2014). Although these reports serve as useful dashboards on the higher education terrain, they tend not to be cognisant of the socio-cultural settings that influence appropriation of technologies in varying contexts. For example, technologies that require high bandwidth would not make entry in context where bandwidth is limited regardless of how much adoption time is given. It follows therefore, that use of ETs for teaching and learning may vary between the Northern and the Southern horizons, as well as resource-rich and resource-poor contexts.

The New Media Consortium use a Delphi-based process where views from groups of experts are analysed for a consensus viewpoint on how emerging technologies would impact on teaching, learning, or creative inquiry in a variety of contexts. The same process was used in Latin American higher education for a five-year period (i.e. 2013–2018) (Johnson, Adams Becker, Gago, Garcia, & Martín, 2013). The report projects that:

- the creation of more flexible learning models will be required;
- most academics are not using new and compelling technologies for learning and teaching, nor for organising their own research;
- appropriate metrics of evaluation lag behind the emergence of new scholarly forms of authoring, publishing, and researching.

The observations suggest that the challenges facing the Latin American higher education sector resonates with some counterpart higher education sectors in Africa. As a useful way of understanding how these projections would impact on the students who will be entering higher education sector in the next five years, a review of the status of primary and secondary education sector, entitled the *Technology Outlook Brazilian Primary and Secondary Education, 2012–2017* (Johnson, Adams Becker, Cummins, Estrada, & Meira, 2012), provides some insight in the NMC Horizon Project regional analysis of Brazilian primary and secondary education.

The review states:

- Education paradigms are shifting to include online learning, hybrid learning and collaborative models.
- The abundance of resources and relationships made easily accessible via the internet is increasingly challenging us to revisit our roles as educators.
- People expect to be able to work, learn, and study whenever and wherever they want.

It can be inferred from these reports that primary and secondary education sectors in Brazil could be more innovative in using emerging technologies for teaching and learning than is the case in higher education sector. The consequences are that students entering institutions of higher learning who might have expectations of being taught and learning with emerging technologies but are likely to be disappointed.

One of the unintended consequences of Horizon Reports could be pressure to play a catch-up game and adopt technologies without following a careful learning design. Notwithstanding these pressures and the limitations of the Delphi-based research method, Horizon Reports are useful benchmark reports for

HEIs to gauge the extent to which emerging technologies are penetrating the education sphere.

Siemens and Tittenberger (2009), in their open source book on Emerging Technologies for Learning, seem to equate ET with social software (see page 42 of their book, where Blogs, Skype, Wikis, *Second Life*, Facebook and Google Reader are described as ETs).[1] They subscribe to the view that technologies are not neutral, but embody philosophies and ideologies in themselves, reflecting particular worldviews. They see technologies as having multiple *affordances*, by which they mean the actual potential of specific technologies, such as the potential of social software to provide emergent learning paths through interaction with peers. Thus, ETs are difficult to define, and for this reason Veletsianos (2010) describes ETs in terms of their characteristics. He contends that ETs are those technologies which match the following five characteristics:

1   ETs may or may not be new technologies. They are technologies that are emerging, but not necessarily new in the sense that they may have been around for some time but are not in use in that particular context. For example, in some parts of the world, Twitter is an established technology in higher education, but its potential in South Africa has yet to be realised or developed. Similarly, in Australia, 3D Virtual Learning Environments (3DVLEs) are a relatively established practice in many higher education institutions (see Wood in Chapter 12 of this volume for examples of this), but they may be considered an ET in South Africa, and may or may not become an ET in other educational contexts.

2   ETs may be considered as evolving or in the state of 'coming into being' and can be seen as being in a continual state of flux and development. For example, Mxit[2] is being used for teaching and learning the South African context and is in a constant state of improvement of its capabilities.

3   ETs go through hype cycles (Gartner Inc, n.d.). The hype cycle is a graphical tool developed by Gartner, a research and advisory group for ICTs. These hype cycles involve a technology trigger, which happens because of access to a presentation or a launch or demonstration such as a workshop that may generate interest by academics to use this technology in teaching and learning. It is then followed by what is known as "the peak of inflated expectations" where there is great enthusiasm that is probably unrealistic, though there are some successful innovative teaching and learning practices, but also many failures in applying the technology. Here people would present their enthusiasm through papers at conferences, seminars and other academic fora. This is followed by the "trough of disillusionment", which happens because the technology has not lived up to the expectations to enhance teaching and learning and the interest in using this to enhance teaching and learning subsides substantially. The "slope of enlightenment" then follows, where those who are really interested in using the technology make a concerted effort to understand how it can be used to improve their pedagogical practice and, finally, the "plateau of productivity" follows where more academics become

convinced of the benefits of using this technology in their own contexts and institutions may decide to make general use of the technology. See Figure 9.1, which shows the Gartner Hype Cycle for Emerging Technologies for 2013. The hype cycle should alert us to remaining sceptical about immediate and lasting transformation of the use of ETs as what may be fashionable at one time may entirely fall from favour at another time or in another context and merely drift into non-use. Veletsianos (2010) notes that educators can become almost evangelical about certain technologies when they are initiated into their use, but the ways in which they use the new technologies may reinforce traditional teaching methods and their knowledge of the affordances. What is also evident from Gartner's hype cycle is that in 2013 most of these technologies are not in use in the South African context.

4   ETs satisfy two 'not yet' criteria:

(a)   ETs are not yet fully understood. They are just starting to be used so their impact on and the implications for teaching and learning are not entirely clear, either for individual educators or for institutions as a whole.

(b)   ETs are not yet fully researched. Some innovators may be starting to research ETs in their own practice, but the findings are at best preliminary. Needless to say, most of these innovative uses of ETs start and end as projects fail to enter the mainstream institutional adoption. The fact that ETs are not properly researched means that evidence of their usefulness may not be there to convince academics or institutional leaders that they could potentially make a good contribution to pedagogical practice in higher education.

5   ETs are potentially disruptive, i.e. they could have an effect of changing traditional approaches to pedagogy, but their potential is mostly unfulfilled. Many definitions of ETs that are found on the web refer to their potential to disrupt common practice. However, the lack of predictability of ETs means that understanding of how they can be profitably used to enhance teaching and learning can only ascertained after some time and this may impede their dissemination (Williams, Karousou, & Mackness, 2011). An example of this is the potential of Open Educational Resources (OER) to change the way publication and copyright are used, however, the potential of this has yet to be developed in higher education research (Veletsianos, 2010).

Further to the above characteristics, Veletsianos (2010, p. 17) sees ETs as transcending academic disciplines and describes ETs as "tools, technologies, innovations, and advancements utilized in diverse educational settings to serve varied education-related purposes". We tend to favour this definition above others, such as those we have discussed by the Horizon Reports (Johnson et al., 2013) as Veletsianos's (2010) definition emphasizes the context-specific nature of ETs, which we regard as particularly relevant for the different geographical contexts, perspectives, disciplines and experiences which are exemplified in this book. It is possible that ETs in these contexts may be different from those that are currently

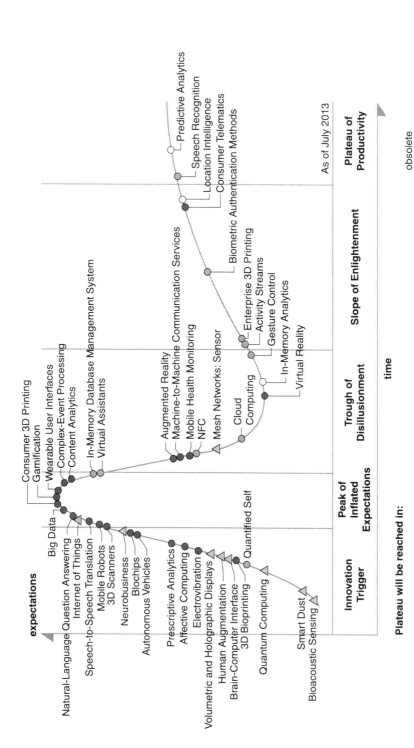

Figure 9.1 The Gartner Hype Cycle for Emerging Technologies for 2013

Source: Gartner's 2013 hype cycle for emerging technologies. Retrieved from http://www.gartner.com/newsroom/id/2575515.

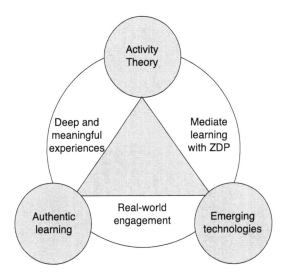

Figure 9.2 Using Activity Theory and ETs

Redrawn from Anderson (2010).

in vogue in other disciplines or in Northern contexts, for example. The definition is also broad enough to incorporate a number of different ways in which tools can be used to transform teaching and learning.

While these categorisations provide a way of understanding emerging technologies in education, the effective uses of technologies requires being cognisant of cultural-historical context in which teaching and learning happens. One of the uses of technologies is mediating student interaction. Anderson (2010) argues that meaningful learning is realised when interactions are fostered in any learning activity. We argue the use of Activity Theory provides a way of visualising the roles of emerging technologies in mediating the interactions as espoused by Anderson (see Figure 9.2). However, meaningful learning as a learning outcome requires that the design of an activity system is conceptualised as an authentic learning task.

In the conception of ETs that we are proposing, technologies are not only seen as tools, but incorporate theories and approaches to teaching and learning in higher education. Thus, the concept 'technology' is viewed in its broadest sense as a craft or art, which is consistent with a cultural historical activity theory perspective as elucidated in Part I of this edited collection.

Mediating transformative learning outcomes

While ETs have potential to transform learning, there is a danger that they can merely be used to promote mundane teacher-centric activities. Anderson (2004) argues that emergent or transformative learning happens when technology is used

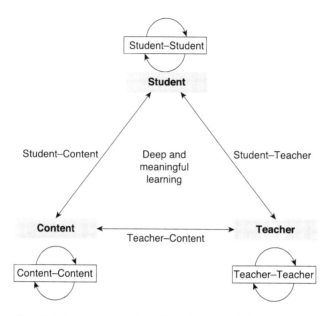

Figure 9.3 Deep and meaningful learning using ETs

to foster high levels of student–student interaction; teacher–student interaction, and student–content interaction, which in turn can lead to deep and meaningful learning. However, for these to mediate higher cognitive function, they need to be wrapped around careful pedagogical design for which authentic learning principles provide a useful framework (see Figure 9.3).

ET changes the way learning happens. For example, students and lecturers used to engage deeply with full texts, but now have access to a deluge of information, and thus need to discern which texts are authoritative and relevant. This means that discernment abilities have become even more important to acquire for transformative learning to happen. The extent that technology can curate resources changes how people learn and broadens access for students and teachers. There are also opportunities for putting ideas across to global communities as access to technology widens access to people. The DIY and maker movement provide participatory ways of learning (Ratto & Boler, 2014).

The role of emerging technologies in CHAT is to mediate learning within a learner's ZPD. The design of activity systems that have potential to realise transformative learning outcomes are governed by authentic learning principles. ETs have affordances that make possible the principles of authentic learning, providing support for engagement with the real-world while creating an archive of a digital trail of student learning. Thus, this framework is consistent with emergent/ transformative learning (Williams et al., 2011).

According to Williams et al., prescriptive learning is based on knowledge that is pre-determined for learners. The contrast is emergent/transformative learning

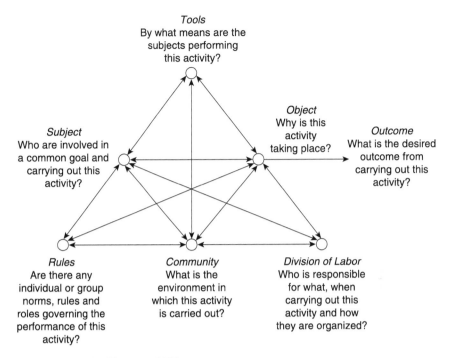

Figure 9.4 Activity Theory and ETs

Redrawn from Zurita and Nussbaum (2007).

which arises out of interactions between a number of people and resources, and is learner-centered. It is typically self-organised and collaborative. It stands to reason that, used effectively; ETs may mediate the learning activities with emergent or transformative outcomes (Figure 9.4). It can be argued that emergent or transformative learning outcomes are higher-order cognitive functions for which the affordances of ETs are well placed to mediate.

Notes

1   Although Siemens and Tittenberger (2009) referred to in this paragraph may be regarded by some as outdated, we still regard them as relevant contributions to conceptualisations of emerging technologies, as they are one of the few full text references dealing with emerging technologies in education.
2   http://en.wikipedia.org/wiki/Mxit.

References

Anderson, T. (2003). Getting the mix right again: An updated and theoretical rationale for interaction. *International Review of Research in Open and Distance Learning, 4,* 2. Retrieved from: www.irrodl.org/index.php/irrodl/article/view/149/230.

Anderson, T. (2004). Toward a theory of online learning. In T. Anderson & F. Elloumi (Eds.), *Theory and practice of online learning*. Edmonton: Athabasca University Press.

Anderson, T. (2010). Theories for learning with emerging technologies. In G. Veletsianos (Ed.), *Emerging technologies in distance education*. Edmonton: Athabasca University Press.

Bozalek, V., Gachago, D., Alexander, L., Watters, K., Wood, D., Ivala, E., & Herrington, J. (2013). The use of emerging technologies for authentic learning: A South African study in higher education, *British Journal of Educational Technology*, *44*(4), 629–638.

Gachago, D., Ivala, E., Backhouse, J., Bosman, J. P., Bozalek, V., & Ng'ambi, D. (2013). Towards a shared understanding of emerging technologies: Experiences in a collaborative research project in South Africa. *The African Journal of Information Systems (AJIS)*, *5*(3), Article 4. Retrieved from: http://digitalcommons.kennesaw.edu/ajis/vol5/iss3/4.

Gartner Inc (n.d.). Research methodologies: Hype cycles. Retrieved from: www.gartner.com/newsroom/id/2575515.

Johnson, L., & Adams, S. (2011). *Technology outlook for UK tertiary education 2011–2016: An NMC Horizon Report regional analysis*. Austin, TX: The New Media Consortium.

Johnson, L., Adams, S. & Cummins, M. (2012). *The NMC Horizon Report: 2012 Higher education edition*. Austin, TX: The New Media Consortium.

Johnson, L., Adams Becker, S., Cummins, M., Estrada, V., Freeman, A., & Ludgate, H. (2013). *NMC Horizon Report: 2013 Higher education edition*. Austin, TX: The New Media Consortium.

Johnson, L., Adams Becker, S., Cummins, M., Estrada, V., & Meira, A. (2012). *Technology outlook for Brazilian primary and secondary education 2012–2017: An NMC Horizon project regional analysis*. Austin, TX: The New Media Consortium.

Johnson, L., Adams Becker, S., Estrada,V., & Freeman, A. (2014). *NMC Horizon Report: 2014 Higher education edition*. Austin, TX: The New Media Consortium.

Johnson, L., Adams Becker, S., Gago, D., Garcia, E., & Martín, S. (2013). *Technology outlook: Latin American higher education 2013–2018: An NMC Horizon project regional analysis*. Austin, TX: The New Media Consortium.

Johnson, L., Levine, A., Smith, R., & Stone, S. (2010). *The 2010 Horizon Report*. Austin, TX: The New Media Consortium.

Ng'ambi, D., & Bozalek, V. (2013a). Editorial: Emerging technologies and changing learning/teaching practices, *British Journal of Educational Technology*, *44*(4), 531–535.

Ng'ambi, D., & Bozalek, V. (2013b). Leveraging informal leadership in higher education institutions: a case of diffusion of emerging technologies in a southern context, *British Journal of Educational Technology*, *44*(6), 940–950.

Ratto, M., & Boler, M. (2014). *DIY citizenship: Critical making and social media*. Cambridge, MA: MIT Press.

Siemens, G., & Tittenberger, P. (2009). *Handbook of emerging technologies for Learning emerging technologies for learning*. Retrieved from: http://ltc.umanitoba.ca/wikis/etl/index.php/Handbook_of_Emerging_Technologies_for_Learning.

Veletsianos, G. (2010). A definition of emerging technologies for education. In G. Veletsianos (Ed.), *Emerging technologies in distance education* (pp. 3–22). Edmonton: Athabasca University Press.

Veletsianos, G. (2011). Designing opportunities for transformation with emerging technologies. *Educational Technology*, *51*(2), 41–46.

Williams, R., Karousou, R., & Mackness, J. (2011). Emergent learning and learning ecologies in Web 2.0. *International Review of Research in Open and Distance Learning*, *12*(3), 39–59.

10 Twenty-first-century pedagogies

Portraits of South African higher educators using emerging technologies

Vivienne Bozalek, Daniela Gachago and Kathy Watters

> I suppose it typifies South Africa in many ways, that we're a country within a country; that there's this first world and third world mix that sort of keeps popping up in sometimes inconvenient settings like higher education.
>
> (Lecturer, Fort Hare University)

Introduction

Across the world, changes in higher education (HE) are driving institutions to explore the use of emerging technologies (ET) to improve their functioning and more particularly, to improve teaching and learning. These challenges include:

- an escalating demand for HE together with dwindling resources and simultaneous calls for widening participation (Burke, 2103);
- the increasing use of distance education and private providers of education and following globalization of education;
- a changing profile and expectations of students;
- new ideas on pedagogy and curriculum design;
- the demand of the "knowledge society" for a different kind of graduate (Johnson & Adams, 2011; Sharples, McAndrew, Weller, Ferguson, FitzGerald, Hirst, & Gaved, 2013, Johnson, Adams Becker, Cummins, Estrada, Freeman, & Ludgate, 2013).

In South Africa, the HE sector faces not only these challenges, but also ones related to the unique circumstances of this country due to its history and current context. South Africa's racially divided past continues to be reflected in access, and more importantly, success in HE, as well as in the configuration of public institutions and their resourcing (Badat, 2012; Council on Higher Education (CHE), 2013; Department of Higher Education and Training, 2013; Leibowitz & Bozalek, 2014). Due to the historical legacy in South Africa, higher education institutions (HEIs) are differently positioned in relation to resources and cultural capital, and yet all of them are required to produce graduates who can contribute to the knowledge economy and the social good in South Africa

(Bozalek & Boughey, 2012; Bozalek & Watters, 2014). Higher education in South Africa is further challenged by a largely dysfunctional and unequal public schooling system, high unemployment coupled with a shortage of key high-level skills, and widespread poverty (Lam, Ardington & Leibbrant, 2011; van der Berg, 2008).

The decreasing cost and consequent increasing availability of technologies are creating new possibilities for their use in education, while pedagogical and social practices are continuously being transformed. Drawing on Veletsianos's (2010) context-aware definition of ET, we view ET in education as "tools, technologies, innovations, and advancements utilized in diverse educational settings to serve varied education-related purposes" (p. 17). Previous research in this field has shown that South African educators use ET creatively to respond to the challenges that they are facing (see Bozalek, Ng'ambi & Gachago, 2013; Ng'ambi, Gachago, Ivala, Bozalek, & Watters, 2012; Ng'ambi, Bozalek, & Gachago, 2013), driven by individual agency and reflexivity in relation to their teaching and learning practices.

This chapter reports on interviews conducted with educators in which they reflect on what drives their innovative practices, within the context of differing and challenging circumstances of their work. In particular, we address the following questions:

1   What drives South African lecturers who use emerging technologies for authentic learning within the complexities of the current HE context?
2   What implications does this have for teaching and learning professional development in higher education?

We argue that common drivers for lecturers we interviewed to use emerging technologies for authentic learning were their heightened awareness of the circumstances with which their students are coping, awareness of the pedagogical affordances of tools, and their interest in developing students as critical agents of the social good and as future professionals.

Methodology

This chapter draws on data collected as part of a larger study that was funded by the National Research Fund (NRF) to investigate how ET can be used to improve teaching and learning in the HE sector. During August and September 2011 a survey was sent to all public HEIs in South Africa to establish the use of ET by academics and support staff to improve teaching. There were 262 responses with representation from all 22 public HEIs in South Africa; this excluded UNISA which only provides distance education. However, the data used for this chapter is based on a subset of 20 responses submitted and was selected for in-depth face-to-face interviews. Respondents were selected who appeared to be using ET for authentic learning. The semi-structured interviews were conducted by five members of the NRF project team and focused on rationale, design, impact, and challenges of the individual teaching intervention(s) using ET and lecturers' underlying teaching and learning beliefs. The interviews were transcribed and then analyzed by the three co-authors for evidence of teacher responses to teaching and learning challenges and the role of technology in responding to these challenges. Data analysis was done in an inductive way, collectively by the three authors, who in a first round of thematic data analysis identified emerging themes across the interviews and then in a second round divided interviews up and selected emblematic verbatim quotes which could best exemplify these themes. To foreground the lecturers' voices in this chapter, we included lengthy quotes in the findings.

The gender of the interviewees was evenly distributed with 11 of the 20 being female. Most of the sample were from the applied sciences (8) while natural sciences (3), education (3), health sciences (3), education (3) humanities (2) and commerce (1) were also represented. Interviewees came from 10 of the 22 HEIs in South Africa. Interviewees represented a range of levels of experience in working at HEIs; six were either associate or full professors, one was a senior lecturer, nine were lecturers and four classified themselves as non-academics. Interestingly only four of the educators had formal teaching qualifications. The research project received ethical clearance from the University of Western Cape.

Findings and discussion

An analysis of the 20 interviews conducted revealed three common themes: (1) lecturers' awareness of the circumstances of their students and how these impact their learning; (2) an awareness of the pedagogical affordances of tools; and (3) their interest in developing students as critical agents of the social good and as future professionals. These three themes are discussed below.

Students in South African higher education

In addition to considering the pedagogical and technological affordances which foster learning, it is important to pay close attention to students' learning needs and experiences (Veletsianos, 2013). South Africa has a low graduation rate of 17 per cent (CHE, 2013), and research has indicated that success, graduation and dropout rates in HE are linked to students in terms of the poverty that they experience (Branson, Garlick, Lam, & Leibbrandt, 2012; Breier, 2010; CHE, 2013). This poverty has a strong influence on student access to the resources required to succeed in HE. A study conducted by the Human Sciences Research Council's Student Pathways study in 2006 and 2007 found that approximately 60 per cent of students dropped out of university and that 70 per cent of families of HE dropouts are poor (Letseka & Maile, 2008). Letseka and Maile (2008) and Breier (2010) suggest that many students who leave institutions prematurely appear to do so because they cannot afford to remain studying.

Lecturers we interviewed demonstrated an understanding of their students in varying ways: one was that they were conscious of the economic and social responsibilities with which many students are encumbered (Bozalek & Carolissen, 2012), as the following quote shows:

> [M]any of our students are head of a child-headed household and they have siblings back home [for whom] they are financially responsible, ... our students just often pitch up in class and they haven't slept and they haven't washed and they haven't eaten.

The lecturers were also aware of the general conditions of poverty and inadequate schooling that students had experienced, and their position as first generation learners as depicted in the following responses by lecturers:

> [M]any of our students come from very poor home backgrounds and also not the best educational backgrounds in terms of their formative schooling.

> [M]ost of our students, and when I say most I'm thinking it's about three-quarters . . . are first-generation students and most of them come from rural areas.

An extreme example of the condition in which students are trying to learn was that one student was found to be squatting in a computer laboratory as she had nowhere to live. The lecturers we interviewed responded empathetically to the contexts of their students and found ways to support them. A lecturer struggling with large groups of students of varying capabilities reported that he structured the groups ensuring that:

> [T]hey have been created not as homogeneous groups but have groups of both students that are quite comfortable and students that are finding themselves out of their depth. They're not confident, and don't speak well [when making presentations in front of students from more resourced HEIs].

Lecturers are not only highly aware of their students' contexts, but this awareness influenced their choice of technologies used in the classroom, resulting in a heightened sensitivity towards the types of technologies accessible to students in their social and professional authentic contexts, as the following lecturers explain:

> I started off using Blackboard and it is a wonderful tool, but since then I found that it's easier and less time-consuming for me to use PDFs, interactive Adobe PDFs. So I've actually taken my textbook off because when students go home and they haven't got the Internet and they can't use the textbook – so I give it to them as a PDF.

> [O]ne of our previous graduates was saying in their office in a very rural setting, they have one computer for eight social workers and no Internet or

email facility. And so the tension here is if I'm investing in them in class and we're taking them to a level of technological advancement or to e-learning and then they're going out to settings where they don't even have cell phone reception or Internet access.

As a response to students' lack of access to technology in the workplace, the lecturer decided to use Facebook as a teaching tool because all of his students had access on their mobile phones and seem to have the skills to use it, as he describes: '[t they seem to be able to use that quite well, their skill-level for Facebook seems to be better than anything else that they do.'

Awareness of pedagogical affordance of tools

It is important that innovations in teaching and learning should be driven by an engagement with pedagogical principles and considerations (Dabbagh & Bannan-Ritland, 2005). Authors such as Herrington, Reeves and Oliver (2010) foreground the affordances of ET to support authentic learning, a pedagogical approach based on social constructivist theorists such as Vygotsky (1978) (see Chapter 5 for more details on authentic learning). This approach has gained momentum globally with its focus on exposing students to real-world contexts and problems in the classroom and as such addressing the increased need of employers for graduates who can respond to the increasingly complex environments they are going to encounter.

The lecturers we interviewed displayed an awareness of pedagogical affordances of tools they experimented with for authentic learning and were not afraid of taking risks, exploring new tools, discarding and replacing them with others, when realizing that they might fit better.

The following quote describes how a lecturer, instead of using multiple choice questions as standard practice in other disciplines, which would reduce his marking time considerably, persisted with essay-type questions, which needed more time to mark but were, in his view, more beneficial to student learning:

I'm sort of envious from a lecturing perspective that . . . colleagues can get an Excel spreadsheet . . . [that] they didn't even have to mark, the computer did it for them. . . . But the negative is ultimately those students are learning how to choose option a, b, c or d as opposed to how to reference properly, how to enter into a proper academic debate, how to see my pencil feedback all over their script.

As students in this course are required to write reports for their professional practice, writing skills are of critical importance to their development, and this lecturer's pedagogical considerations improved the authenticity of this learning experience.

In the following example, one of the lecturers interviewed reflected on how poorly prepared his students were for the demands of studying at an HEI and how he developed strategies to deconstruct complex activities into a series of steps so that each step built on the previous step, thus scaffolding the learning process, which is one of the core elements of authentic learning:

> The one course where I use this approach is the industrial ecology. And in that one they create a hypothetical situation . . . they create a hypothetical factory, they create a hypothetical product. At first year it's design a product, design a factory, design a manufacturing process. And they sit and they start to do a very structured analysis of routing, working out carbon footprints, sources of labour, tax incentives, and then also distribution, packaging, labeling. So that's what we call a very sequential approach to it.

The same lecturer used the affordances of Google translator in an innovative approach to develop students' academic literacy, relating the activity to students' real-life practices and making it authentic and meaningful to their own lives, as he explains below:

> We had a blog and people felt it was very informal, so they used SMS talk. And then we tried to translate SMS into another language using Google translator and I showed them it didn't work. And then I said, but if you used English and you use a Google translator it might actually work and so what you're doing is you're increasing the understanding to a larger number of the population by using simple but structured English.

Another example of authentic learning is where podcasting was used in a student-rather than traditional lecturer-centred way to scaffold learning, is reported in the following quote:

> [W]ith the second years we have used podcasting. The students interview clients but not a real client, a pseudo client . . . So they record it on their cellphones and then they email us the podcast or put it on a disk . . . .[and when they] play it back to themselves, they can actually hear where they went wrong or where they need improving on their interviewing skills.

These interviewing skills are also part of the graduate attributes discussed more fully in the following section that students in the caring professions need to develop.

Focus on graduate attributes

Lecturers who were interviewed identified the importance of graduate attributes of critical scholarship, critical citizenship and lifelong learning to prepare students as agents of social good dealing with the complexity and uncertainty of the twenty-first century (Barnett, 2004). These three graduate attributes are the major ones identified by the University of the Western Cape, but similar ones have been identified by many other higher education institutions (Bozalek & Watters, 2014). The ways in which lecturers developed these attributes can be seen in the examples below.

Critical scholarship

A lecturer working with physiotherapy students identified a disconnect between what it is to be a physiotherapist in practice and what students are expected to do in the classroom. To counteract this, he started to 'model uncertainty' in the comments that were given to students' collaboratively developed lecture notes on Google drive by lecturers and tutors. As he says:

> [W]e model the fact that we don't have all the answers . . . what we are saying to them, now there's no more facts, now what? Because when they graduate they've got no one to give them all the facts and we need to give them the skills now for them to be able to go out into the real world and say, oh, I don't have this answer. Now what do I know? What do I need to find out? How will I find it out? . . .

In this way he was able to develop clinical reasoning skills needed for physiotherapy students, by challenging, as he put it "every single statement that the student makes that is not explicitly guided by a reason".

Critical citizenship and participation

A journalism lecturer reported on a module she had presented that involved developing students to become journalists. She used ideas of critical citizenship and citizen inquiry by fusing collaborative inquiry-based learning with citizen activism (Sharples et al., 2013). She described:

> [her aim of] involving citizens as it boosts democracy by allowing people to voice their own concerns, goes past some of the ideas of gatekeeping and also allows stories to be told from a different perspective.

Strategies included getting citizens – both schoolchildren and those who were unemployed from marginalized communities – to SMS information to community newspapers and radio stations. The lecturer used a modelling process with her students who were first taught to produce text and video sound bites, students then passed on their recently learnt skills to members of the local community:

> It's quite difficult to get ordinary people to contribute video – but I thought most people do have mobile phones and even though the audio on mobile phones is really bad, we could kind of work together with the student so that the student could collaborate with ordinary people . . . to produce completed videos.

The lecturer reported that the finished products were used as a catalyst in local discussion forums and had been posted on YouTube[1] to facilitate sharing on mobile phones among the community.

Lifelong learners

As shown in some of the examples above, where lecturers selected tools and technologies to support students' learning beyond the classroom, student-owned and controlled devices and technologies, such as mobile phones and tablets, become essential tools in building their personal learning environments and preparing them to be lifelong learners (Sharples et al., 2013). We would argue that one of the most important elements of lifelong learning is students' awareness of the importance of using their own devices for accessing information and participating in conversation to develop critical digital literacies beyond the classroom. This makes it important, rather than be punitive with students' use of mobile phones in the classroom, to design learning activities that promote students' use of their mobile devices in and outside the classroom. The following quote shows a lecturer's positive experiences with using mobile phones as active learning devices in his teaching:

> [S]tudents have proved to be very, very resourceful in terms of finding information. I've been surprised at how resourceful. Well, most of them have BlackBerry smartphones, so the access of the Internet is essentially no extra cost. I would say 95 per cent of students now at first year have BlackBerry smartphones.

The above responses show some of the creative ways in which the interviewed lecturers used emerging technologies to promote graduate attributes, such as critical citizenship, scholarship and lifelong learning, and managed to devise innovative ways of developing skills and attitudes in students that would allow them to actively participate as critical citizens in a global world.

Conclusion

This chapter provides an overview of the driving forces that enabled innovative lecturers aiming to create successful authentic learning experiences for their students working with the affordances of emerging technologies, given the complexities of the current South African HE context.

Common threads running across these lecturers' practices were their attentiveness to their students' learning needs, their awareness of the pedagogical affordances of tools and the creative ways in which they developed graduate attributes. Their knowledge of their students' circumstances allowed them to tailor their interventions specifically to match the needs of their students. They developed interventions that were experiential, collaborative, reflexive and student-led. Their approaches showed examples of how one could promote graduate attributes in students using emerging technologies. The importance of students creating their own personal learning environment using their own internet-enabled devices to facilitate their participation in the global world beyond the classroom is of particular relevance for lifelong learning.

Many of these practices can be linked to the elements that are outlined in Herrington et al.'s (2010) authentic learning framework, such as the development of an authentic task, an authentic context, and scaffolding. The technologies that these higher educators chose to use were those which were often not under institutional control, such as social media, podcasting, wikis, Google apps, digital storytelling, blogs and mobile learning. These lecturers, in order to address specific teaching and learning challenges, such as large classes, remote learners, and to facilitate access to learning in resource-poor environments, appropriated these technologies. The technologies selected by this group of higher educators may not be regarded to be the perfect match for what they wanted to achieve. Indeed, the transient nature of these technologies and conflicting needs of lecturers and students meant that they were often in the process of development, experimentation and negotiation with their students about the kind of technologies to use, and thus they may not always yield the desired or expected results. However, these case studies of exemplary lecturers showed the importance of having the confidence to take risks and to continuously seek solutions to improve pedagogy and student learning in the often highly constrained, uncertain and complex South African HE context.

We can conclude that these lecturers were attentive, responsible and imaginative in their dealings with their students – showing a deep sense of care for their students' present and future well-being. The imaginative use of ET represented one way of meeting people across the divides of the differing worlds that South Africans inhabit. The implications for professional practice are that it is important to move away from a discourse of efficiency and an obsession with marks or grades, to a focus on how critical citizenship, scholarship and lifelong learning can be promoted through the use of emerging technologies. Furthermore, it is important to be attentive to the current needs and knowledges of students and to tap into current practices and devices that students have.

Note

1　See more information on the project on www.upstartyouth.com/.

References

Badat, S. (2012). Redressing the colonial/apartheid legacy: Social equity, redress, and higher education admissions in democratic South Africa. In Z. Hasan & M. Nussbaum (Eds.), *Equalizing access: Affirmative action in higher education in India, United States, and South Africa*. New Delhi: Oxford University Press.

Barnett, R. (2004). Learning for an unknown future. *Higher Education Research and Development*, *14*(3), 247–260.

Bozalek, V., & Boughey, C. (2012). (Mis)framing Higher Education in South Africa. *Social Policy and Administration, 46*(6), 688–703.

Bozalek, V., & Carolissen, R. (2012). The potential of critical feminist citizenship frameworks for citizenship and social justice in higher education, *Perspectives in Education, 30*(4), 9–18.

Bozalek, V., Ng'ambi, D., & Gachago, D. (2013). Transforming teaching with emerging technologies: Implications for higher education institutions. *South African Journal of Higher Education, 27*(2), 419–436.

Bozalek, V., & Watters, K. (2014). The potential of authentic learning and emerging technologies for developing graduate attributes, *South African Journal of Higher Education, 28*(3), 1069–1084.

Branson, N., Garlick, J., Lam, D., & Leibbrandt, M. (2012). Education and inequality: The South African case. A Southern Africa Labour and Development Research Unit Working Paper No. 75. Cape Town: SALDRU, University of Cape Town.

Breier, M. (2010). Dropout or stop out at the University of the Western Cape? In M. Letseka, M. Cosser, M. Breier, & M. Visser (Eds.), *Student retention & graduate destination: Higher education and labour market access and success* (pp. 25–40). Cape Town: HSRC Press.

Burke, P. (2013). The right to higher education: Neoliberalism, gender and professional mis/recognitions. *International Studies in Sociology of Education, 23*(2), 107–126. doi: 10.1080/09620214.2013.790660.

Council on Higher Education (2013). A proposal for undergraduate curriculum reform in South Africa: The case for a flexible curriculum structure. In *Report on the task team on undergraduate curriculum structure*. Pretoria: Council on Higher Education.

Dabbagh, N., & Bannan-Ritland, B. (2005). *Online learning: Concepts, strategies, and applications.* Upper Saddle River, NJ: Pearson Prentice Hall.

Department of Higher Education and Training (2013). *Statistics on post-school education and training: 2011.* Pretoria: Government Printer.

Henschke, J. A. (2010). Bringing together personal learning, higher education institutions elements, and global support for a re-orientation towards a focus on lifelong learning and education. In V. Wang (Ed.), *Encyclopedia for using technology in adult and career education.* Hershey, PA: IGI Global.

Herrington, J., Reeves, T. C., & Oliver, R. (2010). *A guide to authentic e-learning.* New York: Routledge.

Johnson, L., & Adams, S. (2011). *Technology outlook UK tertiary education 2011–2016: An NMC Horizon Report regional analysis technology.* Austin, TX: New Media Consortium.

Johnson, L., Adams Becker, S., Cummins, M., Estrada, V., Freeman, A., & Ludgate, H. (2013). *NMC Horizon Report: 2013 higher education edition.* Austin, TX: New Media Consortium.

Lam, D., Ardington, C., & Leibbrant, M. (2011). Schooling as a lottery: Racial differences in school advancement in Urban South Africa. *Journal of Development Economics, 95*(2), 121–136.

Leibowitz, B., & Bozalek, V. (2014). Foundation provision: A social justice perspective. *South African Journal of Higher Education.*

Letseka, M., & Breier, M. (2008). Student poverty in higher education: The impact of higher education dropout on poverty. In *Education and poverty reduction strategies: Issues of policy coherence: Colloquium proceedings*, S. Maile (Ed.) (pp. 83–101). Cape Town: HSRC Press.

Letseka, M., & Maile, S. (2008). High university drop-out rates: A threat to South Africa's future. *Human Sciences Research Council Policy Brief.* Pretoria: HSRC Press.

Ng'ambi, D., Bozalek, V., & Gachago, D. (2013). Empowering educators to teach using emerging technologies in higher education: A case of facilitating a course across institutional boundaries. In *Proceedings of the 8th International Conference on e-Learning*, Cape Peninsula University of Technology, 27–28 June.

Ng'ambi, D., Gachago, D., Ivala, E., Bozalek, V., & Watters, K. (2012). Emerging technologies in South African higher education institutions: Towards a teaching and learning framework. In *Proceedings of the 7th International Conference on e-Learning*. Lam, P. (Ed.). The Chinese University of Hong Kong: 21–22 June (pp. 354–362). Retrieved from: http://academic-conferences.org/pdfs/ICEL_2012-Abstract-booklet. pdf.

Sharples, M., McAndrew, P., Weller, M., Ferguson, R., FitzGerald, E., Hirst, T., & Gaved, M. (2013). *Innovating pedagogy 2013: Open University innovation report 2*. Milton Keynes: The Open University.

van der Berg, S. (2008). How effective are poor schools? Poverty and educational outcomes in South Africa, Centre for European Governance and Economic Development Research Discussion Paper 69.

Veletsianos, G. (2010). A definition of emerging technologies for education. In G. Veletsianos (Ed.) *Emerging technologies in distance education* (pp. 1–22). Edmonton: Athabasca University Press.

Veletsianos, G. (2013). *Learner experiences with MOOCs and open online learning: Hybrid pedagogy*. Retrieved from: http://learnerexperiences.hybridpedagogy.com.

Vygotsky, L. S. (1978). *Mind in society: The development of higher psychological processes*. M. Cole, V. John-Steiner, S. Scribner, & S. Souerman (Eds. and Trans.). Cambridge, MA: Harvard University Press.

11 Emerging technologies in New Zealand

A pedagogical framework for mobile social media

Thomas Cochrane, Vickel Narayan and James Oldfield

Introduction

Authentic learning is concerned with changing higher education pedagogy from its traditional focus upon teacher-delivered content, often involving theoretical concepts devoid of real-world application, towards pedagogies that focus upon transformative learning experiences for students. Unfortunately the predominant pedagogical mode in higher education is still the traditional model of teacher-delivered content, and thus we are presented with the problem of how to enable pedagogical change within our institutions. Hase and Kenyon (2007) argue that pedagogical change requires a catalyst, and we believe that mobile social media (MSM) provides such a catalyst (Kukulska-Hulme, 2010), enabling educators to look beyond the confines of established formal learning and to redefine the role of both the teacher and the learner. We propose that there are three strands involved in designing a curriculum for pedagogical change: (1) developing new pedagogical frameworks; (2) a refocus upon the unique affordances and new opportunities enabled by new technologies (Puentedura, 2006; Kaufman & Sternberg, 2007); and (3) reconceptualizing the role of the teacher and the learner (Danvers, 2003). This involves engaging with new pedagogies and frameworks such as the Pedagogy-Andragogy-Heutagogy (PAH) continuum (Luckin et al., 2010), authentic learning, and other ontological pedagogies (Danvers, 2003) that are focused upon students moving from learning about a subject to *becoming* active members of their chosen profession. We have chosen mobile social media as our pedagogical change catalyst because of the ability to design social constructivist learning environments using social media, and the ubiquitous nature of mobile device ownership provides a democratizing technology that can be used beyond the confines of the classroom and beyond the myopic constraints of institutional learning management systems (Herrington, Reeves, & Oliver, 2005).

Critical success factors for designing and implementing authentic mobile learning

Between them, the authors of this chapter have implemented over 60 mlearning projects, and from evaluating and refining these we have identified six critical success factors (CSF) for implementing mobile social media for enabling pedagogical change (Cochrane, 2012; Narayan & Herrington, 2012):

- the pedagogical integration of the technology into the course and assessment;
- lecturer modelling of the pedagogical use of the tools;
- creating a supportive learning community;
- appropriate choice of mobile devices and Web 2.0 social software;
- technological and pedagogical support;
- creating sustained interaction that facilitates the development of ontological shifts, both for the lecturers and the students.

In the following sections we discuss how our identified critical success factors can be mitigated by using a mash-up of frameworks to guide the design of mobile social media projects.

Mobile learning enabling authentic learning principles

Chapter 5 of this book presents an in-depth overview of authentic learning by Jan Herrington. Herrington et al. (2009) have identified nine design principles for authentic mobile learning (ALP). In this section we briefly explore the implications of these nine principles (highlighted in bold) in light of our identified critical success factors for mobile social media.

1   **An authentic context that reflects the way the knowledge will be used in real life**: Mobile social media leverages the ubiquity of mobile device ownership and enables the formation of professional networks and serendipitous learning.
2   **Authentic tasks**: Focusing upon student-generated e-portfolios created from a mash-up of best-in-class mobile social media platforms enables student creativity and collaboration that is in stark contrast to the typical digital myopia enforced by the reliance upon institutional learning management systems.
3   **Access to expert performances and the modelling of processes**: Lecturers must engage with and model the educational use of mobile social media within the curriculum. This requires reconceptualizing mobile social media from a purely social domain to an academic and professional domain of use.
4   **Multiple roles and perspectives**: Mobile social media allows students to become content generators across both formal and informal learning contexts.
5   **Collaborative construction of knowledge**: Mobile social media is inherently collaborative, but requires a significant rethink of assessment design, utilizing collaborative user-content generation tools such as Vyclone for collaborative video.
6   **Reflection**: Creation of student-generated mobile social media e-portfolios enables curation, critique and reflection.

7   **Articulation**: Mobile social media can utilize a variety of collaborative presentation and interaction tools, such as Prezi, and wireless screen-mirroring via an AppleTV connected to a large screen display.
8   **Coaching and scaffolding**: Mobile learning provides powerful tools for enabling the nurturing of learning communities across varied contexts that previously would have been impossible.
9   **Authentic assessment**: Assessment activities need to leverage the unique affordances of mobile social media.

The affordances of mobile social media

Many mobile learning projects have focused upon the flexibility of access to content via mobile devices but have achieved little in terms of changing pedagogy. Puentedura (2006) provides a simple framework (SAMR) for educational technology adoption and pedagogical change that can be matched to the unique affordances of mobile social media when designing appropriate learning activities and assessments. The SAMR framework defines four levels of technology adoption: Substitution, Augmentation, Modification, and Redefinition (SAMR). Puentedura argues that educators need to move beyond substitution of activities from traditional technologies onto new technologies towards redefining activities and assessments enabled by the affordances of new technologies. We argue that flexibility of content access via mobile learning represents substitution of teacher-generated content, whereas mobile social media enables redefining learning around student-generated content, for example, using the built-in camera of smartphones for students to capture and share experiences beyond the classroom, geolocate activities, and collaborate via Twitter and Google Plus across geographical and timezone barriers.

As educators we value the development of creativity within our students as one of our key learning outcomes. The SAMR framework aligns closely with Kaufman and Sternberg's (2007) definition of three levels of creativity: reproduction (Substitution and Augmentation), incrementation (Modification), and reinitiation (Redefinition). This reinforces a focus upon the unique affordances of mobile social media when designing appropriate activities and assessments for learning.

Ontological pedagogies

Thinking differently about teaching and learning is predicated upon a reconception of the role of the teacher and the learner. This represents an ontological shift or reconception of roles from a prior category to another. Danvers (2003) argues that the creative professions require pedagogies that focus upon role reconception or ontological pedagogies. One such ontological pedagogical framework is the Pedagogy-Andragogy-Heutagogy (PAH) continuum proposed by Luckin et al. (2010). Luckin et al. argue that heutagogy, or student-directed learning, need not be the sole domain of post-graduate education, but can be achieved at any

Table 11.1 The characteristics of three levels of pedagogy

	Pedagogy	*Andragogy*	*Heutagogy*
Locus of control	Teacher	Learner	Learner
Education sector	Schools	Adult education	Doctoral research
Cognition level	Cognitive	Meta-cognitive	Epistemic
Knowledge production context	Subject understanding	Process negotiation	Context shaping

educational level, and define the characteristics of three levels of pedagogy (Table 11.1).

Hase and Kenyon (2007) argue that heutagogy builds student capability: "Capability is a holistic attribute and concerns the capacity to use one's competence in novel situations rather than just the familiar . . . having appropriate values, being able to work in teams, and knowing how to learn" (p. 113). We propose that mobile social media provides the tools to enable lecturers to design learning environments for heutagogy, such as student-directed projects, providing a rich set of collaborative and student content generation tools.

A mobile social media framework for authentic learning

Activity Theory has been used as a theoretical foundation for designing mobile learning projects by many mobile learning researchers, however, we agree with Pachler, Bachmair and Cook (2010) that Activity Theory presents a barrier to mobile learning for the average lecturer who may be an expert teacher in their field but does not necessarily have the depth of educational technology theory needed to operationalize the complexities of Activity Theory.

> Activity Theory (AT) is characterised by a number of features and weaknesses, which make it unsuitable for our purposes . . . We would argue that as with Engeström's original model, the level of abstraction is too high for it to be readily operationalisable and, therefore, the model is arguably of limited value for policy makers and practitioners.
>
> (Pachler et al., 2010, p. 163)

Based upon our experiences of implementing mobile learning in a range of educational contexts we believe that widespread adoption of mobile learning requires a more pragmatic foundation than AT, and therefore we have developed a framework based upon our goals of enabling new pedagogies by designing new learning experiences using mobile social media. Our mobile social media framework is a mash-up of associated frameworks that work together to achieve creative social-cultural pedagogy, mapped onto the pedagogy-andragogy-heutagogy continuum (Luckin et al., 2010). The goal of this framework is to provide a simple guide to the types of activities and assessment strategies that focus upon authentic learning enabled by mobile social media. Thus, we leverage the three strands: (1) developing new pedagogical frameworks (Herrington et al., 2009); (2) a refocus upon the unique affordances and new opportunities enabled by new technologies (Puentedura, 2006; Kaufman & Sternberg, 2007); and (3) reconceptualizing the role of the teacher and the learner (Danvers, 2003). The framework also indicates how our six critical success factors are met (Cochrane, 2012).

We propose that our mobile social media framework provides a guide for educators to design appropriate learning activities and assessment strategies to create authentic learning environments. In the following sections we illustrate the application of this framework within three different case studies.

Mobile social media case studies

This chapter uses three case studies in three different higher education contexts to illustrate how authentic mobile learning can be achieved using our mobile social media framework. Having collaborated on implementing many mobile social media projects together, the three authors chose one example each to illustrate how a common framework can implemented in different contexts. In these three cases the mobile device used was the iPad, however, we have also previously implemented mobile social media projects with a wide range of mobile devices including smartphones such as the iPhone, Android, Palm, and Symbian-based smartphones. The iPad is merely the most popular choice of new mobile device at the time of our three selected projects. In the discussion of these case studies, we bring together Herrington et al.'s nine principles with Cochrane's six critical success factors guided by a selection of learning frameworks as outlined in Table 11.2. In each case study an educational technology researcher partnered and collaborated with a group of lecturers within a department to form a community of practice (Lave & Wenger, 1991) that would support the exploration and integration of new pedagogical practices enabled by mobile social media. Table 11.2 provides a summary of the types of changes brought about in the curriculum by the mobile social media framework and provides a potentially transferable mobile social media framework for a variety of contexts.

Case study 1 Product Design

The context of the first case study was the third year of a Bachelor of Product Design at AUT University – New Zealand's newest university. Prior to the implementation of the mobile social media project, the AUT Product Design course used an institutionally hosted version of Mahara as a student e-portfolio, and all student projects and portfolios were required to be submitted as printed hard copies of written reports viewable by the student and their lecturer only, reinforcing a reluctance by students to share their designs. The participants of the

Table 11.2 Changes effected by the mobile social media framework

	Pedagogy	*Andragogy*	*Heutagogy*
Locus of control	Teacher	Learner	Learner
Course timeframe and goal	Initial establishment of a course project and induction into a wider learning community	Early to mid-course: Student appropriation of mobile social media and initial active participation	Mid to end of course: Establishment of major project where students actively participate within an authentic community of practice
Activity Types	Content delivery Digital assessment Teacher delivered content Teacher defined projects	Teacher as guide Digital identity Student-generated content Student negotiated teams	Teacher co-learner Digital presence Student-generated contexts Student negotiated projects
Cognition Level	Cognitive	Meta-cognitive	Epistemic
SAMR	Substitution & Augmentation: Portfolio to eportfolio PowerPoint on iPad Focus on productivity Mobile device as personal digital assistant and consumption tool	Modification: Reflection as VODCast Prezi on iPad New forms of collaboration Mobile device as content creation and curation tool	Redefinition: In-situ reflections Presentations as dialogue with source material Community building Mobile device as collaborative tool
Creativity	Reproduction	Incrementation	Reinitiation
Knowledge production context	Subject understanding: lecturers introduce and model the use of a range of mobile social media tools appropriate to the learning context	Process negotiation: students negotiate a choice of mobile social media tools to establish an eportfolio based upon user-generated content	Context shaping: students create project teams that investigate and critique user-generated content within the context of their discipline. These are then shared, curated, and peer-reviewed in an authentic COP
Supporting mobile social media affordances	Enabling induction into a supportive learning community	Enabling user-generated content and active participation within an authentic design COP	Enabling collaboration across user-generated contexts, and active participation within a global COP

(Continued)

Table 11.2 (Continued)

	Pedagogy	*Andragogy*	*Heutagogy*
Alignment with critical success factors	CSF 1, 2, 3	CSF 4, 5	CSF 5, 6
Alignment with authentic learning principles	ALP 1, 2, 3, 4	ALP 5, 6, 7	ALP 8, 9
Ontological shift	Reconceptualizing mobile social media: from a social to an educational domain	Reconceptualizing the role of the teacher	Reconceptualizing the role of the learner
Self-perception	Learning about	Learning to become	Active participation within a professional community

mobile social media project initiated in 2012 included 24 students, two lecturers, and two researchers. The project builds on previous mobile social media projects within the context of Product Design implemented at the researcher's previous institution which informed the initial development of a transferable mobile social media framework (Cochrane & Withell, 2013) that we extend in this chapter (see Table 11.2). As we are interested in pedagogical change and better graduate outcomes, a participatory action research methodology was used (Swantz, 2008). This allowed the participating lecturers to modify iterations of the project based upon student feedback. Students undertake team-based design projects in the first half of their final year of the Product Design course, and in 2012 a partnership was established with the Auckland Transport (AT) Company designed to provide student teams with an authentic experience of producing a project for AT as the client. The project involved designing an enhanced experience for commuters using AT buses in Auckland. Because mobility was a key part of the project specification we chose students' mobile devices to record their experiences and collaborate while experiencing bus travel throughout Auckland. As the goal of the project involved improving public experience, social media (such as Posterous and Twitter) was leveraged to interview bus patrons and publicize the student projects. A survey of the 2012 third year Product Design students at AUT University indicated that fewer than 40 per cent of the students owned smartphones and none owned tablet devices. Thus, the first iteration of the project in 2012 utilized only a basic set of mobile social media tools. Therefore, to take the project to a higher level in 2013 we required appropriate mobile devices for the participants. The authors applied for and secured a grant from Vodafone New Zealand to supply all third-year Product Design students with an iPad mini and 2GB per month mobile broadband data to utilize during the 2013 iteration of the project to investigate and design an enhanced commuting experience for public transportation on Auckland buses. An acceptable use policy was created and signed by all participating students that outlined the project expectations and use of the iPad Mini. Students also signed ethics consent forms consenting to anonymous use of data associated with the project for research publication. Students were expected to use their mobile device on a number of social media platforms for collecting data, collaborating in their teams, and sharing their project designs, including: Wordpress, Google Plus, YouTube (for recording Video reflections or VODcasts) and Twitter. The project was introduced and supported by several mobile social media tutorials in March 2013 and run by the researcher in partnership with the course lecturers, and these tutorials were curated via Evernote (http://tinyurl.com/b5d97vr). The project enabled a refocus from teacher-directed pedagogy towards student-directed heutagogy. Students were assessed on their application of the Design Thinking processes throughout the project. Project criteria included: planning and management, analysis, research, synthesis, communication, and appropriate use of mobile social media.

Students used their Wordpress blogs as the hub of their e-portfolios for the AT bus project, embedding YouTube videos and a variety of social media into their blogs. These were aggregated via RSS feeds using Google Reader as a news reader for automatically collating new student blog posts and media uploads, and curated by the students via the Flipboard App for reading and following one another's progress on their iPads. Analysis tools included the use of Surveymonkey for student feedback, discourse analysis of participant blog posts using collated word clouds, and transcription of participant reflective videos that had been uploaded to YouTube and embedded in their blogs. This enabled identification of emerging themes, and this was triangulated against the observation and identification of critical incidents from focus group discussions with selected students. Another rich source of comparative data indicating the pedagogical change initiated by the project was the use of Google Docs for collaborative comparison of previous course assessments with those developed as outcomes of the project.

Results

The initial rollout of iPad minis for the students was met with unsurprising enthusiasm, with the most immediate impact being most noticeable in a significant higher level of engagement with blogging as student design journals. A survey of the 24 participating students at the end of the first semester of the project asked the students to indicate what activities they had used the iPad for, shown in Figure 11.1 as percentages of students who used a range of mobile social media tools.

The survey also asked students to rate the most useful affordances of the iPad (Figure 11.2).

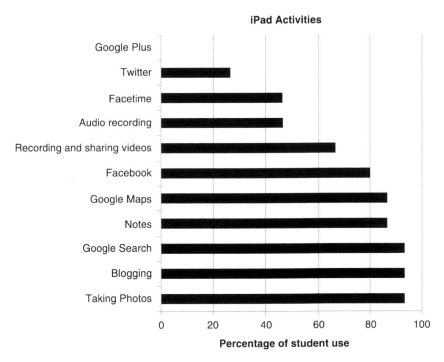

Figure 11.1 Types of iPad activities

Figure 11.1 indicates that students used the iPad mini to document their design processes and record the design activity associated with their projects. Less used were the communication affordances of the iPad, with Twitter being used by only 26 per cent of the students for collaborating on their projects, and none utilizing Google Plus. Some 80 per cent of students did, however, make use of Facebook on their iPad. Facetime (video calling) and audio recording were used by a significant number of students, mostly for free video calling between team members, and recording of interviews with industry experts and public transport patrons used to gather feedback on the Auckland Bus transportation system. One of the highest uses the iPad was for blogging, including blogging in situ while reflecting on their experiences. On average, student blog posts increased 500 per cent after the introduction of the iPad in 2013 in comparison to the average number of blog posts per student during 2012. Students also began embedding YouTube video reflections on their blogs for the first time after the introduction of the iPad.

> Since we received the iPads, my laptop has been collecting dust unless I need to do something involving Adobe CS, Solidworks or some lengthier writing. Being able to access the Internet from anywhere, in an intuitive and impressive visual format has been incredibly helpful . . . The addition of the iPad seems

to make the capturing and storing or transferring [of information] completely seamless, allowing me to not only go back and reflect on my thoughts or experiences, but also share them with others.

(Student blog post, March 2013)

Figure 11.2 indicates that the experience was a positive enhancement across a range of activities for students, with no direct negatives identified. Most valued by the students was the mobility and ubiquitous connectivity of the iPad, particularly allowing them to reflect and critique in-situ experiences that previously required separate documentation and subsequent recording and evaluation. They were able to record and critique the implementation of their bus trip enhancement designs while on location and coordinate intricate real-time experiments. A visual summary of student feedback was represented as a word cloud of collated student reflections on their iPad experience posted to their course blogs. The student reflective posts were copied, collated, and pasted into Wordle to provide a visual indication of the most cited terms in student comments – Wordle uses font size to represent the most frequently occurring terms. The creative, serendipitous and empowering nature of mobile blogging featured strongly in student feedback, as well as the temptation to procrastinate.

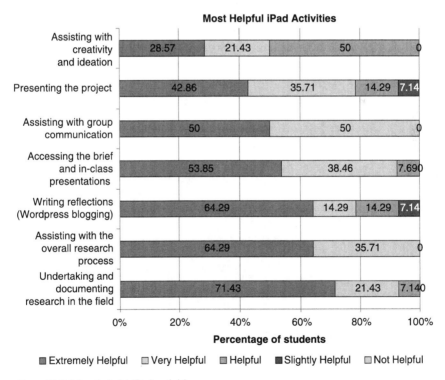

Figure 11.2 Most helpful iPad activities

The iPad project followed a process similar to Puentedura's (2006) SAMR model (Substitution, Augmentation, Modification, Redefinition) of educational technology transformation. Students initially used the iPad to replicate or replace activities they used their laptop computers for, but then progressively found creative affordances that enabled new ways of working that enabled them to modify and even redefine team activities and collaboration. Table 11.3 provides a summary of the types of changes brought about in the curriculum by the mobile social media project and provides a potential mobile social media framework for a variety of contexts. One of the initiatives of the course had been the development of a Design Thinking Toolbox (DTT) to provide students with a set of guidelines for good design. Initially the DTT had been developed as a set of Flash-based tutorials accessible on a computer from the institutions Learning Management System (Blackboard). As an outcome of the mobile social media project the DTT was redesigned as HTML5 for access via mobile devices. The project also initiated a new culture around the benefits of collaborative design and sharing of student work.

Case study 2 Journalism

Case study 2 was situated within the Journalism course at AUT University during 2012 to 2013. Social media tools such as Twitter, Facebook and YouTube coupled with the ubiquitous of a mobile device empowers the user to be a creator of digital content on the move (Sharples, Milrad, Arnedillo, & Vavoula, 2007; Whitworth, 2008). In an age where almost every person is equipped

Table 11.3 Potential mobile social media framework for a variety of contexts

	Pedagogy (pre 2012)	*Andragogy (2012)*	*Heutagogy (2013)*
Activity types	• DTT delivered • Digital assessment • Teacher-delivered content • Teacher-defined projects	• DTT as guide • Digital identity • Student-generated content • Student-negotiated teams	• DTT inherent • Digital presence • Student-generated contexts • Student-negotiated projects
SAMR	Substitution and Augmentation • Portfolio to eportfolio • PowerPoint on iPad • Focus on productivity • Mobile device as personal digital assistant and consumption tool	Modification • Reflection as VODCast • Prezi on iPad • New forms of collaboration • Mobile device as content creation and curation tool	Redefinition • In situ reflections • Presentations as dialogue with source material • Community building • Mobile device as collaborative tool

(International Telecommunication Union, 2013) with an Internet-enabled device, set up on at least one social media platform and can capture a picture, audio and video, this drastically impacts on the way news is collected, edited and reported (Newman, 2009). More importantly, the role of a journalist, the relationship with the audience, interaction and the identity are heavily influenced or enhanced by mobile and social media tools and its affordances (O'Sullivan & Heinonen, 2008).

The researchers worked with a group of 46 third-year journalism students with the aim of introducing mobile social media into the learning process for enhanced learning. Authentic learning and the six critical success factors for mobile learning were used as a framework to guide the design and facilitation of the course. Prior to the redesign of the course, the final grade was informed by the ten stories students wrote in the semester. Each story was pitched to the lecturer, written and submitted in print format. As such, every activity that students undertook in the semester-long course was confined within the four walls of the classroom. In extreme cases where a student had done extraordinary work, the story was pitched to a newspaper editor.

Using the principles of authentic learning (Herrington, 2006) and keeping mobile social media affordance in mind (Cochrane, 2012), a third-year journalism paper was redesigned in mid-2012. Table 11.4 outlines the use of authentic learning principles (ALP) and integration of MSM in the learning process.

A participatory action research (PAR) methodology (Kemmis & McTaggart, 2000) was used in this project. Data in this project was collected at various times and form. A pre-project survey was run to ascertain the type of mobile device ownership and what social media tools the students were already using. Qualitative data was collected from weekly reflections and discussions from volunteering students in class on the processes and learning experience over 12 weeks of the semester. Student blog posts and digital artefacts were also used as data in this project. A post-project survey using Google form was used to gather student data on the learning process. The data was transcribed into digital format (such as reflective video posts, hand-written notes taken by the researcher and weekly verbal feedback given by the students in class) and analysed using the process of data reduction, data display, conclusion drawing and verification (Miles & Huberman, 1994) to identify the themes and attributes for the approach taken. The impact of the design and implementation of the project on learning and teaching is further summarized later in the chapter.

Case study 3 Accountancy Law and Finance

Case study 3 involved a series of mobile learning projects within the Unitec Institute of Technology Bachelor of Business Undergraduate Degree Programme since the iPad was first introduced to New Zealand in 2010. Each of these projects was informed by the six critical success factors for implementing mobile social media for enabling pedagogical change (Cochrane, 2010). These projects initially focused primarily on the use of the iPad as a web-enabled tool to support the

Table 11.4 Authentic learning principles (ALP) and integration of MSM in the learning process

ALP		How they were implemented in the course
1	Authentic tasks have real-world relevance	The course was designed with an 'open' philosophy, meaning the students were given the freedom to choose and write stories on topics or leads they had discovered from their own sources. This allowed the students to act and behave like a journalist in real context. The integration of MSM in the process also gave the students an audience unlike before where it was between the student and the teacher only.
2	Authentic tasks are ill-defined	The open curriculum encouraged student participation lead to problems being defined and created by the student rather than the teacher.
3	Authentic tasks are complex in nature	The redesign of the course required the students to be active agents in the learning process simulating complex learning scenarios.
4	Enables multiple perspective	The use of mobile social media was embedded in the learning process. Students were required to set up a Twitter, Storify and WordPress (blog) accounts. Every story created had to be shared using the class hashtag on Twitter (#monlec). This enabled peer critique and feedback on the stories written.
5	Enables collaboration	Peer feedback was encouraged using social media. Students commented on stories written using a rubric for critiquing the quality and standard of the news reported in the post.
6	Provides opportunity for reflection	The peer feedback had to be taken into consideration and a justified of the actions taken had to be written by the student.
7	Is cross-disciplinary	The redesign and integration of MSM in the course had learning implications on taking pictures (how, angle and quality) and also impacted on the digital skills such as the use of videos, pictures and other multimedia in the write-up of the story.
8	Has embedded assessment	The ten stories posted on the blog effectively took the form of an eportfolio. The eportfolio became a living collection of digital stories or news the student had created or worked on.
9	Creation of polished products	The creation of an eportfolio at the end on the course for moderation and assessment purposes.

students' access to and creation of content in a socially constructed learning environment. One particular project was conducted in a first-year introductory information systems course in semester 2 of 2010. The course was spread across two streams, (one day stream and one night stream), each of approximately 30 students. The students in the day stream were equipped with first-generation

Table 11.5 Example affordances of the mobile devices

Mobile device capability	Supporting social constructivist pedagogy	Example application of affordances
eBooks	Background reading that formed the basis of class discussions	Individual access to material enabling students to be informed in their interaction with each other
Polling	A springboard for generating class conversations	Gathering and sharing of student thoughts, questions and answers. www.polleverywhere.com
Blogging	Peer critique and collaboration via commenting	Student ePortfolio creation. www.wordpress.com
Mind mapping	Concept linking and sharing of learner-generated content (Bruns, 2008)	Student idea creation and sharing. www.mindmeister.com

iPads and the students in the night stream were equipped with Dell netbooks. Both devices provided students with Internet connectivity via Wifi connection and supported the student learning experience to varying degrees. Each group of students made use of a range of web-based tools, such as blogging, mind mapping, collaborative documents and eBooks. The student learning experience was evaluated and compared between those who used the iPad and those used the netbooks. Students displayed a preference for the iPad over the netbook as it was easier to carry, read from and annotate (Cochrane, Narayan, & Oldfield, 2013). Example affordances of the mobile devices utilized in the initial 2010 Bachelor of Business mlearning project are outlined in Table 11.5.

Three years on from the initial iPad project, the information systems course in the first year of the Bachelor of Business course has been completely re-written to follow a model of authentic mobile learning. This re-write was informed by a combination of reflections on these initial projects and the theories of authentic learning (Herrington & Oliver, 2000; Herrington et al., 2010), cognitive tools (Jonassen & Reeves, 2004) and the mobile learning critical success factors developed by Cochrane (2010) and refined in (Cochrane, 2012), and is illustrated in Table 11.6.

All 65 students in the course have access to an iPad for the duration of the course. A number have their own, and those who do not were given the choice of borrowing either an iPad2 or an iPad mini (both the wifi-only 16GB version). The course follows a blended model with face-to-face teaching coupled with online access to materials and activities via an institutionally hosted Moodle course. All course material is provided in the iBook format, incorporating a variety of multimedia content with interactive elements, such as online polls and links to web-based content. Students reflect on their learning and experiences with the technologies used in the course via their own Wordpress blog. This blog is also used

Table 11.6 A model of authentic mobile learning

iPad capability	Supporting social constructivist pedagogy	Example application of affordances
Interactive iBooks	Background reading, multimedia, activity prompts and interactive elements that formed the basis of class discussions and activities	Individual access to material enabling students to be informed in their interaction with each other. www.apple.com/nz/ibooks-author/
Polling	A springboard for generating class conversations	Gathering and sharing of student thoughts, questions and answers, www.polleverywhere.com
Blogging	Reflection, peer critique and collaboration via commenting	Student eportfolio creation, www.wordpress.com
Collaborative mind mapping	Concept linking and sharing of learner-generated content (Bruns, 2008)	Student idea creation, brainstorming, sharing and collaboration. www.mindmeister.com
Collaborative documents	Provision of a virtual space for synchronous and asynchronous student collaboration on documents	Student group work platform enabling collaboration and communication. www.drive.google.com
Online presentations	Provision of a virtual space for synchronous and asynchronous student collaboration on presentations	Student group work platform enabling collaboration and remote presentation of content. www.prezi.com
VoIP Communication	Enabling communication at any time or place	Student group communication via smart device or PC. www.google.com/hangouts
Augmented reality	Enabling creation of rich digital content that augments and redefines interaction	Student creation of augmented reality enhanced authentic content. www.aurasma.com

as an eportfolio of their work, which they can use as evidence of the learning experience and capabilities later in life.

The learning environment for the course is based on a simulated company in which the students work as graduate interns. The company (Animal Adventures) is an adventure tourism company, which specializes in animal-themed adventure tours. The students' learning experience is guided by the completion of a series of authentic tasks, all set within the context of the Animal Adventures Company. The iPads are used to provide a more immersive simulation of the working environment. This is achieved through the use of ongoing characters (in varying roles, including managers and sales representatives) that are "brought to life" in audio interview excerpts embedded in the iBook materials. The iPads enable the students to perform these tasks in an authentic manner by creating business outputs, such as project plans, presentations and reports. Collaboration is a huge part of the course, as students spend the majority of their time working in groups on tasks, which are both formative and summative. The affordances of the iPad support students to work collaboratively both in and out of the classroom as they make use of collaborative tools (Apps in most instances) such as Google Drive, Prezi, Mindmeister and Google Hangouts. This helps to simplify the group work process as they can work together even when they are not physically in the same location.

Students undertake authentic assessment throughout the course, while acting in multiple roles, where they develop authentic content and articulate it in a variety of ways under simulated real-world circumstances. As systems analysts, they develop reports, which must be presented to the Animal Adventures management team, utilizing their iPads and other cognitive tools, such as Prezi and polleverywhere.com. As marketing materials developers, they develop marketing materials such as posters or presentations using tools such as Word and PowerPoint, augmented using Aurasma. As systems developers, they build a database and spreadsheet system the advantages of which they must demonstrate and defend to the Animal Adventures management team.

Students provided feedback on their learning experience through semi-structured interviews. All students found that the use of the iPad and the mobile learning techniques employed in the course had a positive effect on their learning experience.

A design-based research (Reeves, 2006) project has been used to develop and evaluate this course. Two iterations of experimentation with the course have been run with lecturer and student feedback gathered during and at the end of the course. Student reflections throughout the course are examined along with interviews staged after the course has completed. Initial discussions amongst teaching staff and lecturer reflections have been gathered to complement the student perceptions.

Conclusion

Each of the preceding three case studies was located within a different educational context, and each had a different focus upon the unique mobile social media affordances that supported their context. However, each had a common implementation methodology informed by our six critical success factors and the nine principles of authentic mobile learning, and therefore shared a common theoretical foundation focused upon a desire to enable new pedagogies. In each of these examples we have seen a significant change in pedagogical strategies and the integration of mobile social media in ways that move beyond merely substituting prior activities onto new technologies. By focusing upon a goal of transforming education from teacher-delivered content to enabling authentic collaborative experiences for our students, we have leveraged the unique affordances of mobile social media to achieve this within different educational contexts. Critical to this has been the establishment of collaborative communities of practice of lecturers and educational researchers who have modelled the use of mobile social media in their own teaching practice. Reconceptualizing the role of the teacher and the learner has enabled a focus upon ontological pedagogies rather than traditional teacher-directed pedagogies. Future research will explore the transfer of this framework within other higher education institutions throughout New Zealand.

Our case studies illustrate that mobile learning empowers authentic learning and can support collaborative curriculum design that focuses upon student-generated content and student-generated contexts. We have applied this approach to three different higher education contexts developing a potentially transferable mobile social media framework for enabling authentic learning.

References

Bruns, A. (2008). *Blogs, Wikipedia, Second Life, and beyond: From production to produsage.* New York: Peter Lang Publishing.

Cochrane, T. (2010). Exploring mobile learning success factors. *ALT-J, Research in Learning Technology, 18*, 133–148.

Cochrane, T. (2012). Critical success factors for transforming pedagogy with mobile Web 2.0. *British Journal of Educational Technology* (in pre-print doi:10.1111/j.1467-8535. 2012.01384.x).

Cochrane, T., Narayan, V., & Oldfield, J. (2013). iPadagogy: Appropriating the iPad within pedagogical contexts. *International Journal of Mobile Learning and Organisation, 7*(1), 48–65.

Cochrane, T., & Withell, A. (2013). Augmenting design education with mobile social media: A transferable framework. *Journal of the NUS Teaching Academy (JNUSTA)*, in review.

Danvers, J. (2003). Towards a radical pedagogy: Provisional notes on learning and teaching in art & design. *International Journal of Art & Design Education, 22*, 47–57.

Hase, S., & Kenyon, C. (2007). Heutagogy: A child of complexity theory. *Complicity: An International Journal of Complexity and Education, 4*, 111–118.

Herrington, J. (2006). Authentic e-learning in higher education: Design principles for authentic learning environments and tasks. In T. Reeves & S. Yamashita (Eds.), *World conference on E-learning in corporate, government, healthcare, and higher education.* Chesapeake, VA: AACE.

Herrington, J., & Oliver, R. (2000). An instructional design framework for authentic learning environments. *Educational Technology Research and Development, 48*(3), 23–48.

Herrington, J., Herrington, A., Mantei, J., Olney, I., & Ferry, B. (Eds.) (2009). *New technologies, new pedagogies: Mobile learning in higher education.* Wollongong: Faculty of Education, University of Wollongong.

Herrington, J., Reeves, T., & Oliver, R. (2005). Online learning as information delivery: Digital myopia. *Journal of Interactive Learning Research, 16*, 353–367.

Herrington, J., Reeves, T. C., & Oliver, R. (2010). *A guide to authentic e-learning.* London: Routledge.

International Telecommunication Union. (2013). *Measuring the information society.* Geneva, Switzerland: ITU.

Jonassen, D. H., & Reeves, T. (2004). Learning with technology: Using computers as cognitive tools. In D. H. Jonassen (Ed.), *Handbook of research on educational communications and technology.* New York: SP.

Kaufman, J. C. & Sternberg, R. J. (2007). Creativity. *Change: The Magazine of Higher Learning, 39,* 55–60.

Kemmis, S., & McTaggart, R. (2000). Participatory action research. In N. K. Denzin & Y. S. Lincoln (Eds.), *Handbook of qualitative research* (pp. 567–605). London: Sage.

Kukulska-Hulme, A. (2010). Mobile learning as a catalyst for change. *Open Learning: The Journal of Open and Distance Learning, 25,* 181–185.

Lave, J., & Wenger, E. (1991). *Situated learning: Legitimate peripheral participation.* Cambridge: Cambridge University Press.

Luckin, R., Clark, W., Garnett, F., Whitworth, A., Akass, J., Cook, J. et al. (2010). learner-generated contexts: A framework to support the effective use of technology for learning. In M. Lee & C. McLoughlin (Eds.), *Web 2.0-based e-learning: Applying social informatics for tertiary teaching* (pp. 70–84). Hershey, PA: IGI Global.

Miles, M. B., & Huberman, A. M. (1994). *Qualitative data analysis: An expanded sourcebook* (2nd ed.). Thousand Oaks, CA: Sage.

Narayan, J., & Herrington, J. (2012) Mobilising authentic learning: Understanding the educational affordances of the iPad. In M. Brown, M. Hartnett, & T. Stewart (Eds.), *Future challenges, sustainable futures: Proceedings of Ascilite 2012* (pp. 723–727). Wellington: Ascilite Massey University.

Newman, E. (2009). Latest OECD broadband statistics highlight NZ data caps. Weblog Retrieved from: www.tuanz.org.nz/blog/e379f711-b2b6-4423-9e32-4a8bf9f301db/cc7d9b67-8aa2-4674-a967-3bdd9fdaa241.html.

O'Sullivan, J., & Heinonen, A. (2008). Old values, new media: Journalism roles' perceptions in a changing world. *Journalism Practice, 2*(3), 357–371.

Pachler, N., Bachmair, B., & Cook, J. (2010). *Mobile learning: Structures, agency, practices,* London: Springer.

Puentedura, R. (2006). *Transformation, technology, and education* [Online]. Hippasus. Retrieved from: http://hippasus.com/resources/tte/puentedura_tte.pdf (accessed 18 February 2013).

Reeves, T. (2006). Design research from a technology perspective. In J. Akker, K. Gravemeijer, S. McKenney, & N. Nieveen (Eds.), *Educational design research.* London: Routledge.

Sharples, M., Milrad, M., Arnedillo, S. I., & Vavoula, G. (2007). Mobile learning: Small devices, big issues. In N. Balacheff, S. Ludvigsen, T. de Jong, A. Lazonder, S. Barnes, & L. Montandon (Eds.), *Technology enhanced learning: Principles and products.* Berlin: Springer.

Swantz, M. L. (2008). Participatory action research as practice. In P. Reason & H. Bradbury (Eds.), *The Sage handbook of action research: Participative inquiry and practice* (2nd ed., pp. 31–48). London: SAGE.

Whitworth, A. (2008). Learner generated context: Critical theory and ICT education. *The 6th Panhellenic Conference on Information and Communication Technologies in Education.* Retrieved from: http://www.etpe.gr/files/proceedings/23/1236077186_09. 20 p 62_70.pdf.

12 The affordances of three-dimensional virtual worlds as authentic learning environments

Denise Wood

Introduction

Joanne Hardman's and Alan Amory's introduction to Cultural-Historical Activity Theory (CHAT) and the associated case studies presented in Part I of this book provide the foundations for understanding the role of technology-enhanced learning within complex activity systems. Hardman and Amory argue that teaching and learning with technology are culturally situated, historically informed and imbued with power and control. These factors impact on the ways in which technologies are employed and their effectiveness in supporting transformative approaches to teaching and learning. Their discussion of tool mediation focuses more specifically on the role that tools (both material and/or cognitive) play in mediating between subject and object in fulfilling an activity within activity systems. This chapter builds on these foundations by exploring three-dimensional virtual worlds (3DVWs) and *Second Life (SL)* in particular, as emerging technologies with affordances that can support transformative learning through authentic learning activities. The chapter describes the experience of trialling *SL* in *Accessible Interactive Media (AIM)*, which is a final year media arts course offered by the School of Communication, International Studies and Languages at the University of South Australia. The analysis of the technology-enhanced learning activities employed in the course draws on CHAT with a particular focus on the affordances of *SL* as a mediating tool, and Herrington, Reeves and Oliver's (2010) authentic learning framework to discuss the potential benefits and challenges in the use of 3DVWs as material and cognitive tools for facilitating transformative pedagogical approaches within the undergraduate curriculum.

Three-dimensional virtual worlds as emerging technologies

Three-dimensional virtual worlds are online multi-user virtual environments, which incorporate many of the features characterising social networking applications, such as communication, collaboration, and co-production (Obasanjo, 2004). As such, they support the establishment of networks of friends as individuals and as members of virtual communities. Communication within 3DVWs occurs via the personal 3D avatar representations of the individuals using text chat, instant messages, notecards and animated gestures, and/or through voice. Such communication mediated by the customised avatar personae of individuals can be effective in creating a sense of presence for users who may be separated geographically. Virtual worlds, such as *SL*, are built by the users (also known as residents) and are based on the principles of social constructivism and user-generated content. Such virtual worlds are therefore distinguishable from simulation games with fixed rules and goals because of their affordances for flexibility and creativity (Ondrejka, 2007). Educators have adopted both commercial 3DVWs such as *SL* and open source platforms such as *OpenSim*, as educational tools for facilitating communication (Robbins, 2007), exploratory learning, collaboration and constructivism (Clark & Maher, 2003), problem solving, as 'safe' environments for simulations (McDonald et al., 2012), and transformative approaches to enhancing students' understanding of cultural diversity (Lee & Christopher, 2006).

At the time the course described in this chapter was first trialled in *SL* in the second half of 2009, virtual, augmented, and alternate realities were regarded as one of the emerging technologies likely to be adopted by Australian and New Zealand educational institutions within two to three years (Johnson et al., 2009). The final Part of this book further elaborates the concept of emerging technologies. However, for the purposes of this discussion, *SL* can be described as emerging if the definition of emerging technologies proposed by Veletsianos (2010) is adopted. This definition suggests that technologies that are evolving are subject to hype cycles, satisfy the 'not yet' criteria, and are potentially disruptive, even though their potential is mostly unfulfilled (p. 17). Three-dimensional worlds can also be regarded as new and emerging ('coming into being'), having peaked on the Gartner hype cycle for emerging technologies in 2007 (Gartner, 2007), then progressing to the trough of disillusionment by 2009, and more recently, beginning to plateau as educators gain a greater understanding of their potential as mediating tools (see Figure 9.1 on p. 110). Also consistent with Veletsianos's description of emerging technologies, 3DVWs are still not yet fully understood or well researched, and continue to be regarded as potentially disruptive even though their potential has yet to be fully realised (Veletsianos, 2010, p. 17).

Tool mediation and the affordances of 3D virtual worlds

Hardman and Amory introduce the term 'affordance' in their introduction to CHAT and tool mediation. As they explain, the term has been attributed to Gibson (1979) who differentiated between the 'action possibilities in the environment in relation to the action capabilities of an actor' and the 'actor's experience, knowledge, culture, or ability to perceive' (Soegaard, 2003). Gibson argues that objects or environments have existing properties that impact on how an actor will use or act on that object. In the context of educational technology, an affordance is defined as the perceived and actual properties of the technology that determine how that technology can be used for learning (Salomon, 1997, p. 51).

Savin-Baden and colleagues (2010) describe three major affordances of 3DVWs: (1) scenarios, simulations and role-plays; (2) teamwork or team-building enhanced through the sense of presence and co-presence created by avatar representations of students; and (3) as the focus of the activity (for example, programming, 3D construction or modelling). Dalgarno and Lee's (2010) framework for matching the affordance requirements of learning tasks with the affordances of 3DVWs identifies five primary affordances of the educational use of 3DVWs: (1) enhancing spatial knowledge representation of the explored domain; (2) enabling experiential learning activities that would be impractical or impossible to undertake in the 'real world'; (3) facilitating intrinsically motivating learning tasks; (4) providing learning opportunities that support the transfer of knowledge and skills to 'real' situations through contextualisation of learning; and (5) facilitating rich and effective collaborative learning tasks. It is evident from Savin-Baden et al.'s (2010) discussion, and Dalgarno and Lee's (2010) framework, that 3DVWs have potential as material and cognitive tools which, if used in ways that maximise their affordances, can support collaborative, intrinsically motivating, authentic learning activities and also facilitate the transfer of knowledge from the 3DVW environment to 'real' situations.

Elements of authentic learning

The design of the course described in this chapter aimed to provide an authentic learning approach using the affordances of the *SL* platform as the mediating tool. As Jan Herrington elaborates in Chapter 5 of this book, the principles of authentic learning are based on theories of situated cognition and cognitive apprenticeship (Brown, Collins, & Duguid, 1989). Herrington, Reeves and Oliver's (2010) authentic learning framework provides a detailed heuristic to guide academics in the design of learning activities based on the principles of authentic learning. This heuristic describes nine elements of authentic learning and these elements provided the foundation guiding the design of the course discussed in this chapter. These elements include: (1) authentic contexts; (2) authentic tasks; (3) access to expert performances and the modelling of processes; (4) multiple roles and perspectives; (5) collaborative construction of knowledge; (6) reflection to enable abstractions to be formed; (7) articulation to enable tacit knowledge to be made explicit; (8) coaching and scaffolding; and (9) authentic assessment of learning.

The next section of this chapter describes the design of the course incorporating these elements of authentic learning and the strategies employed to maximise the affordances of *SL* to support the program.

Design of the course

Accessible Interactive Media (AIM) is an advanced Web design course focusing on the skills required of designers to assess websites for accessibility compliance, develop an accessibility policy and apply advanced techniques in accessible design. The course is a final-year capstone for students enrolled in the University of South

Australia's Bachelor of Media Arts program as well as students enrolled in multi-media and computing courses offered by the School of Computer and Information Science. The assessments in the course involve students undertaking service learning with community organisations as their clients and working in project teams with those clients throughout the semester in the process of developing an accessibility policy and designing an accessible website for their client.

Students enrolled in the semester two 2009 offering of the course were given the option of undertaking their service learning project with health- or disability-related support groups in *SL*. Of the 21 students enrolled, seven opted to work with *SL* groups including: 'Health Support Coalition', communities of people with HIV/AIDS and Attention Deficit Disorder, a group of leaders of the various support groups, and an organisation known as 'Virtual Helping Hands'. The remaining students undertook service learning projects with 'not-for-profit' organisations recruited through the South Australian Government's Office for Volunteers. The objects of the activity were for students to develop a greater understanding of cultural diversity and to enhance their communication skills, to complement the development of the technical skills they required to create accessible websites. The students met with their clients on a regular basis in *SL* and they also met with the course coordinator each week, as well as with the coordinator of the Health Support Coalition (HSC) for debriefing sessions.

The primary use of the 3DVW was as a venue for students to communicate with clients, research their client's needs and to provide them with access to debriefing sessions conducted by members of the *SL* community. Some students chose to meet their clients via Skype or communicated primarily via email due to the challenges of synchronising meeting times, given the different time zones of their clients. Most students attended the weekly debriefing sessions with the coordinator and the periodic sessions with the coordinator of the HSC.

The design of AIM sought to provide an authentic context through which students could meet their clients in the *SL* virtual world. The tasks involved students communicating with their clients in *SL* to identify their needs, preparing a web accessibility policy and, finally, designing an accessible website to meet their client organisation's needs. The process exposed students to multiple perspectives and cultural diversity with the *SL* environment. The regular debriefing sessions within *SL* provided students with mentoring and access to experts via the support provided by the HSC coordinator and *SL* mentors. While the learning activities involved collaboration and communication with clients, the assessment tasks were individual rather than collaborative. Reflective practice was integral to the course, with students reflecting on their experiences with their clients and in *SL* throughout the semester via personal blogs. Although the assessment activities were based on an authentic learning approach in so far as students met with their clients through the *SL* platform, the actual assessment tasks (preparing design specifications, writing an accessibility policy and designing a website for their clients) were undertaken outside the *SL* environment using a reflective journal (a blog) and web design tools.

Drawing on CHAT as the heuristic, the object of the course motivating the activities was for an authentic learning task designed to facilitate the development of students' communication skills, and to enhance their understanding and appreciation of cultural diversity; skills that they could apply in professional practice upon graduation.

The mediated activities involved the use of *SL* as both a *material* and *cognitive tool*, enabling students to investigate how disability support groups were using *SL*, as a conduit for situated information, a medium for meetings with clients, and as a supportive environment through which students were mentored by the teacher as well as the HSC coordinator via regular debriefing sessions. The *subjects* were the students enrolled in the course who chose to undertake the *SL* option, as well as their clients. The *activities* mediated by the *SL* technologies were both *explicit* (i.e. 'meet regularly with your clients in *SL* to learn about their organisation's operations, identify their target audience, agree on design specifications and review milestones'), and *implicit* (i.e. 'in doing so and through the mentoring support provided through the tutorials, develop your understanding of different cultures within *SL*').

The *community* that developed through this course within *SL* comprised the students, teacher, their *SL* clients and the HSC coordinator, and through that community, *SL* became a medium to scaffold students developing their understanding and awareness of cultural diversity. The mentoring component of the *SL* interactions via the community is consistent with Vygotsky's (1978) concept of the Zone of Proximal Development, which is the distance between what an individual can achieve on their own and what they can accomplish when guided by more capable peers or adults through social interactions that take place in a cultural and historical context.

Within that community, there was a *division of labour*, with students as learners, apprentice designers and peers; the teacher as facilitator, mentor and peer; the clients as 'customers' of the apprentice designers, but also implicitly their mentors; and the HSC coordinator as mentor.

The activity system itself was subject to the *rules* of the University policies and procedures, the rules of the course itself and the rules imposed by the *SL* service (Linden Labs Terms of Service).

As we learned in Part I, CHAT is represented visually using a pyramid to illustrate the various components of the activity system. Figure 12.1 represents a CHAT analysis of the activity system for the case study described in this chapter. Third-generation CHAT also recognises the interaction between two or more activity systems. In this case study there are at least two activity systems evident: the activity system of the course itself and the students and teacher with their clients as representing one activity system, as well as the activity system of the *SL* 3DVW. The *SL* activity system is depicted in Figure 12.2.

Methodology for evaluating student s' experiences in the course

Students were invited to complete an anonymous online evaluation at the conclusion of the semester. This evaluation included questions aimed at identifying

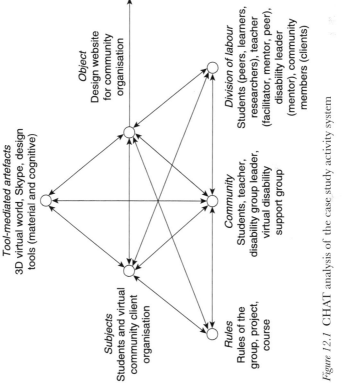

Tool-mediated artefacts
3D virtual world, Skype, design tools (material and cognitive)

Object
Design website for community organisation

Outcomes
- Demonstrated understanding of principles of usability and universal design
- Demonstrated understanding of the social and ethical issues of web design and their impact on different user audiences
- Apply World Wide Web Consortium's web accessibility guidelines to design of accessible web site
- Develop policies and accessibility guidelines for client groups
- Demonstrate professional communication skills

Division of labour
Students (peers, learners, researchers), teacher (facilitator, mentor, peer), disability leader (mentor), community members (clients)

Community
Students, teacher, disability group leader, virtual disability support group

Subjects
Students and virtual community client organisation

Rules
Rules of the group, project, course

Figure 12.1 CHAT analysis of the case study activity system

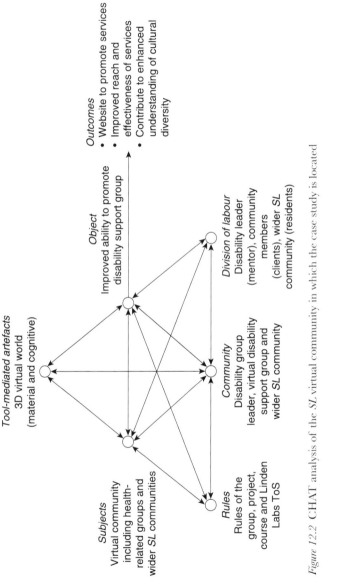

Figure 12.2 CHAT analysis of the *SL* virtual community in which the case study is located

students' familiarity with and use of Web 2.0 and 3DVW technologies, and to assess the extent to which the *SL* platform was perceived by students as supporting the objectives of the course and their learning. The evaluation included a mix of Likert-scale (five-point scale ranging from 1 strongly disagree to 5 strongly agree) and open-ended questions.

Findings

All seven students participated in the online evaluation. Of those respondents, five were male and two female. Ages ranged from 18 to 34 years. All of the respondents were enrolled in degrees in computer science and/or media arts. Four of the seven respondents reported that they rarely use online 3D computer games, one reported that he/she had never used online 3D computer games and two described themselves as occasional users. No respondents were frequent users of either online 3D virtual games or 3D virtual worlds such as *SL*. All reported that they had access to a high speed broadband connection at home.

More than half of the students (43%, n = 3 strongly agreed; 14%, n = 1 agreed) reported that they were willing to put the effort needed to complete the learning activities. Most students (14%, n = 1 strongly agreed; 43%, n = 3 agreed) that they liked using *SL* in the course and would recommend the instructor continue using *SL*. Five students (28%, n = 2 strongly agreed; 43%, n = 3 agreed) reported that the activities in *SL* offered opportunities for interaction and communication.

Positive experiences reported by students through their qualitative comments to the open-ended questions in the anonymous online evaluation suggested that some students enjoyed the creative aspects of the *SL* environment as reflected in one student's comment who stated he/she enjoyed having 'The ability to combine my IT abilities with my artistic passion.' Similarly, other students indicated that they liked the affordances that the environment provided for enabling them to customise their appearance, as suggested by one student who stated 'I liked the possibility of customisation' and another who stated that they enjoyed 'Changing their user appearance'. Other students commented on the benefits they gained from experiencing the diversity of people they met within the virtual world as indicated by one student who noted that 'Learning about the world of *Second Life*, affected me personally after meeting with my client. I learned that there is more to *Second Life* than idiots buying land that they cannot even step on.' Another student stated that he/she benefited from gaining insight into 'Understanding why people might engage in such an environment'. Other students suggested that having access to expert mentors was beneficial to their learning experience as reflected in the comment that 'I was able to source out influential people and gain a lot from different events based around accessibility' and another noted that 'The weekly meetings provided a very helpful tutorial environment for this directed study course.'

Less positive experiences reported by students suggested that even though they did see some benefit in the use of the 3DVW in the course, they would not want to participate in the environment in a more sustained way. As one student commented:

> I did not mind using Second Life as a component of my course. However, I do not think I would have enjoyed using it as a basis for any course. I do understand the need for such communication mediums, however, it is not something I would use personally. I am just not a big fan of Second Life anyway, which is why some of my answers may seem harsh.

Similarly, another student suggested that:

> The experience was a good one, but it is one I would not like to repeat again, I found it difficult to communicate with certain people due to time differences and I just couldn't get into the program like so many other people have.

Another student suggested that 3DVWs were not yet ready for the mainstream as reflected in the comment that 'I think in time it will not seem as foreign as it does now and that if you stick with it, it can be a powerful learning tool.'

One student's comment highlighted the potential contradictions experienced by students undertaking their course in an environment where there are inconsistencies in the rules of their course and the *SL* cultural context. As this student reflected,

> It was an overall good experience for me. Although I felt I was treated harshly when my avatar was wearing a 'koolade man' costume by the HSC representative, the first time I met her I asked if what you wear matters since it is an online world, (i was dressed as a robot). She said no its fine. . . then grilled me about the koolade man costume. . . I thought that was rather strange.

Discussion

As the comments by students suggest, some students were very positive about the learning experience with comments indicating the authentic learning activities were effective in challenging their assumptions about diverse cultures within the *SL* environment, as suggested by the student who commented that the experience affected him/her personally after meeting with their client. Despite the positive comments, some students indicated that they did not enjoy the experience even though they saw the value. The observation by one student that in time the environment might not feel so foreign, suggests that at the time this case study was conducted, *SL* did represent an emerging technology; one that had not yet reached wide adoption and acceptance.

The concerns expressed by one student who he felt he was treated harshly by the HSC coordinator regarding his chosen avatar appearance 'koolade man' costume reflects the tensions that can arise when students undertake authentic learning activities that involve two or more activity systems through which contra-dictions arise. Engeström's (2001) concept of expansive learning recognises the multi-voicedness and historicity of activity systems inevitably lead to contradic-tions within and between activity systems. By analysing the case study through the lens of Cultural-Historical Activity Theory, the complexity of the activity system becomes readily apparent. It is evident that students undertaking the activities (subjects) relied on both the material and cognitive tools afforded by the *SL* plat-form to act on the object in order to achieve the desired learning outcomes. However, complicating this activity system are three additional layers as apparent in Figure 12.1. The first is that there are rules governing students' actions within the *SL* environment, including the rules established by the teacher and the group. The second factor impacting on students' actions in *SL* relate to the diversity of the community with which students must interact, including each other, the teacher and other residents of *SL*. There is a division of labour within that com-munity, with the teacher taking on the role of facilitator and mentor, the health coalition leader acting as mentor, and students in the role of learners and peers (and potentially mentors). At the same time, there are contradictions between the two activity systems along each of these dimensions, which impact on the effectiveness of *SL* as a mediating tool.

For example, the comments of the student who noted his confusion over being advised by the HSC coordinator that his attire was inappropriate after she had previously advised that any avatar appearance is acceptable in the SL environ-ment, suggest that he was unaware that the 'Koolaide Man' costume he was wear-ing has a particular cultural connation within *SL*. The HSC coordinator evidently did not appreciate that that students who had no previous experience in *SL* would be unaware of some of the cultural taboos within the virtual world. In this par-ticular case, the avatar appearance chosen by the student ('Koolaide Man') is also a representation used by people in *SL* who are 'griefers' (a form of cyber bullying in the 3DVW). However, as Engeström argues, it is in exposing these contradic-tions that transformative learning can occur. This episode would have been an opportunity for the teacher to discuss the varying cultures and sub-cultures evident within SL virtual worlds, and in doing so the student would have been able to use that experience to further develop his understanding of diversity in virtual worlds.

CHAT analysis highlights the many considerations that need to be taken into account when designing learning activities that seek to provide immersive experiences within a platform such as *SL*. As the figures reflect, students need to negotiate not only the mastery of the mediating tools, but also how to interact with a community that is more diverse than their own learning community. Analysis of the interplay between all components of such an activity system can assist in the design of authentic learning activities that maximise the affordances of the platform, and open up opportunities for transformative learning experiences.

As with any 'real-life' situation, students encountered many challenges in the course. For example, while students had assignment deadlines they needed to meet, they also had to manage their interactions with clients who did not always deliver content within negotiated timelines. Students also learned that timely response to client emails or Instant Messages (IMs) was critical to the timely delivery of content, particularly since many of their clients had other 'real-life' constraints limiting their ability to be available for consultation when it suited the students. The students also had to negotiate the complexities of multiple time zones and various preferred methods of communication; some clients preferred email correspondence, others IMs through *Second Life* and others wanted to meet with the students via Skype.

Conclusion

Despite the limited scope of the study reported in this chapter, the trial of AIM in *SL* provides valuable insights into the benefits and challenges of the use of 3DVWs such as *SL* as mediating tools to support the learning outcomes of a course. Analysis through the lens of Cultural-Historical Activity Theory highlights the complexity of the activity systems within which the students were required to operate to achieve the desired learning objectives. Despite those challenges, observations of students' interactions with their clients, the group meetings held with the Health Support Coalition coordinator and regular debriefing sessions with students suggest that they benefited from learning first-hand about the life-experiences of people with disabilities through their *SL* experiences, while completing their assignment requirements.

It is evident from the discussion of the features of authentic learning tasks embedded in the activities undertaken in *SL* that more effective use could have been made of the affordances of the platform. For example, while there were opportunities for collaboration, the assessment tasks were all individual assignments. Moreover, while the *SL* platform provided the conduit for communication with their clients, the assessment tasks were undertaken outside the *SL* environment. Some students could not see the direct relationship between the activities undertaken in the virtual world and the articulation of those skills in professional practice, indicating that further strengthening of the alignment of the learning objectives, design of the course and the elements of authentic learning is required.

Exposing the contradictions that were evident from the trial of AIM in *SL* represents what Engeström (2001) refers to as an expansive learning opportunity. As CHAT analysis reveals, such contradictions inevitably arise when students undertake authentic learning activities within cultural contexts that are vastly different from their own prior experiences provide rich opportunities for discussion, reflection, and ultimately represent opportunities for innovation and more transformative approaches to teaching and learning. *SL* is still very much an emerging technology, with affordances that have yet to be fully realised in higher education. The case study reported in this chapter demonstrates the potential of such environments for supporting more transformative approaches to technology-enhanced learning by maximising the affordances of the technologies in ways that support a more authentic learning approach.

References

Brown, J. S., Collins, A., & Duguid, P. (1989). Situated cognition and the culture of learning. *Educational Researcher, 18*(1), 32–42.

Clark, S., & Maher, M. L. (2003). The effects of a sense of place on the learning experience in a 3D virtual world. In *Communities of practice research: Proceedings of the 10th Association for Learning Technologies Conference (ALT-C2003)* (pp. 82–101). Sheffield, UK: University of Sheffield.

Dalgarno, B., & Lee, M. J. W. (2010). What are the learning affordances of 3-D virtual environments? *British Journal of Educational Technology, 41*(1), 10–32.

Engeström, Y. (2001). Expansive learning at work: Toward an activity theoretical reconceptualization. *Journal of Education and Work, 14*(1), 133–156.

Gartner Inc. (2007). Gartner says 80 percent of active internet users will have a 'Second Life' in the virtual world by the end of 2011'. Available from: http://gartner.com/it/page.jsp?id=503861.

Gibson, J. (1979). *The ecological approach to visual perception*. Hillsdale, NJ: Lawrence Erlbaum Associates.

Herrington, J., Reeves, T., & Oliver, R. (2010). *A guide to authentic e-learning*. New York: Routledge.

Johnson, L., Levine, A., Smith, R., Smythe, T., & Stone, S. (2009). *The Horizon Report: 2009 Australia–New Zealand Edition*. Austin, TX: The New Media Consortium.

Lee, J. J., & Christopher, M. H. (2006). Ugly in a world where you can choose to be beautiful: Teaching and learning about diversity via virtual worlds. In *Proceedings of the 7th International Conference on Learning Sciences*. Bloomington, IN: International Society of the Learning Sciences.

McDonald, M., Ryan, T., Sim, J., James, J., Maude, P., Scutter, S., & Wood, D. (2012). Multidiscipline role-play in a 3D virtual learning environment: Experiences with a large cohort of health care students. *Future changes: Sustainable futures. Proceedings of ASCILITE 2012*. Wellington, New Zealand, 25–28 November.

Obasanjo, D. (2004). Dare Obasanjo aka Carnage4Life: Social Software is the platform of the future. Available at: http://www.25hoursaday.com/weblog/PermaLink.aspx?guid=06ff2206-27a3-4d55-81d8-bbee37073d6d (accessed 16 December 2008).

Ondrejka, C. (2007). Collapsing geography: Second Life, innovation, and the future of national power. *Innovations, Summer*, 27–54.

Robbins, S. (2007). A futurist's view of Second Life education: A developing taxonomy of digital spaces. In D. Livingstone & J. Kemp (Eds.), *Proceedings of the Second Life Education Workshop Community Convention* (Vol. 2007, pp. 27–33). Chicago Hilton: The University of Paisley.

Salomon, G. (Ed.) (1997). *Distributed cognitions: Psychological and educational considerations*. Cambridge: Cambridge University Press.

Savin-Baden, M., Gourlay, L., Steils, N., Tombs, G., & Mawer, M. (2010). Situating pedagogies, positions and practices in immersive virtual worlds. *Educational Research, 52*(2), 123–133.

Soegaard, M. (2003). *Affordances*. Retrieved from: http://www.interaction-design.org/encyclopedia/affordances.html (accessed 25 November 2013).

Veletsianos, G. (2010). A definition of emerging technologies in education. In G. Veletsianos (Ed.). *Emerging technologies in distance education* (pp. 3–22). Edmonton: Athabasca University Press.

Vygotsky, L. S. (1978). *Mind in society*. M. Cole, V. John-Steiner, S. Scribner, & E. Souberman (Eds.). Cambridge, MA: Harvard University Press.

Part IV

Case studies

13 The case studies

CHAT in use

Joanne Hardman, Alan Amory, Irina Verenikina,
Lotte Latukefu, Najma Agherdien, Rita Kizito,
Nomakhaya Mashiyi, Roisin Kelly-Laubscher,
Daniela Gachago, Veronica Barnes and Eunice Ivala

Introduction

This chapter draws on six case studies of pedagogy with technology in Higher Education. The studies are chosen because they illustrate how the use of technology impacts on pedagogy in these contexts. While the cases are drawn from different levels of higher education (undergraduate to postgraduate) they are woven together by a shared framework: namely, the use of CHAT to explore pedagogical innovation with technology. One of the significant strengths of CHAT, all studies will argue, lies in its ability to situate goal-directed action within the larger context of a motive-directed activity. That is, its explanatory power lies in situating pedagogy (in the instances reported here) socially, taking it out of the realm of the teacher/student dyad to enable a more nuanced understanding of how learning actually happens as a complex activity.

CASE STUDY 13.1 DESIGNING AN EFFECTIVE UNDERGRADUATE VOCAL PEDAGOGY ENVIRONMENT: A CASE OF CULTURAL-HISTORICAL ACTIVITY APPROACH IN A SINGING COURSE

Irina Verenikina and Lotte Latukefu

Context

This case exemplifies the application of Cultural-Historical Activity Theory (CHAT) to vocal education at an Australian University. It represents an overview of a five-year study which aimed to develop and critically evaluate an innovative undergraduate classroom environment based in collaborative vocal pedagogy (Latukefu, 2010). The 'technology' used was an innovative undergraduate vocal classroom environment aimed at enhancing vocal students' self-regulated learning. The case study presented in this chapter is focused on the ways that cultural-historical activity theory (Engeström, 1999) were used to re-conceptualise tertiary vocal education and develop an innovative model of collaborative teaching of singing.

Background

Vygotskian (1978) cultural-historical theory was applied to underpin the study by using a number of concepts such as socially and culturally mediated teaching, co-construction of knowledge, self-regulated learning (Latukefu & Verenikina, 2013) and concept formation (Latukefu & Verenikina, 2011).

One-to-one tuition in higher vocal education is considered the most powerful mode for instrumental and vocal training (Gaunt, 2011). However, the amalgamation between drama and music teaching at the university made the formerly offered one-to-one lessons unsustainable. This change provided an opportunity to look for an effective alternative to this traditionally predominant way of vocal training. This is particularly important as the one-to-one vocal training model (also known as a master-apprentice model) has a number of limitations (Jorgenson, 2000).

Collaborative learning has been extensively employed by educators to promote student learning (e.g. Ioannou & Artino, 2010; Johnston, Johnston, & Smith, 2007; Main, 2010; Latukefu &Verenikina, 2013). It is seen as "an accepted, and often the preferred, instructional procedures at all levels of education" (Johnston, Johnston, & Smith, 2007, p. 15). However, peer learning in relation to learning singing at a tertiary level has been under-researched (Latukefu, 2009; 2010). This study was undertaken in response to the lack of research of vocal pedagogy in an environment that is not the traditional one-to-one learning model.

Socio-cultural approaches to teaching can be used in relation to vocal education, both in one-to-one tutoring and in a teacher's work with a group of music students where self-directed learning and self-evaluation can be facilitated by peer support. The role of the teacher in peer support is that of "the director of the social environment in the classroom, the governor and guide of the interactions" (Vygotsky, 1997, p. 49). To be effective, peer support needs to be carefully orchestrated so the students are working together on a joint task which is within their reach (Daniels, 2001).

Question

How does an innovative undergraduate vocal classroom environment enhance vocal students' self-regulated learning?

Approach

The study employed design-based research methodology (DBRC, 2003) to design an innovative undergraduate vocal classroom environment which enhances vocal students' self-regulated learning. Improving educational practice, designing a learning environment and at the same time developing learning theories in the real situation of the singing course were central to the study (Gravemeijer & Cobb, 2006).

Vygotsky's (1978) cultural-historical approach was systematically applied to inform the design. The theory provided the means to alter the traditional vocal education relationship between the teacher and the student offered by master-apprentice relationship where the master is considered a role model and a source of identification for the student (Jorgenson, 2000). In this relationship where the predominant focus was on the transfer of skills and knowledge from the teacher to the learner, the students are often not actively involved in their learning and the responsibilities for improvement are shifted to "the teachers, who have to take on the role of omnipotent master" (Zhukov, 2007, p. 124).

The main purpose of the developed design was to encourage students to take more responsibility for their own learning of singing and move toward the goal of self-regulated learning. Student reflection, collaborative peer learning and assessment aimed at students taking control of their learning and the co-construction of knowledge with peers and the teacher as a mentor. Introducing the students to the scientific concepts concerning vocal technique and new vocal exercise as well as the musical knowledge complemented this. The purpose of this was to integrate musicianship and aural skills into the authentic environment of singing and not separate theory from practice.

The transformation of the classroom environment was constructed collaboratively over five years in consultation with the staff members and used the reflective journals that students and the teacher wrote during that time as a way of refining and changing the design. This was achieved by analysing the reflective journals for recurring themes, which were then taken into account and incorporated into the design of the next iteration. Revisiting the theoretical framework, the student feedback from formal teacher evaluations and focus groups with students also influenced the design.

Findings and discussion

The sociocultural approach used in this study, combined with design-based research methodology, resulted in a number of design principles that emerged from the constant reflection back to theory during iterations of the design. These principles are transferable to other contexts even if the local context is different from the one where the principles were developed.

* *Design principle 1*: Students self-regulate their own singing when they understand how their voice works scientifically in relation to their bodies. Students may not always grasp the scientific concepts of singing immediately, but they gain a deeper understanding of meaning in relation to their singing as they progress with their study. Unlike models of learning singing, which are often prescriptive of content, this model allows practitioners flexibility to choose scientific concepts of singing that they will teach their students. The essential point is

that scientific concepts themselves become a mediating tool for learning if combined with the everyday concepts students hold about singing.

- *Design principle 2*: Interaction with peers motivates reflection and further learning. The dominance of the one-to-one lesson in the conservatoire means that students do not get as much chance to learn from each other as they do using a socio-cultural approach. It was found that the students in the study placed a high value on watching the development of others and learning with them. While advocating for the continued need for one-to-one lessons in the conservatoire, this study questioned whether at an undergraduate level, a balance between group teaching of concepts that are basic for vocal development and one-to-one lessons, was more beneficial because of the peer learning culture that develops.
- *Design principle 3*: Transformation of practical activity through reflection benefits learning. This study demonstrated that formal reflection by students on their vocal development assisted students in their learning. It achieved this by providing the students with an opportunity to diagnose a problem, think of a solution, carry out the solution through their practice and then refine the solution if necessary. Some students used the reflections to bring together all the perspectives about the voice that they learnt and to work out the ones which worked best for them.
- *Design principle 4*: Singing students must be able to critically discern quality in singing. To become self-regulated learners capable of continuing with their learning after graduation, students must be capable of thinking critically about their own singing. It was demonstrated that the introduction of peer assessment into the course helped the students to reflect on their own practice by having to make the effort to interact with the criteria given in order to properly assess a peer. Students co-constructed the assessment-related knowledge, which they were able to appropriate as their own and apply to self-assessment.
- *Design principle 5*: Multiple perspectives are important for learning singing. There is a culture of protection of students from multiple perspectives that exists in many conservatoires as it might be confusing for students to have different teachers tell them different things (Jorgenson, 2000). The present study supported the case for multiple perspectives being highly beneficial to singing students as they transferred the vocal work that they were doing from one class to the other.

The activity theory model (Engeström, 1999) served as an analytic framework to exemplify the teacher-learner relationship from the perspective of a teacher as a subject of teaching activity. The model allowed for conceptualisation of teaching activity within the social context which included the rules and responsibilities of people involved.

In relation to the one-on-one master–apprentice model, the teacher was the focus of attention as a desirable model. The object and the desirable outcome of the teacher's activity were that the student should be able to render a passable imitation of the phrasing and interpretation of the song by the teacher. The tools in such activity were limited to the teacher's knowledge, and division of labour was mainly one-way communication from the teacher to the student. The rule of this classroom was that the student should follow the teacher's instruction without question and accept the vocal techniques that were usually based on somatic feelings that the teacher had when singing, which were translated into words for student to imitate (Latukefu & Verenikina, 2013).

In contrast, the modelling of the teacher's activity within the designed learning environment required the use of multiple models following the richness of the object and desirable outcomes of teaching activity – the development of the students' self-directed learning and the complex involvement of the students in collaborative learning (Latukefu & Verenikina, 2013).

Recommendations for future use/advice for practitioners

The present research study begins addressing the lack of empirical and systematic research on how students develop singing skills in an environment that is not the traditional one-to-one learning model. Documentation of the processes involved in the development of the model, the experience of the students and their perceptions of how their singing develops help to explain the evolution of the model.

The principles that emerged from the study provide insights into strategies that students can develop for self-directed learning and this in turn can act as a framework for teachers so they can organise the content of their singing teaching. For more experienced teachers who find themselves having to adjust the way they teach because of economic pressures or as part of curriculum renewal and review, the theoretical concepts of how students can learn using a different model of teaching will be useful as they develop their own models of teaching suitable to their local context.

CASE STUDY 13.2 TOWARDS AUTHENTIC LEARNING FOR PROFESSIONAL DEVELOPMENT AT THE CENTRE FOR ACADEMIC TECHNOLOGIES (CAT)
Najma Agherdien

Context

This case study explores the use of the theoretical framework adopted by the Centre for Academic Technologies (CAT), part of the Academic Development and Support division at the University of Johannesburg. The study focuses on the combined use of Cultural-Historical Activity Theory (CHAT), Authentic Learning (AL) and Vygotsky's tool mediation concept (Amory, 2012) as the underlying framework for professional development. Traditionally, the professional development approach at CAT was one of technical training and support. This approach required major transformation and comprised a shift away from a fixation on "fragmented and meaningless" information dissemination (Garrison & Archer, 2000, p. 7) to the co-construction of meaning and growth. This study aims to explore the use of the framework to promote Teaching and Learning Consultancy as part of academic development. While the framework allowed us to rethink our approach and realign our services, tensions exist within its application.

Background

The CAT Framework includes Cultural-Historical Activity Theory/CHAT (C), Authentic Learning (A) and Technologies as Tools (T). Tool-mediated learning – as part of CHAT (C) – states that Tools (T) or artefacts are used to mediate between a subject and an object (Vygotsky, 1978; Amory, 2012). The object (motive) then is transformed into an outcome by means of engagement in Authentic Learning (**A**) tasks. I will briefly explore each framework component.

Cultural-Historical Activity Theory

For the purposes of this case study, an activity system comprises: (1) the subject (person or group); (2) the tool (physical, symbolic, cultural or psychological); (3) the object (the objective of the activity) which is transformed into an (4) outcome; (5) the community – those who share the object; (6) division of labour – the engagement in the work – and; finally (7) the rules or standards and conventions that govern the activity (Engeström, 2001) (see Figure 1.3, on p. 16). When technology serves as a physical *Tool* (**T**) and not the *Object*, the desired '*learning with*' *technology* is the end result and production is enabled (Jonassen & Reeves, 1996). If students are to construct knowledge, authentic tasks must be given that are socially embedded. According to Vygotsky's general genetic law (1978), development first happens on a social level with others before it is internalised on an individual level. The implication is that learning, in the sense of cognitive change, cannot be an individual activity.

Through tool-mediated learning, subjects gain a tacit understanding of the world and the tools that they use (Brown, Collins, & Duguid, 1989). Additionally, learning tasks or activities are seen as always being *social* and *cultural* in nature and it is therefore the context that determines how actors use the tools. The historically evolving nature of the activity is just as vital (Engeström, 1987; Roth & Lee, 2007; Stetsenko, 2008; Edwards, 2012). CHAT– in Stetsenko's words (2008, p. 485) – provides a vision of "what is, how it came to be, how it ought to be, and how all of this can be known".

Engeström's (2001) more recent claim states that new objects produced during human activity are sometimes unintended outcomes of several activities. This notion of "expansive learning" holds that tensions in two adjoining activity systems lead to transformation. These tensions, also called "dramatical collisions" (Veresov,

2007) can occur in and/or between any of the CHAT components within an activity or across activities, thereby impacting on the activity system. These contradictions are potentially sites of dynamic change.

Authentic learning

Authentic learning involves taking into account students' perspectives and real-life experiences (Anderson & Anderson, 2005). Simply stated by Brown, Collins and Duguid (1989, p. 34), authentic activities involve "ordinary practices of the culture" and can be achieved through collaborative activities, questioning, simulations, and through the use of authentic learning material. Tasks are authentic when they are ill-defined and include subtasks; have real-world relevance, are complex; provide opportunities to consider different perspectives; are collaborative and reflective; are integrated across subject areas; have integrated assessments; generate products that have multiple iterations, and cater for competing answers (Reeves, Herrington, & Oliver, 2004).

Technology as tools

Through a CAT framework where a "learning with technology" approach (Amory, 2012) is adopted, actors actively produce an artefact as opposed to consuming ideas. Amory (2011; 2012) suggests that ICTs (Tools) can be used in teaching and learning to facilitate the delivery of information and communication between participants, convert information from one form to another, enable teamwork, and last but not least, provide tools specific to a profession.

Question

How does the use of the CAT framework enable or constrain the professional development of academic staff at the University of Johannesburg?

Approach

In a bid to develop lecturers' ability to engage in and construct authentic learning tasks, workshops were held to change lecturers' pedagogical practices. The workshop entails two parts: the first part is where the lecturer works as a student. Participants engage in collaborative reading of research papers and then use an evaluation instrument to evaluate the papers. The collaborative opportunity aligns with a CHAT perspective that views learning as a social activity (Engeström, 1999; Tinto, 1999; Vygotsky, 1978). The evaluation instrument (Tool) – with built-in AL principles mediates the learning of AL (object). The concept of tool mediation is illustrated in this way. The ratings are submitted and accessed via a Gmail account. After a discussion (articulation), the ratings are transformed into a different format using Excel graphs and mind maps. In this way, the technology (Tool) is used to mediate the understanding of the AL principles.

In the second part of the workshop, the lecturer acts as a designer, producing a polished product through collaborative engagement in authentic learning tasks. Participants read a newspaper article and design AL activities within their disciplines around the article. Articulation of the activity design concludes the workshop.

Findings and discussion

While many of the academic staff are experts in their respective fields, a number of them have a deprived educational backgrounds and consequently are not familiar with good pedagogical practices. They find it easier to disseminate information than to focus on the learning process. Despite the fact that complexity is sought, taking staff too far out of their comfort zones can cause paralysis. Many staff members indicate that they find the content and approach too complicated. One of the lecturers explains: "I am of the opinion that the workshop is experienced by many lecturers as a shock as they were not prepared for this giant leap."

Academic staff do not see the practical value of the framework. Moreover, the framework is seen as something that might work with smaller student numbers, and it is not for academics who are not technologically savvy. A lecturer argues: "In my experience, I feel that most of our lecturers have not yet 'moved on' and accepted this approach and need more scaffolding and guidance in this paradigm shift."

Finally, moving on to technology as tool, vast numbers of staff are not technologically savvy and therefore are scared to embrace technology, let alone integrate it into their T&L practice.

Recommendations for future use/advice for practitioners

I propose using the nine authentic learning characteristics to guide future implementation of the CAT framework. Table 13.1 outlines how to develop AL activity with the help of the nine AL characteristics originating from the work of Herrington and Herrington (2008).

Characteristic no. 3 states that access to expert performances and/or modelling processes must be put in place. I suggest that lecturers start pilot projects with some volunteers and then showcase the framework in action to illustrate its applicability. Characteristic 5 alludes to collaborative construction of knowledge. Lecturers should therefore cultivate Communities of Practice by using academic technologies as enablers of collaboration. A Google group or social media could be used for this purpose. Characteristic 8 talks of coaching and scaffolding and I suggest on-going support beyond the one-day workshop is thus advisable. Last but not least, characteristic 9 – authentic assessment is one that staff in general battle with. Lecturers should provide assistance with setting assessment activities that require the production of artefacts as opposed to the regurgitation of information. In conjunction with examining the framework using the AL characteristics, conflicts

Table 13.1 Authentic learning characteristics

	AL characteristic	Guide to framework usage
1	Authentic context	Physical environment reflects knowledge usage and resources to accommodate multiple views
2	Authentic activities	Tasks are done over a longer period and correspond with Reeves et al.'s authentic tasks
3	Access to expert performances and modelling processes	Embark on pilot projects with volunteers and showcase the framework in action
4	Multiple roles and perspectives	Seek input from different stakeholders
5	Collaborative construction of knowledge	Form communities of practice with enabling network opportunities
6	Reflection	Reflection in a social environment is built in.
7	Articulation	Staff have opportunities to defend positions
8	Coaching and scaffolding	Provide on-going support throughout task completion
9	Authentic assessment	Staff create products

Source: Adapted from Herrington and Herrington (2008).

between activity systems need to be addressed. Focus group interviews would be suitable in order to access the voices of participants. As suggested by Garraway (2009), identifying conflicts between activity systems could present opportunities for mutual development.

In conclusion, the CAT framework for professional development has much to offer by way of academic development. Lecturers have opportunities to work differently and transform their practices. However, the way the framework is used is not without tensions. By considering the context of academic staff, a more inclusive and equitable professional development experience can be enabled.

CASE STUDY 13.3 WHERE ACTIVITY THEORY AND AUTHENTIC LEARNING PRINCIPLES INTERSECT: KICK-STARTING LEARNING ACTIVITY DESIGN FOR MATHEMATICS TEACHING

Rita Kizito

Context

Reform efforts in mathematics teaching recommend that the changes needed for successful student learning will require transformation in teaching practices (Boaler, 2013). One of these practices is learning activity design. The majority of our students struggle to learn mathematics because mathematical knowledge is isolated from personalised forms of experiences (Kizito, 2012). Often, there is a gap between a student's intuitive knowledge and the formal world of mathematics (Tall, 1991).

Proponents of authentic learning maintain that the abstraction and de-contextualisation of the type of knowledge taught in schools and universities from real-world contexts is problematic (Herrington & Oliver, 2000; Resnick, 1987). To compound this effect, new lecturers are not trained to develop tasks that address social and cultural aspects of learning. They lack sufficient exposure to opportunities promoting learning activity design principles that could make learning more accessible to students.

With the onset of online technologies, it is now possible to design authentic learning environments using web-based technologies such as the blog to engage and support learners in contexts similar to real-world contexts (Herrington, 2009). Despite this, examinations of the social-cultural dimensions of the authentic e-learning interactions afforded by the new technologies are limited. Cultural-historical activity theory (CHAT) (Engeström, 1999; Leontiev, 1978; Vygotsky, 1978) could offer a methodological frame of reference for this examination.

In this case study, the CHAT theoretical framework was used to analyse the contributions of two teaching assistants (TAs) in a Science Extended Curriculum Programme (ECP). The two TAs participated in a pilot program designed to prepare future science lecturers. The learning outcomes of the program included: examining the learning context; designing authentic learning activities; facilitating learning in the classroom; marking and assessing student work and identifying a small research project. The reports on the tasks completed were combined in a portfolio of evidence.

Experienced university academics trained the TAs in workshops and gave them learning tasks to complete. These tasks were uploaded onto a common blog space. The TAs were learning by examining how to teach in a way that could promote deep mathematical understanding. They reported their experiences and findings in the blog for sharing and discussion, and they were participating in knowledge creation of how to teach math to promote mathematical thinking. This project was designed to provide support for collective knowledge construction as the TAs learnt how to teach in a way that could promote deep mathematical understanding. Each TA developed a blog (with links to the main blog), for completing the assigned tasks as blog entries for comments and feedback. Flexibility was important as the pilot program was not formalised. It had to fit into tight TA workload structures combining postgraduate study and teaching functions.

Background

Reality in authentic learning activities refers to real-world situations, as well as situations where students can solve problems in a manner similar to experts operating in real-world contexts (Herrington & Oliver, 2000). I would argue, then, that learning math should involve learning to think and act like mathematicians.

To some extent, authentic learning imitates the traditional apprenticeship model where the apprentice watches and learns from the expert. According to Hardman (Chapter 1 in this volume), the "presence of a culturally more competent other opens up a unique learning space that Vygotsky called the Zone of Proximal Development (ZPD)" (p. 14). Learning facilitation ensues when there is a deliberate effort to "act" and create a link between what students know and what they need to learn. These acts of scaffolding learning development are always mediated by artefacts (tools and signs) in a social-cultural milieu (Vygotsky, 1978).

A web presence does not equate to authentic learning (Herrington, 2009). Preferably, authentic e-learning environments should "provide realistic sets of situated opportunities allowing each learner expressions of forms of personal knowledge that fit or correspond with finding appropriate solutions to the given tasks" (Zualkerman, 2006, p. 200). Authentic learning tasks challenge students to think and solve problems like real-world professionals (Herrington & Herrington, 2006).

Herrington (2009) identifies four authentic e-learning pedagogical benefits: (1) situating learners in realistic contexts which prepare them for professional work; (2) engagement with complex, realistic tasks that challenge them to think like real professionals; (3) production of real artefacts with a real value; and (4) exposure to the use of technologies as cognitive tools (Jonassen, 2000). In these constructivist learning environments, provisions are made for students to access expert performances and a variety of sources (Herrington & Oliver, 2000). Students are also allowed to co-construct knowledge within situated opportunities (Lave & Wenger, 1991). Despite this, it is not clear how the interdependence of social and individual processes is given prominence in the 'authentic activity'. CHAT could provide a lens for this investigation.

Originating from Soviet psychology and philosophy, CHAT adopts a philosophical perspective whereby human consciousness is viewed as a product of practical activity, inseparable from material states of human existence (Marx, 1971). Bakhurst (1991) translated this to mean that people transform themselves and their surrounding environments culturally and historically as they *act on* and transform materials. This notion of 'activity' as people function in everyday contexts, combined with a practical, critical method of analysing its historical and cultural changing *course of action* can contour an understanding of learning.

The fundamental elements of the activity unit of analysis include a subject, an object, tools, rules, a community and division of labour (Engeström, 1987; Kuutti, 1996) (see Figure 1.3, on p. 16).

All activities are socially and culturally mediated (Leontiev, 1978). There are rules mediating the relationships between the subject and the community, and forms of organisation (division of labour) to ensure that the activity goals are met. Activity elements and neighbouring activities influence and are influenced by each other. Social and historical factors such as prior knowledge, or personal and cultural predispositions affect activities. Internal contradictions and tensions among the activity elements and activity systems lead to transitions and transformations.

CHAT has been used as a heuristic for designing learning experiences or courses (Amory, 2012), or to evaluate teaching and learning (Hardman, 2005). A common CHAT-based research aim is to determine "how participants transform objects and how the various system components mediate this transformation" (Barab et al., 2002, p. 79). In this case study, the authentic e learning model provided a framework for designing learning activities while CHAT was used to characterise and explain blog-mediated learning activity design.

Questions

1   What elements of blog-mediation affect the TAs learning process?
2   How does the blog-mediated learning activity change over time?
3   How can the information gained in questions (1) and (2) inform future learning activity design for mathematics teaching?

Approach

Primary data sources were blog posts of the two Master of Science (Mathematics) TAs and a questionnaire. (TA$_1$) had taught for one year while (TA$_2$) had five years of teaching experience. TA$_1$ supported pre-calculus teaching while TA$_2$ assisted with the calculus module. This case study analyses the first learning activity.

The analyses focused on four goals: (1) understanding the subjects and their motivations and interpretations of the tasks; (2) describing the structure of the blog-supported environment; (3) identifying mediating processes between the activity system elements and indicating potential tensions within and between the elements; and (4) outlining the resulting developmental transformation of the activity system.

Findings and discussion

Two questions from the questionnaire were used to solicit TAs' perceptions about mathematics learning. The TAs attributed motivational factors (willingness to learn and confidence) to student ability to understand mathematics. This is illustrated in their responses to the question: "When you are teaching, what do you focus on to make sure your students understand you?"

> [E]ncouraging the students to learn Mathematics beyond x and y . . . to the joy you get knowing the exact interpretation of x and y, something unknown to people who hate Mathematics subject
>
> (TA$_1$)

> [I]t's very important to build confidence in their ability to deal with maths by giving them an opportunity to express themselves and participate in the class.
>
> (TA$_2$)

When asked about key challenges faced by the students, TA₁ thought it was "the time it takes them to grasp the some concepts" while TA₂ believed that students "are not able to recall what has been taught in the previous stages due to their poor background in math". Both TAs recognised the importance of learning activity design.

The elements of activity were used to form an AT checklist such as Hardman's (2005) further analysis (Table 13.2).

The blog provided a platform for presenting the tasks, recording responses and feedback, as well as communication between participants. The language (English)

Table 13.2 An Activity Theory checklist

AT concepts	Questions	Descriptions	Analytic dimensions
Object	What is the purpose of the activity? What are the TAs working on? Why are they working on these tasks?	To use the blog as a learning tool for displaying completed tasks and for receiving feedback on completed tasks in order to improve them	What are the characteristics of the object and how is it being transformed?
Tools	Which tools are used? Non linguistic Linguistic	Non-linguistic (blog) Linguistic (English language)	Does the tool **restrict** the learning activity or does it **enrich** it? If so, in what ways?
Rules	What kinds of rules are used (instructional, evaluative, pacing)? Can they be regarded as social order rules, for disciplinary use, for communication, or foe interaction?	Rules for • Populating the blog • Completion and presentation of tasks • Interacting with each other • Co-constructing knowledge	Are they facilitator-led or TA-lead?
Division of labour	What community is involved? What group of people work on the object and how is power distributed?	Co-ordinators, the researcher and academics set the direction, assessment of the learning tasks while the TAs comment on and complete the given tasks	Is the power distribution symmetrical or asymmetrical?
Outcomes	What is produces (as learning) on part of the TAs?	A better understanding of the principles influencing good teaching practice, the context in which the occurs and the roles of the TAs	Are the outcomes localised or specialised?

was another tool used for articulating learning, communicating and developing a shared understanding of the tasks. Even though the TAs attended a workshop on blogging, they took time to adjusting to working with the blog. They concentrated on responding to the tasks individually and did not comment on each other's work as had been initially suggested. There were tensions around rules for populating the blog and using it as a collaborative learning tool. While the facilitator should provide direction, it is also important for the TAs to initiate meaningful collaboration.

The community included the TAs and facilitators (coordinators, academics and the researcher investigating the process). The facilitators presented the learning tasks while the TAs completed the tasks. Pacing for task completion was problematic and deadlines for submitting task responses were not adhered to. Feedback on task activities was also not promptly given. This loose arrangement could be attributed to the informal nature of the pilot project. There were tensions around rules of engagement in a space where the social norms were not made explicit.

An analysis of the responses to task 1b: "What principles guide the teaching of your subject area?" revealed that the principles expressed by the more experienced TA closely resembled Chickering and Gamson's (1987) seven principles for good practice in undergraduate education. The less experienced TA identified two ideas which needed further interrogation. Interaction between the two TAs could have assisted collaborative knowledge construction.

Information about the roles and responses to the tasks has informed the construction of a model for blog-mediated learning activity design (Figure 13.1). Learning activity 1 has been reformulated as a more authentic task.

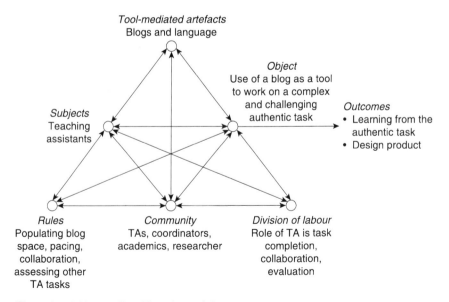

Figure 13.1 A blog-mediated learning activity

Recommendations for future use/advice for practitioners

The blog is a useful resource for participants' real accounts of their learning experiences. However, using the blog to facilitate collaborative learning can be constrained if the rules of engagement are unclear. Some time should be allocated to the adoption of the blog as a learning tool. An understanding of what students need to master at the operational and action levels is required to achieve the intended outcomes of blog-mediated learning.

CASE STUDY 13.4 UNDERSTANDING THE IMPLEMENTATION OF CURRICULUM INNOVATION FROM AN ACTIVITY THEORY PERSPECTIVE

Nomakhaya Mashiyi

Context

A few South African higher education institutions have identified and embedded graduate attributes into the curriculum in order to increase the employability of graduates and promote life-long learning. Graduate attributes are defined as:

> the qualities, values, attitudes, skills and understandings that a particular university sets out as being important for students to develop by the end of their studies. These attributes are both intended to equip them for future employment and as critical and responsible citizens, contributing to the social and economic well-being of society.
>
> (UWC Charter of Graduate Attributes Document, 2009)

The University of the Western Cape has developed a Charter of Graduate Attributes and subsequently, faculty-level and discipline-specific attributes. The study used the central tenets of CHAT and authentic learning to establish how the interacting components of the activity system in an Accounting lesson contributed to participatory learning, the development of graduate attributes and achievement of learning outcomes.

The Foundation Programme (FP) enables under-prepared students who have not met all the entrance requirements to pursue degree studies and study the three-year Commerce degree programme over a period of four years. During the first two years, FP students are provided with foundational knowledge and skills that enable them to meet the academic demands of the programme.

Background

The lineage of the three generational model of the Cultural-Historical Activity Theory (CHAT) can be traced back to Soviet psychology and philosophy.

Vygotsky (1978) asserted that the development of higher psychological processes came about as a result of mediated interactions within one's socio-cultural context. Through the scaffolding provided by the 'more knowledgeable other' and collaboration, learners can be assisted to reach the Zone of Proximal Development (ZPD).

In the second generation of CHAT, Leontiev (1978) expanded Vygotsky's theory which emphasised the subject–object–tool triad and focused on the notion of "object-orientedness". Through the subject's activity, the object is transformed into mental operations (cognition) and actions during the process of internalisation, resulting in an outcome. Leontiev conceptualised human activity as a system within a system of social relations. In the third generation of CHAT, Engeström (1999) embraced the relevance of the preceding stages and used activity triangles to represent the structure and internal relationships within an activity system. An activity is the unit of analysis in CHAT (see Figure 1.3, on p. 16). CHAT has been used as a tool to design learning (Issroff & Scanlon, 2002; Puustinen, Baker, & Lund, 2006) and as a heuristic to evaluate learning and teaching (Barr, Noble, & Lund, 2006, in Amory, 2012).

During a teaching-learning event, students become subjects, the content/topic under discussion becomes the object and the outcome is the final product that the student attains. The students internalise and appropriate the object in different ways e.g. through problem solving and cooperative learning. Learning can be tool-mediated, that is, physically and psychologically. CHAT emphasises the importance of context and conceives of learning as a collective community activity in which everyone has a role to play and is governed by implicit and explicit rules and regulations.

Authentic learning

Newman, Marks and Glamorgan (1996) define an authentic learning environment as "a pedagogical approach that allows for the construction of meaning grounded in real-life situations and the learner's own personal experience". The notion of authentic learning does not support a transmission style of teaching and highlights the importance of active learning, student engagement, responsibility for one's own learning, and knowledge construction on the part of the student. By creating authentic learning environments and designing authentic teaching and assessment activities, lecturers aid students' learning and sense-making, and thus the development of higher-order thinking skills.

Reeves, Herrington and Oliver (2000) state that authentic learning activities have the following characteristics: they mirror the real world, are ill-defined, complex and value laden, require students to use multiple perspectives to solve the problems, require students to collaborate in solving the problems, encourage interdisciplinary perspectives, create authentic products, and allow a range and diversity of outcomes that lead to multiple solutions. In short, solving such complex problems would require structured scaffolding on the part of the teacher, cooperation among students and lecturers, using different tools effectively to arrive at solutions and thinking outside of the proverbial box.

Questions

1   How did the Foundation Programme lecturer promote transformative learning in the Accounting lesson?
2   How were the teaching and learning activities used to promote the achievement of learning outcomes and UWC graduate attributes?

Findings and discussion

The findings are discussed below according to the study questions.

Question 1 How did the Foundation Programme lecturer promote transformative learning in the Accounting lesson?

Accounting students tackled Accounting transactions that they had been given as homework by their lecturer the previous day. These were contextualised problems that required them to apply theory to solve real-world problems that had been harvested from an Accounting textbook. Some of the problems were slightly adjusted to suit different scenarios in the South African context or were based on the lecturer's corporate experience. Problem solving and discussion were employed as teaching-learning strategies to help students achieve lesson outcomes. Mayo, Donelly, Nash and Schwartz (1993 in Killen 2000, p. 131) maintain that "problem-solving is a strategy for posing significant, contextualised, real-world situations, and providing resources, guidance and instruction to learners as they develop content knowledge and problem-solving skills". According to Killen (2000), problem-solving can be used as part of a lesson, as a theme for several lessons, or to structure the whole curriculum. Discussion as a teaching-learning strategy can be used with the whole class or in small groups to solve a problem, answer a question, enhance learner understanding, or reach a decision (Killen, 2000).

The lecturer displayed the problems to be solved on the screen and took the students through the problems using Accounting rules and the five-step process of solving Accounting problems. He provided structured support to the students by asking open-ended questions to help them arrive at the correct answers through whole-class discussion. Individual students who were experiencing problems at the different stages of solving the problems posed questions to the lecturer who in turn directed focused questions to the rest of the class to make it possible for the students to make sense of challenging aspects in the activities. There was *production and consumption* of knowledge as the *subjects* engaged in problem-solving, i.e. transformed the *object* in order to achieve the *outcome*.

The lecturer and students fulfilled distinct but complementary roles. The lecturer guided the teaching-learning encounter by discussing the Learning Outcomes and Assessment Standards, identifying problems to be solved, putting the students at ease at the introductory stage of the lecture, tapping into the students' prior knowledge, taking students through the activities and referring them to theory, rules and procedures that would help them solve the Accounting problems. Students completed the homework exercises individually, and through collaboration with peers contributed to a whole-class discussion, thus giving them an opportunity to reflect on their individual responses and adjust their responses.

Question 2 How were the teaching and learning activities used to promote the achievement of learning outcomes and UWC graduate attributes?

The *object* in this study was Accounting problems that had to be solved individually as homework, and then collaboratively in class by the students through the lecturer's assistance. Through problem solving and multiple engagements in the form of questions and answers between the lecturer and students and student-to-student interaction, the object was transformed, and the students were assisted to reach the ZPD. They created authentic products such as financial statements, and comprehensive income and change statements. Teaching was mediated through the use of discipline-specific terminology and technology (laptop and the interactive whiteboard). In this lesson, technology was used as an "enabler of communication", "information stream" and "transformation tool" (Amory, 2012) to enhance learning.

The Accounting problems displayed all the characteristics of authentic activities suggested by Reeves, Herrington, and Oliver (2004). Although text-book-based, the teaching-learning activities mirrored the real world, were ill-defined, complex and value-laden.

Students were required to use inter-disciplinary perspectives to solve the problems. For example, they used their knowledge of mathematics, in particular percentages, to work out depreciation and appreciation and created authentic products such as statements of financial position. The authentic products that had been created presented evidence to the lecturer that learning outcomes had been achieved.

Recommendations for future use/advice for practitioners

The study indicates that AL and CHAT are useful heuristics for understanding how situated learning contributes to knowledge construction and the achievement of learning outcomes. Elements of the CHAT system and AL work in concert in interactive student-centred teaching to develop the *skills and competencies* that the university and employers expect of graduates, namely, a critical attitude towards knowledge, critical citizenship and the social good, and a commitment to lifelong learning. They lay the foundation for the development of *overarching skills and abilities*, namely, "inquiry-focused and knowledgeable, critically and relevantly literate, autonomous and collaborative, ethically, environmentally and socially aware and active, skilled communicators, flexible and confident people" (UWC Charter of Graduate Attributes, 2009, pp. 2–4).

Authentic teaching-learning activities promoted student engagement and teamwork, instilled confidence in the students and prompted them to ask and answer questions, make informed judgements, unpack difficult concepts, evaluate their own understanding and engage in active learning. Student-centred teaching encompasses all the elements mentioned above, thus creating a climate that is conducive to the development of graduate attributes.

CASE STUDY 13.5 A WIKI FOR MEDIATING LEARNING IN ANATOMY

Roisin Kelly-Laubscher

Context

Anatomy is the study of the structure of living things. Future health sciences professionals, such as doctors, nurses, physiotherapists, occupational therapists, and also some science students, study human anatomy at the university level. Anatomy teaching methods have traditionally focused on lectures and laboratory dissections. More recently, there has been a shift towards including technology in anatomy teaching (Biasutto, Ignacio Caussa, & Esteban Criado del Río, 2006; Lewis, 2003; Pereira et al., 2007) as well as towards more integrated pedagogical models such as problem-based learning (Yiou & Goodenough, 2006). However, none of these have addressed the issue of academic literacy within the subject of anatomy. Furthermore, there have been concerns regarding students' focus on memorisation of vast numbers of anatomical structures without a clear understanding of the underlying concepts (Miller, Perrotti, Silverthorn, Dalley, & Rarey, 2002).

Background

The Intervention Programme (IP) is an extended curriculum for Health and Rehabilitation Sciences students at the University of Cape Town, similar in background and design to that described by Alexander, Badenhorst, and Gibbs (2005). Instead of students being selected for the programme based on their year 12 scores, all students first enrol in the mainstream physiotherapy and occupational therapy programmes. Both programmes follow a traditional curriculum format with lectures and practicals. After this semester, any students who have failed one or more subjects are asked to enter IP for one year. During the initial stages of IP, topics covered in the first semester of the mainstream programme are revisited. Therefore, since the students have already been taught using traditional anatomy lectures and laboratory dissections, the Anatomy Wiki was created to allow students to engage with this material in a different way.

Another important aim of this activity was to allow the students to practise skills in academic literacy within the subject of anatomy. There is a recent move away from generic academic literacy classes towards a more integrative approach. According to Lea and Street (1998): "Academic literacy practices – reading and writing within disciplines – constitute central processes through which students learn new subjects and develop their knowledge about new areas of study." The amount of overlap between the literacy practices of the student and the literacy practices within the discipline they are trying to access, ultimately determines their success (McKenna, 2010). Therefore, it is imperative that any extended programme includes opportunities for students to engage and become familiar with the literacy practices of these disciplines.

Therefore, the Anatomy Wiki project sought to provide the opportunity for students to become more familiar with underlying concepts in anatomy and practice skills in academic literacy within the subject of anatomy. This activity is based on the nine broad design elements of authentic learning, which are outlined in Chapter 5 of this book. Here we conceptualise the Anatomy Wiki project as part of an activity system (see Chapter 1) and discuss its role in tool mediation (see Chapter 1) in student learning.

Approach

A wiki was chosen as the central tool for this activity. A wiki is an online collaborative writing space. It is normally unstructured but since there were specific learning aims for this course, a model wiki page was provided along with a wiki page template for each student. The model wiki page was used to model the processes of finding information, identifying reliable sources versus unreliable sources, deciding which information to include and combining the information to form a complete paragraph. Besides describing the basic anatomy of a muscle, students also had to describe the importance of the muscle for their future careers and find and add links to interactive media to their wiki page. Before writing their own wiki page, the students needed to research the topic using the Internet and textbooks. After collating their research, they created a wiki page about each topic. Based on this work, students gave constructive criticism on their peers' wikis. Finally they had to present the information in their wiki to the class, both individually and in groups, over the course of the semester. Students also needed to be able to answer questions about their presentation. Each paragraph and presentation of the Anatomy Wiki project were assessed separately using a purpose-made rubric to evaluate student progress.

The Anatomy Wiki project, in conjunction with traditional lectures, mediated student engagement with the content (Figure 13.2). The subject of this activity is the student who, through the use of several mediating tools, acts on the object, in this case, anatomy. These tools allowed the student to actively engage with anatomy in an authentic context. The way the students used these tools to act on the object would be determined by their background, beliefs and preferences. For example, the section on "relevance to future career", allowed students the freedom to draw

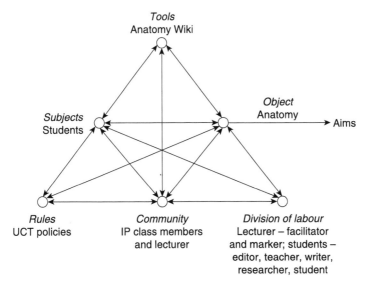

Figure 13.2 The Anatomy Wiki Project as an activity system

on theories and techniques from their profession specific courses. The approaches taken by physiotherapy students and occupational therapy students were different and this was reflective of the differences in their future career paths (Brown & Greenwood, 1999). Other members of the community may also influence them.

Findings and discussion

The wiki as a central tool and sign

Although there were many tools and signs involved in this activity, the wiki acted as a central mediator to which all the other tools and signs were related. This was not the same as a learning management system where tools can be placed together and accessed from one place. Instead, the wiki provided the stimulus for the use of other tools and signs. For some students this might have been a disadvantage because they might have focused on the wiki instead of on anatomy.

A tool itself should not be the object of the activity, but should mediate the transformation of the object. Gillespie and Zittoun (2010) describe how non-reflective tool use can become reflective when difficulties arise with the tool. In this situation, the tool rather than the object becomes the focus. To avoid this, students were initially instructed on how to use a wiki and given scheduled time in the computer lab to start their projects. This meant that if they had problems with either the wiki platform or the assigned task, they could immediately ask for help. These sessions were reduced and eventually removed as the year progressed. The other tools involved in this activity included the Internet and textbooks, interactive media, empty feedback sheets, and a PowerPoint presentation. Introductory sessions on the use of each of these tools were also provided. It is possible, due to the students' lack of experience in presenting, that their focus in the initial presentations might have been on the tool rather than the object. However, since the students did a total of six presentations over the two semesters it is hoped that their focus would have eventually shifted back to the object.

As highlighted in Chapter 1, tools can also act as signs depending on the context and that seemed to be the case for most of the tools used in the Anatomy Wiki project. As a sign, the wiki acted as a stimulus for dialogical activity between (critiques and presentations) and hopefully within (reflection) the students, which should further mediate learning. Since it is difficult to give sufficient feedback without engaging with and reflecting on what one is critiquing, the wiki pages acted as a stimulus for the students to interrogate their own knowledge. Likewise, it is difficult to ask or answer questions on a presentation without comparing it to the knowledge the student already possesses. Each student was given some time to address and implement the feedback provided in the completed feedback sheets before being marked. Comparing one's own wiki page with its feedback and implementing the feedback should have prompted reflection on the students' own thinking, thus incorporating reflective mediation. The reflection here was different to that mentioned above, because the students were reflecting on the anatomy content and/or ways of writing about anatomy, i.e. they were reflecting on the object of the activity. By comparing their own writing and content knowledge to the feedback comments, they would have been assessing the relation between their ideas and those of their peers. It was hoped that the students would eventually internalise the process of assessing one's work in terms of the standards provided in the feedback sheet and their own existing knowledge.

Explicit and implicit mediation in the Anatomy Wiki project

Many of the tasks in the project involved both explicit and implicit mediation. The initial task of creating a wiki explicitly mediated via the provision of a wiki page with a built-in template and model wiki page. The creation of presentations was also explicitly mediated by the use of the PowerPoint package and clear instructions on what should be included in the presentations. However, the presentations themselves also acted as a sign which implicitly mediated learning by stimulating conversations through the co-creation of presentations and the discussions that ensued during and after the presentations. The critiquing of each other's wiki pages also mediated both explicitly and implicitly as described above, however, provision of an oral critique instead of a written feedback sheet may have provided more opportunity for discussion of content and ideas.

The utility of the Anatomy Wiki as a cultural tool for learning is very dependent on the subject's aims. If their aims do not align with those of the lecturer or the community, the tools and signs may mediate differently. In the current learning activity, individual marks were awarded for all parts of the project. Assignment of a group mark for the whole project might have encouraged greater collaboration in terms of group presentations and constructive criticism.

Overall, the Anatomy Wiki project used both explicit and implicit non-reflective mediation to facilitate learning of anatomy and the application of academic literacy within anatomy. The structure of the project could be used in any subject. The final wiki was released in Open Educational resources and so it may continue to serve as a tool and/or sign to mediate learning.

CASE STUDY 13.6 FROM CONSUMPTION TO PRODUCTION OF KNOWLEDGE: USING DIGITAL STORYTELLING TO ENHANCE AUTHENTICITY OF INDUSTRIAL DESIGN STUDENTS' LEARNING

Daniela Gachago, Veronica Barnes and Eunice Ivala

Context

Technology 1, an introductory course within the Industrial Design qualification at a South African University of Technology, provides students with theoretical knowledge and practical experience of the materials and processes used in the manufacture of products.

This course makes use of industrial design's studio-based education, which is rooted in a cognitive apprenticeship model (Duggan, 2004; Tucker & Reynolds, 2006) and subscribes to a teaching and learning approach that is interactive, project-based and has a strong link to real-world problems (Docherty, Sutton, Brereton, & Kaplan, 2001). Brill, Kim, and Galloway (2001) describe the cognitive apprenticeship model as an authentic learning environment – with goal-orientated activities to solve real-world problems.

However, in this course, assessment methods often follow the traditional academic patterns, such as essays and other written work, which some authors consider less authentic. Allen (2009) and McLaren (2007), for example, argue that traditional approaches to assessment such as essays, tests, student-centred discussions and presentations will begin to appear inauthentic if they do not, to some extent at least, recognise and embrace multi-modal, Internet-enabled knowledge networking. As McLaren (2007, p. 10) argues: "Greater creativity is needed to help devise multi-dimensional, multi-expression assessment strategies which celebrate the complexity and influence pedagogy appropriate for learning in the 21st century."

Therefore, following Allen and McLaren's argument, this study explored whether an alternative learning activity using a specific tool, namely digital storytelling, could mediate students' appropriation and production of knowledge in a more authentic way than in an individual essay. This case study presents a reflection on the introduction of this digital storytelling project in Technology 1 using Cultural-Historical Activity Theory as a heuristic (Engeström, 1987), and explores whether and how the move from activity system 1 (essay task) to activity system 2 (digital storytelling project) transformed students' learning experience.

Approach

Previously, students wrote a conventional essay as part of the timber module assessment (Figure 13.3). The students were assessed on their content knowledge, analysis and application of the knowledge, and academic writing conventions (e.g. in text referencing). As an activity system, this essay task (object) often promoted a consumption of content by the individual student (agent). Rules were pre-established by the lecturer, the community (here including the essay audience) limited to the student and the lecturer, and a clear division of labour between these two was established (student producing the essay, the lecturer marking it and providing feedback). The tools used in the development of the essay were the library, the Internet, word processing software and textbooks. Outcomes were theoretical content knowledge and varied levels of academic literacy skills, e.g. searching for information, academic referencing and writing. Increasingly digitally aware students meant a change of approach was needed – focusing, not only on textual literacy and reasoning that predominate in schools and universities, but on an approach that facilitates the development of a full range of digital literacies necessary for twenty-first-century graduates (Hull, 2003).

In 2011, the research essay was replaced with a digital storytelling project. Digital storytelling is an innovative teaching, learning and assessment practice (Barrett, 2011). Digital stories are usually short movie clips, created with off-the-shelf equipment and techniques, combining text, images, videos, music and narration (Lundby, 2008). They are not professionally produced, but are self-made media. Lecturers use digital storytelling as an alternative means to appropriate knowledge in and outside the classroom. By creating the digital story, students acquire, interpret and produce content in different ways, using different multimodal tools (e.g. textual, visual and aural media). Consequently, digital storytelling facilitates the development of a full range of digital literacies, including more traditional literacies such as research, writing, but also more innovative multimodal literacies (e.g. shooting and editing digital movies). These literacies require students to know *how* and *when* to use tools and technologies.

The digital storytelling brief had specific requirements in terms of content and deliverables (e.g. topic and length of movie), but was broad in terms of processes, allowing students freedom and creativity. Students had a rubric to guide them in their project. The task was a group project, with three to four students randomly assigned to a group.

Findings and discussion

The brief in the digital storytelling project (object) mirrored an industrial designer's real-world scenario, which involves a client defining the requirements of a task, specifying materials and target group and limitations in terms of time and financial

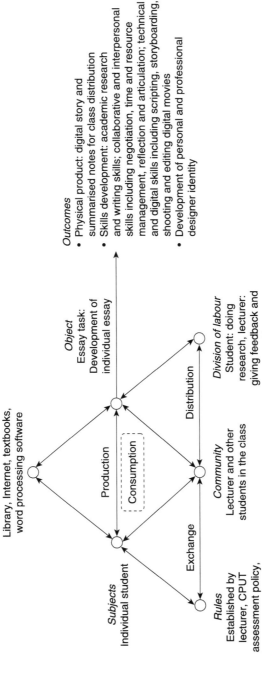

Figure 13.3 Activity system for the research essay task

resources. Apart from broad timelines and suggestions for milestones, the possibility to schedule a meeting with lecturers, students were responsible for negotiating roles and responsibilities for their project within their group (division of labour). Students were grouped randomly, in preparation for the real world, where students had to work and collaborate with a diverse group of colleagues (actors). This meant setting up rules of engagement in a negotiated exchange between the group and the community, which involved planning the project, ascertaining the skills of each group member, distributing tasks of research, using group brainstorming for communicating the information, prop building, script writing, filming, editing, and other tasks (division of labour).

Because of the openness of the brief and the diverse skill set involved in developing a digital story, students approached the wider community of friends and families to support them in carrying out the tasks (e.g. using a brother as movie actor, sourcing necessary equipment or asking friends for editing assistance). Students interviewed experts (e.g. workers at lumber mills) in their own environment, helping them to establish networks of experts, an essential skill for their future career.

Students had the opportunity, through negotiating group tasks and decision-making, to articulate their growing understanding of the tools and technologies they engaged, both through reflection-in-action and reflection-on-action (Schön, 1987).

A public screening to show the digital movies took the form of an Oscar ceremony, awarding prizes for different categories (e.g. best film, best special effects). Team members introduced their movie and group. Screening their stories to an authentic audience (of their peers) played a major role in the students' motivation to produce a high quality end product. Using a rubric enabled the lecturer to evaluate the presentation using criteria such as the introduction of the film, logic and sequencing, the visual impact of the film and content. Marks were given for the whole group, but students also rated their group members' contribution, which influenced individual student's final marks. Peer critique and peer marking are important elements of the reflective process, and important skills for students to be able to give and receive critique in the workplace.

The first author of this chapter, in his introductory chapter, introduced Wertsch's (2007) notion of implicit and explicit mediation. Explicit mediation refers to a conscious thinking about the tool/sign while undertaking an activity. During non-reflective activity, the subject/actor concentrates on the particulars of a task without thought of the tool/sign, resulting in an object of unconscious reflection. As an outcome of this project, students developed a polished product (the digital story) and the skills needed to produce the story (e.g. scripting, storyboarding and movie editing), which were intentionally introduced and, one could argue, students consciously thought about during the process of engaging with this task. However, this project also unintentionally mediated the development of a range of skills during the process of students collaboratively creating their stories. These skills were: crucial intra- and interpersonal skills (e.g. negotiation, leadership, collaboration, time and resource management) (Hull, 2003; Kajder, 2004), networking and development of personal and professional identity.

The introduction of an authentic task (object), using digital technologies (tools) to develop a digital story (outcome) among groups of Industrial Design students (actors), disrupted the way students negotiated their rules of engagement (rules), involved their community, and divided their tasks (division of labour), which mediated or resulted in an expanded outcome (Figure 13.4). Digital storytelling in this activity system was thus a tool (the tools and technologies needed to develop a digital story), which created an object (the authentic task of developing a digital story) and outcome (the physical digital story).

Recommendations for future use/advice for practitioners

This study explored introducing a pedagogical innovation as an alternative assessment methodology in a first-year module in the Industrial Design qualification. Digital storytelling technologies were chosen as a tool to allow or mediate authentic acquisition, interpretation and production of content. From the lecturer and the students' perspective, this project demonstrated that trusting students' collective abilities can help achieve complex projects with minimal support from lecturers, instead relying on students' own resourcefulness. This project showed that students developed intrinsic motivation through the challenge, relevance, interest and involvement in the digital storytelling project. Students' responses revealed a strong sense of ownership and pride in their final product, and a sense that the project was relevant to their own lives as individuals, as students and future professionals — all elements of authentic pedagogy (Snape & Fox-Turnbull, 2013). However, we argue that complex projects such as this one need sufficient time, and may also require provision of digital training and technology to less well-resourced students. Combining a digital story with short referenced notes by the students to be distributed in class may allow for broad transfer of content. Considering these factors, the digital storytelling project proved to be an authentic and meaningful learning experience for students, with a wider range of conscious and unconscious learning outcomes, which included the acquisition of crucial interpersonal and digital literacy skills, allowing professional identity development in students.

Conclusion

This Part of the book has introduced CHAT as a potential framework for understanding the complexities involved in teaching/learning in higher educational settings. The power of CHAT, especially in the South African context, lies in its understanding of activity as complex and multi-faceted, imbued with historical traces and socially situated. The case studies discussed in this chapter seek to animate the theoretical heuristic provided by CHAT, illustrating how this theory provides a powerful language of description, capable of

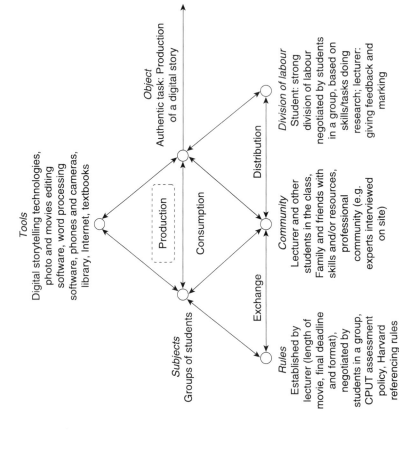

Figure 13.4 Activity system for the digital storytelling task

Tools

Digital storytelling technologies, photo and movies editing software, word processing software, phones and cameras, library, Internet, textbooks

Object

Authentic task: Production of a digital story

Outcomes

- Physical outcome: Physical digital story and summarised notes for class distribution
- Academic research and writing skills
- Skills outcome: Collaborative and interpersonal skills including: negotiation, time and resource management, reflection and articulation
- Skills outcome: Technical and digital skills including: scripting, storyboarding, shooting and editing digital story
- Skills outcome: Development of personal and professional identity as designer

Production

Consumption

Distribution

Exchange

Subjects

Groups of students

Rules

Established by lecturer (length of movie, final deadline and format), negotiated by students in a group, CPUT assessment policy, Harvard referencing rules

Community

Lecturer and other students in the class, Family and friends with skills and/or resources, professional community (e.g. experts interviewed on site)

Division of labour

Student: strong division of labour negotiated by students in a group, based on skills/tasks doing research; lecturer: giving feedback and marking illuminating teaching with technology in higher educational settings in South Africa and Australia. The cases illustrate how CHAT provides an explanatory framework that situates individual actions within the activity in which they unfold over time. Findings indicate that novel technology has the potential to transform pedagogy in higher education, depending on how it is used and the nature of the object it is used to work on. That is, we might conceive of novel technology as a tool, capable of mediating learning, if that is indeed the object of the activity. The understanding of technology as a mediating tool is elaborated in Chapter 14 in relation to authentic learning.

References

Allen, M. (2009). Authentic assessment and the internet: contributions within knowledge networks. In T. Bastiaens (Ed.), *Proceedings of World Conference on E-Learning in Corporate, Government, Healthcare, and Higher Education 2009* (pp. 1505–1510). Chesapeake, VA: AACE.

Alexander, R., Badenhorst, E., & Gibbs, T. (2005). Intervention programme: a supported learning programme for educationally disadvantaged students. *Med Teach. 27*(1): 66–70. DOI:10.1080/01421590400016472.

Amory, A. (2011). Pre-service teacher development: A model to develop critical media literacy through computer game-play. *Education As Change, 15*(1), 111–122.

Amory, A. (2012). Tool-mediated authentic learning in an educational technology course: A design-based innovation. *Interactive Learning Environments,* 1–16.

Anderson, S. B., & Anderson, I. (2005). Authentic learning in a sociocultural framework: A case study on non-formal learning. *Scandinavian Journal of Educational Research, 49*(4), 419–436.

Bakhurst, D. (1991). *Consciousness and revolution in Soviet philosophy: From the Bolsheviks to Evald Ilyenkov.* New York: Cambridge University Press.

Barab, S. A., Barnett, M., Yamagata-Lynch, L., Squire, K., & Keating, T. (2002). Using activity theory to understand the systemic tensions characterizing a technology-rich introductory astronomy course. *Mind, Culture, and Activity, 9,* 76–107.

Barret, M. (2005). Musical communication and children's communities of musical practice. In D. Miell, R. MacDonald, & D. J. Hargreaves (Eds.), *Musical communication* (pp. 261–281). Oxford: Oxford University Press.

Barrett, H. (2006). Digital stories in eportfolios: multiple purposes and tools. Retrieved from: http://electronicportfolios.org/digistory/purposes.html (accessed 25 January 2011).

Biasutto, S. N., Ignacio Caussa, L., & Esteban Criado del Río, L. (2006). Teaching anatomy: cadavers vs. computers? *Annals of Anatomy-anatomischer Anzeiger, 188*(2), 187–190.

Boaler, J. (2013). *Experiencing school mathematics: Traditional and reform approaches to teaching and their impact on student learning.* New York: Routledge.

Brill, J., Kim, B., & Galloway, C. (2001). Cognitive apprenticeships as an instructional model. In M. Orey (Ed.), *Emerging perspectives on learning, teaching, and technology.* Retrieved from: http://projects.coe.uga.edu/epltt/.

Brown, T. G., & Greenwood, J. (1999). Occupational therapy and physiotherapy: similar, but separate. *The British Journal of Occupational Therapy, 62*(4), 163–170.

Burdett, J. (2007). Degrees of separation: Balancing intervention and independence in group work assignments. *Australian Educational Researcher, 34*(1), 55–71.

Chickering, A. W., & Gamson, Z. F. (1987). Seven principles for good practice in undergraduate education. *AAHE Bulletin*, 3–7.

Daniels, H. (2001). *Vygotsky and pedagogy*. New York: Routledge.

Design-Based Research Collective (DBRC). (2003). Design-based research: an emerging paradigm for educational inquiry. *Educational Researcher, 32*(1), 5–8.

Docherty, M., Sutton, P., Brereton, M., & Kaplan, S. (2001). An innovative design and studio-based CS degree. In *Proceedings of the Thirty-second SIGCSE Technical Symposium on Computer Science Education* (pp. 233 237). Retrieved from: http://delivery.acm.org/10.1145/370000/364591/p233-docherty.pdf?ip=155.238.4.86&acc=ACTIVE SERVICE&CFID=112074168&CFOKEN=62779657&__acm__=1339752696_0ad3 3a393cce77ead9421744bc40a7b5.

Duggan, F. (2004). The changing nature of the studio as an educational setting. Retrieved from The Centre for Education in the Built Environment.

Edwards, A. (2012) The role of common knowledge in achieving collaboration across practices. *Learning Culture and Social Interaction, 1*(1), 22–32.

Engeström, Y. (1987). *Learning by Expanding: an activity-theoretical approach to developmental research*. Helsinki: Orienta-Konsultit.

Engeström, Y. (1991). Non scolae sed vitae discimus: Toward overcoming the encapsulation of school learning. *Learning and Instruction, 1*, 243–259.

Engeström, Y. (1999). Activity theory and individual and social transformation. In Y Engeström, R. Miettinen & R. L. Punama (Eds.) (pp. 29–38). *Perspectives on Activity Theory*. Cambridge: Cambridge University Press.

Engeström, Y. (2000). Activity theory as a framework for analysing and re-designing work. *Ergonomics*, 960–974.

Engeström, Y. (2001). Expansive learning at work: Toward an activity theoretical reconceptualization. *Journal of Education and Work, 14*(1), 133–156.

Engeström, Y. (2005). *Developmental work research: Expanding Activity Theory in practice*. Berlin: Lehmans Media.

Falchikov, N. (2007). The place of peers in learning and assessment. In D. Boud & N. Falchikov (Eds.), *Rethinking assessment in higher education learning for the longer term* (pp. 134–142). London: Routledge.

Garraway, J. (2009). Higher education and the world of work. In *Higher Education in South Africa: A scholarly look behind the scenes*. Stellenbosch: Sun Media.

Garrison, D. R., & Archer, W. (2000). *A transactional perspective on teaching and learning: A framework for adult and higher education*. Oxford: Pergamon.

Gaunt, H. (2011). Understanding the one-to-one relationship in instrumental/vocal tuition in higher education: Comparing student and teacher perceptions. *British Journal of Music Education, 28*(2), 159–179.

Gillespie, A., & Zittoun, T. (2010). Using resources: Conceptualizing the mediation and reflective use of tools and signs. *Culture & Psychology, 16*(1), 37–62.

Gravemeijer, K., & Cobb, P. (2006). Design research from a learning perspective. In J. von der Akker, K. Gravemeijer, S. McKenney, & N. Nieveen (Eds.), *Educational design research* (pp. 17–51). London: Routledge.

Hardman, J. (2005). Activity Theory as a potential framework for technology research in an unequal terrain. *South African Journal of Higher Education, 19*(2), 378–392.

Herrington, A., & Herrington, J. (2006). *Authentic learning environments in higher education*. Hershey: PA. New Media Consortium.

Herrington, A., & Herrington, J. (2008). What is an authentic learning environment? In: *Online and Distance Learning: Concepts, Methodologies, Tools, and Applications, Information Science Reference* (pp. 68–76).

Herrington, J., Herrington, A., Mantei, J., Olney, I. and Ferry, B. (Eds.), *New technologies, new pedagogies: Mobile learning in higher education*. Faculty of Education: University of Wollongong.

Herrington, J. & Oliver, R. (2000). An instructional design framework for authentic learning environments. *Educational Technology Research and Development, 48*(3), 23–48.

Herrington, J., Oliver, R., & Reeves, T.C. (2004). A development research agenda for online collaborative learning. *Educational Technology Research and Development, 52*(4), 53–65.

Herrington, J., & Reeves, T. C. (2003). Patterns of engagement in authentic online learning environments. *Australian Journal of Educational Technology, 19*(1), 59–71. Retrieved from http://www.ascilite.org.au/ajet/ajet19/herrington.html

Hull, G. A. (2003). At last: youth culture and digital media: new literacies for new times. *Research in the Teaching of English, 38*(2), 229–233. Retrieved from: http://www.jstor.org/stable/pdfplus/40171638.pdf?acceptTC=true.

Ioannou, A., & Artino, A. (2010). Learn more, stress less: Exploring the benefits of collaborative assessment. *College Student Journal, 44*(1), 189–199.

Issroff, K., & Scanlon, E. (2002). Using technology in higher education: An Activity Theory perspective. *Journal of Computer Assisted Learning, 18*(1), 77–83.

Johnson, D. W., Johnson, R. T., & Smith, K. (2007). The state of cooperative learning in postsecondary and professional settings. *Educational Psychology Review, 19*(1), 15–29.

Jonassen, D. (2000). *Computers as mindtools for schools: Engaging critical thinking.* Upper Saddle River, NJ: Merrill/Prentice Hall.

Jonassen, D., & Reeves, T. C. (1996). Learning with technology: using computers as cognitive tools. In D. H. Jonassen (Ed.), *Handbook of research on educational communications and technology* (pp. 693–719). New York: Macmillan.

Jonassen, D. H., & Rohrer-Murphy, L. (1999). Activity Theory as a framework for designing constructivist learning environments. *ETR&D, 47*(1), 61–79.

Kajder, S. B. (2004). Enter here: Personal narrative and digital storytelling. *The English Journal, 93*(3), 64–68. Retrieved from: http://www.jstor.org/stable/pdfplus/4128811.pdf?acceptTC=true.

Killen, R. (2000) *Teaching Strategies for Outcomes-based Education*. Lansdowne: Orchard Publishing.

Kizito, R. N. (2012). Realistic Mathematics Education (RME) as an instruction design perspective for introducing the relationship between the derivative and integral via distance education. (Unpublished doctoral dissertation). Stellenbosch University.

Kuutti, K. (1996). Activity Theory as a potential framework for human-computer interaction research. In B. Nardi (Ed.), *Context and consciousness: Activity Theory and human–computer interaction* (pp. 17–44). Cambridge, MA: MIT Press.

Latukefu, L. (2009). Peer learning and reflection: Strategies developed by vocal students in a transforming tertiary setting. *International Journal of Music Education, 27*(2), 128–142.

Latukefu, L. (2010). The constructed voice: a socio-cultural approach to teaching and learning singing (manuscript). PhD thesis, University of Wollongong, Australia.

Latukefu, L., & Verenikina, I. (2011). Scientific concepts in singing: do they belong in a student toolbox of learning? *British Journal of Music Education, 28*(2), 181–194.

Latukefu, L., & Verenikina, I. (2013). Expanding the master-apprentice model: Tools for orchestrating collaboration as a path to self-directed learning for singing students. In H. Gaunt & H. Westerlund (Eds.), *Collaborative learning in higher music education* (pp. 101–109). Surrey: Ashgate Publishing.

Lave, J., & Wenger, E. (1991). *Situated learning: legitimate peripheral participation* Cambridge: Cambridge University Press.

Lea, M. R., & Street, B. V. (1998). Student writing in higher education: An academic literacies approach. *Studies in Higher Education, 23*(2), 157–172.

Leontiev, A. N. (1978). *Activity, consciousness, and personality.* Englewood Cliffs, NJ: Prentice-Hall.

Lewis, M. J. (2003). Computer-assisted learning for teaching anatomy and physiology in subjects allied to medicine. *Medical Teacher, 25*(2), 204–207.

Lundby, K. (2008). *Digital storytelling, mediatized stories: Self-representations in new media.* New York: P. Lang. Retrieved from: www.seminar.net/index.php/reviews-hovedmeny-110/72-reviews/157-digital-storytelling-mediatized-stories-self-representations-in-new-media.

Main, K. (2010). Teamwork – teach me, teach me not: A case study of three Australian preservice teachers. *Australian Educational Researcher, 37*(3), 77–93.

Marx, K. (1971). *A contribution to the critique of political economy.* London: Lawrence & Wishart.

Mayo, P., Donelly, M. B., Nash, P. P., & Schwatrz, R. W. (1993). Student perceptions of tutor effectiveness in problem-based surgery clerkship. *Teaching and Learning in Medicine, 5*(4), 227–233.

McLaren, S. V. (2007). An international overview of assessment issues in technology education: Disentangling the influences, confusion and complexities. *Design and Technology Education: An International Journal, 12*(2), 10–24. Retrieved from: http://ojs.lboro.ac.uk/ojs/index.php/DATE/article/view/Journal_12.2_0707_RES1.

McKenna, S. (2010). Cracking the code of academic literacy: An ideological task1. *Provision of Extended Curriculum Programmes in South Africa,* 8.

Miller, S. A., Perrotti, W., Silverthorn, D. U., Dalley, A. F., & Rarey, K. E. (2002). From college to clinic: Reasoning over memorization is key for understanding anatomy. *The Anatomical Record, 269*(2), 69–80.

Oblinger, D. G. (2008). *Growing up with Google: What it means to education.* Retrieved from: http://partners.becta.org.uk/upload-dir/downloads/page_documents/research/emerging_technologies08_chapter1.pdf.

Olney, I., Herrington, J., & Verenikina, I. (2009). Digital story telling using iPods. In *New technologies, new pedagogies: Mobile learning in higher education* (pp. 36–44). University of Wollogong. Retrieved from: ro.uow.edu.au/newtech.

Pereira, J., Merí, A., Masdeu, C., Molina-Tomás, M,. & Martinez-Carrio, A. (2013). Using videoclips to improve theoretical anatomy teaching. *European Journal of Anatomy, 8*(3), 143–146.

Puustinen, M., Baker, M., & Lund, K. (2006). GESTALT: A framework for redesign of educational software. *Journal of Computer Assisted Learning, 22*(1), 34–46

Reeves, T. C., Herrington, J., & Oliver, R. (2002). Authentic learning and online learning. *HERDSA* (pp. 562–567).

Reeves, T. C., Herrington, J., & Oliver, R. (2004). A development research agenda for on-line collaborative learning. *Educational Technology Research and Development, 52,* 53–65.

Resnick, L. (1987). Learning in school and out. *Educational Researcher, 16.* 3–20.

Roth, W. M., & Lee, Y. J. (2007). Vygotsky's neglected legacy: Cultural-historical activity theory. *Review of Educational Research. 77,* 186–232.

Schön, D. (1987). *Educating the reflective practitioner.* San Francisco: Jossey-Bass.

Snape, P., & Fox-Turnbull, W. (2011). Perspectives of authenticity: Implementation in technology education. *International Journal of Technology and Design Education.* doi:10.1007/s10798-011-9168-2.

Stetsenko, A. (2005). Activity as object-related: Resolving the dichotomy of individual and collective planes of activity. *Mind, Culture, and Activity, 12*(1), 70–88.

Stetsenko, A. (2008). From relational ontology to transformative activist stance on development and learning: expanding Vygotsky's (CHAT) project. *Cultural Studies of Science Education, 3*(2), 471–491.

Tall, D. O. (1991). Setting the Calculus straight. *Mathematics Review, 2*(1), 2–6.

Tinto, V. (1999). Taking retention seriously: Rethinking the first year of college. *NACADA Journal, 19*(2), 5–9.

Tucker, R., & Reynolds, C. (2006). The impact of teaching models, group structures and assessment modes on cooperative learning in the student design studio. *Journal for Education in the Built Environment, 1*(2). Retrieved from: http://dro.deakin.edu.au/eserv/DU:30003698/tucker-impactofteaching-2006.pdf.

University of the Western Cape. (2009). Charter of Graduate Attributes. http://www.uwc.ac.za/TandL/Pages/Graduate-Attributes.aspx#.U4C-4ViSxbw

Verenikina, I. (2012). Facilitating collaborative work in tertiary teaching: A self-study. *The Australian Educational Researcher, 39*, 477–489.

Veresov, N. (2007). Sign mediation: Magic triangle: sign-mediated action and behind. Fourth Nordic Conference on Cultural and Activity Research, 15–17 June 2007 Oslo, Norway.

Vygotsky, L. S. (1978). *Mind in society; The development of higher psychological processes*. M. Cole, V. John-Steiner, S. Scribner, & S. Souberman (Eds. and Trans.). Cambridge, MA: Harvard University Press.

Vygotsky, L. S. (1986). *Thought and language*. E. Hanfmann & G. Vakar (Eds. and Trans.). Cambridge, MA: MIT Press.

Vygotsky, L. S. (1987). *The collected works of L.S. Vygotsky*, Vol. 1: *Problems of general psychology*. R. W. Rieber & A. S. Carton (Eds.), N. Minick (Trans.). New York: Plenum Press.

Vygotsky, L. S. (1997). *Educational psychology*. Boca Raton, FL: St Lucie Press.

Wells, G. (1999). *Dialogic inquiry. Towards a sociocultural practice and theory of education*. Cambridge: Cambridge University Press.

Wertsch, J. V. (2007). Mediation. In H. Daniels, M. Cole, & J. V. Wertsch (Eds.), *The Cambridge companion to Vygotsky* (pp. 178–192). New York: Cambridge University Press.

Yiou, R., & Goodenough, D. (2006). Applying problem-based learning to the teaching of anatomy: The example of Harvard Medical School. *Surgical and Radiologic Anatomy, 28*(2), 189–194.

Zhukov, K. (2007). Student learning styles in advanced instrumental music lessons. *Music Education Research, 9*(1), 111–127.

Zualkernan, I. A. (2006). A framework and a methodology for developing authentic constructivist e-Learning environments. *Educational Technology & Society, 9*(2), 198–212.

14 The case studies

Authentic learning

Jan Herrington, Veronica Mitchell,
Michael Rowe and Simone Titus

Introduction

Moving from theory to practice in higher education is deeply challenging. While exploring pedagogical models in the literature may lead to tacit understanding of general principles, actually implementing these principles in practice can be an entirely different matter.

Authentic learning is a pedagogical model that is sometimes misunderstood, such as when teachers believe that in order for authenticity to be achieved, learning must occur outside the classroom in the real world. In fact, authenticity – as described in this model – can readily be achieved within the regular classrooms and lecture halls of the university environment. Providing examples of successful cases of such authentic learning environments offers an opportunity to explore the practical application of a theoretical model, and provide concrete instances of implementation in different subject areas. This chapter provides three such cases.

The cases presented here provide international examples of authentic learning in practice across different discipline areas, using different technologies, and focusing on different aspects of the approach. The first case (Case study 14.1) describes the use of reflective analysis and role play in the study of obstetrics, using the model of authentic learning described in Chapter 5 (Herrington, 2014). It focuses on the use of technology as a mediating vehicle for authentic learning through the use of practice dilemmas. The second case (Case study 14.2) describes specific tasks developed within an authentic learning environment, using characteristics of authentic tasks (Herrington, Reeves, Oliver, & Woo, 2004). This case describes the use of complex contexts and the development of case notes in the study of physiotherapy. The final case (Case study 14.3) explores the use of wikis and blogs to medicate authentic learning in sport science education.

All the cases represent authentic learning in action, and include details of the context, the tasks, and the problems that inevitably arise when teachers necessarily relinquish their more traditional role to allow students to take primary responsibility for learning. They are also effectively works in progress, where solutions are refined and improved in successive iterations. But above all, they are visible and tangible exemplars of theory in action.

CASE STUDY 14.1 TRANSFORMING OBSTETRIC EXPERIENCES THROUGH STUDENTS' CONSTRUCTION OF COLLABORATIVE CRITICAL INSIGHTS

Veronica Mitchell

In medical education, much emphasis is placed on the scientific grounding of evidence-based practice and the achievement of measurable and assessable learning outcomes. However, the curriculum as designed differs from the enacted curriculum. Forces that play out as students engage in their curricular tasks weather the linear and predictable nature of a systematically organised accredited curriculum. These dynamic, fluid and complex influences underpin what and how students are learning. Consequently unpredictable outcomes result from the additional social aspects of interrelationships in the learning contexts, which impact on each individual student's learning (Barnett & Coate, 2005, p. 44).

Students' clinical encounters beyond the classroom introduce uncertainty, ambiguity and at times dissonance, challenging their developing professional identities. Students sometimes face conflicting behaviours, attitudes and values, especially and surprisingly in the discipline of obstetrics. At the University of Cape Town (UCT), the student community is a vulnerable population working within a weak public health system amidst the hierarchy of medicine in practice and university structures. There appears to be a mismatch between insights gained by students to practise medicine in a socially accountable manner and their observations of human rights violations in the workplace (Vivian, Naidu, Keikelame, & Irlam, 2011; Mitchell, 2012).

This case example draws on the problematisation of the medical curriculum and calls for change, and an authentic curricular task in the Department of Obstetrics and Gynaecology is explained as a design-based research project (Reeves, 2006). The reflective element of authentic learning is strongly valued as students are provided with a forum to articulate and recognise their emotional dissonance. Through the affordances of technology, students' workplace challenges are surfaced and shared, fostering a collaborative effort to delve into the real-life problems encountered in our healthcare delivery. Yet, as Herrington and Kervin (2007) claim, "Experiences that put technology into the hands of the students challenge the traditional roles of teachers and students and their associated relationships" (p. 233).

Background

Shifting paradigms are occurring not only from the perspective of medical education as a discipline, but also from students' expectations. A brief theoretical background will lead to an explanation of this authentic learning case study in obstetrics. In addition to the educational changes spurred on by emerging technologies, there are strong calls for rethinking practices in medical education, emphasising a focus on transformative learning and interrelationships and a shift away from the apprenticeship approach and competency-based curricula

(Dall'Alba & Barnacle, 2007; Frenk et al., 2010; Taylor & White, 2000). The limitations imposed by a focus on competence to practise has devalued the importance of taking a reasoning, critical stance in the curriculum, embracing and sharing multiple perspectives (Kneebone, 2002; Savin-Baden, 2009; Zembylas, 2013).

There is increasing recognition of more curricular focus on the developing professional identity of future doctors and the health needs of communities in which they work (Jarvis-Sellinger, Pratt, & Regehr, 2012). Furthermore, the complexity of the curriculum with "multiple variables [which] are interacting simultaneously" confirms the stance to move away from reductionist and binary concepts (Mennin, 2010, p. 27). Reflective practices contribute to an expanded approach. Yet reflection is not generally favoured by students and remains a challenging process for educators to motivate and to facilitate (Bozalek & Matthews, 2008). Herrington, Reeves and Oliver (2010) point out that "learners need to work at times beyond their comfort zones and to take risks as they seek to develop their solutions as part of the learning process" (p. 127). Students expect their teachers to be good role models, yet frequently they witness professional lapses (Vivian, Naidu, Keikelame, & Irlam, 2011; Mitchell 2012). There is a tendency to silence criticism. Ruch's (2002) research with social workers highlighted the professional ethos that "expects workers to be unaffected by the experiences they encounter and able to operate regardless of their emotionally toxic professional context" (p. 207).

Students' meaning-making from their curricular experiences reflects their individual social constructs. Within a diverse student population, this richness of multiple knowledges offers a multi-coloured bouquet of understandings. Such learning towards real-life relevance is fundamental to authentic learning and provides an opportunity for meaningful engagement especially appropriate in a discipline like obstetrics which is characterised by tension and uncertainty.

Question

How can educators better prepare students for the complexities of practice and facilitate advocacy in promoting women's health?

Approach

The elements of authentic learning included in this case study are outlined in terms of the nine characteristics identified by Herrington, Reeves and Oliver (2010, p. 18):

1   *Authentic contexts*: Students reflect on their delivery experiences in the Maternal Obstetric Units (MOUs).
2   *Authentic activities*: Fourth-year students share and interrogate their obstetrics experiences. They interpret and prioritise what they wish to present to the class at the end of their eight-week learning block.

3   *Expert performances*: Students have access to experts such as midwives and clinicians, also learning from senior students in tutorials. The Internet offers wider learning opportunities.

4   *Multiple roles and perspectives*: A reflective online tool is used in preparation for the classroom interactive workshop. Through probing questions in the spiral tool (see Figure 14.1), the perspective of the different players is illuminated: the student, midwife, doctor and patient. By seeking to understand the forces that play out in obstetrics, students are opened to shifting frames of reference.

5   *Collaborative construction of knowledge*: Students post reflective commentaries online, engaging with a critical friend and developing group presentations.

6   *Reflection*: Reflective enquiry is on-going and facilitated within a visual framework.

7   *Articulation*: Students converse with each other during the block and in preparing for their interactive workshop. Critical dialogue is encouraged online and in the classroom.

8   *Coaching and scaffolding*: Sharing personal experiences and reflections can be challenging. This is acknowledged throughout the process. Student queries are responded to either online or in person. Notes of encouragement are

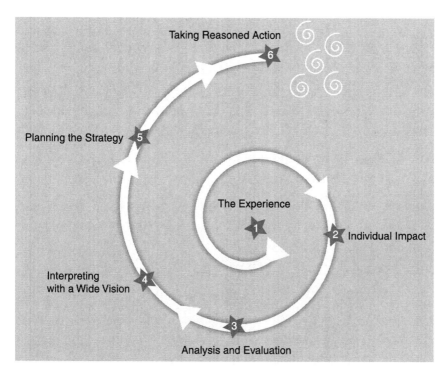

Figure 14.1 Reflective task: Six step spiral for critical reflexivity

Source: Mitchell (2013)

offered on the Faculty Learning Management System (LMS), over e-mail or in class.

9   *Authentic assessment*: Assessment happens through performance rather than judgement. Students create an authentic product in the form of a presentation, with multimedia, role-play or other elements.

The obstetrics class activity is described below in terms of the tasks, resources and support implemented in the environment. The time frame incorporates three stages: a brief introduction with the students in the computer centre, an online element, and a face-to-face interactive classroom activity.

At the obstetrics introductory session, an environment of trust and respectful sharing is created. The facilitator introduces the task with motivation that students' voices are being valued. Students then post prior insights online, initially on the institutional LMS course forum (but now Google Drive is the preferred option). Comments include personal narratives heard from colleagues including some difficult situations. Expressions of emotion are encouraged. This is an exciting curricular moment when students often feel they are becoming real doctors.

Students are then introduced to the Six Step Spiral for Critical Reflexivity (SSS4CR) available on the LMS, the Google Drive folder and the Faculty Open Content repository. Students explore this new multi-layered visual tool with its probing questions (see Figure 14.1). Students are requested to choose an incident during their practical block, to then 'unpack' it using the probing questions connected to the spiral, and to post their text online.

At the end of the learning block, subgroups of approximately 12 students present a component of their reflections to the rest of the group as a role-play, multimedia presentation or case discussion. Preparation for this final presentation is crucial. It involves students sharing their experiences with each other, towards producing a meaningful message or enquiry to present to their colleagues, the facilitator and an outside expert.

The resources develop incrementally as students post their personal narratives and unpack their delivery experiences online. Guided by the spiral, their comments create the resource material, co-constructed knowledge which also acts as feedback from the curricular task. The LMS Forum and the sharing of Google documents enable a collaborative approach, as insights are visible for other students and educators to read and to respond to where appropriate.

Support and scaffolding are offered at key points. For instance, in the introductory session, an appreciation of students' vulnerability within the institutional hierarchy and with online postings is acknowledged. Later, uploading a previous student's reflection contributes to the scaffolding. Students are invited to interact with their clinical partner as a critical friend. This fosters shared insights enabling students to compare and contrast their experiences, ideas and actions. Students may submit their reflections individually or as partners. Some students choose the privacy of sending the facilitator their reflective commentaries by e-mail. These are acknowledged with encouraging responses.

Findings and discussion

The creative inclusion of technology has effectively drawn the students into the process with favourable outcomes. This curricular task has been valued particularly in terms of the authentic learning elements of articulation, reflection and collaboration.

First, articulation occurs across several layers of interactions. In the introductory session, students glimpse the real world of obstetrics in Cape Town clinics where their taken-for-granted expectations are questioned. By engaging online and face-to-face at the different stages during the block, a collective approach is fostered promoting students' capacity to become change agents. Students are expressing and sharing their tensions in their postings and conversations. Clearly, "responsibility for learning rests with the learner" rather than the teacher (Herrington, Reeves, & Oliver, 2010, p. 190). Students' online engagement has encouraged them to explore beyond their individual boundaries of meaning-making. Progressively more students have shared their comments in the collaborative spaces. When students prepare for the end-of-block presentations, they draw on each other's experiences and explore the Internet to explain the legal, social, political and personal realities that play out in the local clinics. Technology enables their enquiry and sharing. Multimedia presentations include video clips where students present scenarios. Issues such as inequality, vulnerability and discrimination are illuminated. A special guest is invited to these presentations, contributing expertise and critique to the dialogue.

Second, feedback indicates that the SSS4CR introduces a novel structured approach for debriefing and making sense of experiences. It promotes reflexivity referred to as "looking for the social in the individual account, asking how particular events, categories and assumptions might have been produced through discourse, culture, political affiliations, and/or social practice" (Bozalek et al., 2010, p. 1026). Originally the spiral aimed to assist students debrief from abuse witnessed in the workplace. Later editing introduced new questions to also probe positive practices. This iterative approach demonstrates how design adaptation and improvement have furthered teaching, a necessary element of authentic learning (Herrington, Herrington, & Mantei, 2009).

Third, the collaborative element of the task is evident and continues to play an important role in giving value to the students' voices. Beneficial consequences beyond the students' engagement include reports by the departmental head to the Health Department and to facility managers leading to workshops for midwives, and to policy changes towards creating a formal Code of Practice. The website published on UCT OpenContent is an Open Educational Resource (Mitchell, 2013).

Recommendations for future use/advice for practitioners

A trusting environment is needed for students to develop their capacity to overcome their vulnerability in critiquing observed practices. Encouragement, support and openness assist the process. For educators, willingness to take risks and traverse uncertainty and discomfort is required. Departmental buy-in facilitates shifting the pedagogy away from a linear predictable approach.

This case explains how technology has provided a mediating vehicle for an authentic learning initiative in obstetrics. By constructing knowledge online drawn from students' own social networks, perspectives and experiences, the students have engaged in dialogue on difficult issues expanding their understanding of practice dilemmas. Through online interaction relating their real-life events, students are acknowledging the complexities of their roles and responsibilities. Moreover, the collaborative sharing of students' experiences has acted as a collective vehicle to catalyse policy changes in the health system. The take-up of these messages is demonstrating the beneficial impact of moving towards curricula for relevance and change. In essence the outcomes from this authentic learning task have proved beneficial to students, facilities and women in labour.

CASE STUDY 14.2 USING GOOGLE DRIVE TO FACILITATE A BLENDED APPROACH TO AUTHENTIC LEARNING

Michael Rowe

While technology has the potential to create opportunities for transformative learning, it is often used simply to reinforce teaching that aims to control access to expert knowledge. Instead, educators should consider using technology to enhance communication and provide richer, more meaningful platforms for the social construction of knowledge. By using technology to engage in shared learning experiences that extend beyond the walls of the classroom, we can create opportunities to develop the patterns of thinking that students need to engage with complex, real-world situations.

An authentic task framework was used to guide the design and implementation of a case-based learning module in a South African physiotherapy department. Google Drive was used as a collaborative online authoring environment in which small groups of students used clinical cases to create their own content, guided by a team of facilitators. This case describes an approach to healthcare education using authentic learning as a guiding framework, and Google Drive as an implementation platform. This approach led to the transformation of student learning practices, altered power relationships in the classroom and facilitated the development of critical attitudes towards knowledge and authority.

The study was conducted in a physiotherapy department at the University of the Western Cape, South Africa. Following feedback indicating that final year students displayed a lack of critical thinking during clinical exams, the department moved to address these problems. A second-year module was selected, in which students learn the pathology, clinical presentation, and therapeutic management of common health conditions found in the South African healthcare system. In the past, they had been given course readers that covered the major concepts, and a lecturer went through the concepts with the students, using a lecture-based format.

We made a series of changes to the module, including a move from lectures to case-based learning to promote critical thinking and problem-solving, as well as using technology to facilitate different forms of communication. Both of these changes were informed by social constructivist and situated theories of learning. We also moved from having one lecturer in the classroom to having 6–8 facilitators, with students working collaboratively in small groups.

Background

One of the challenges in higher education is to create an environment that does not separate the "learning" from the "doing", and where students are not constrained in the activities that would lead to personally meaningful learning opportunities. When knowledge and context are separated, knowledge is seen by learners as a product of education, rather than as a tool they can use (Brown, Collins, & Duguid, 1989).

While technology has the potential to create opportunities for transformative learning, it is often used simply to reinforce didactic teaching that aims to control access to knowledge. In contrast to authentic learning spaces that are informed by learning theories, the predominant use of technology in higher education emphasises teachers generating content, gathering resources, grouping and sequencing information, and then passing that information on to students (Herrington, Reeves, & Oliver, 2010). Such an emphasis on higher education as a content delivery mechanism has the potential to damage the perception of the use of technology in education, as well have a negative influence on student learning. Educators should therefore consider using technology to enhance communication and provide richer, more meaningful platforms for the social construction of knowledge rather than use systems that envision higher education as closed-off silos of content.

Question

How can we use a collaborative online environment to create an authentic learning space that aims to facilitate the development of critical thinking in undergraduate physiotherapy students?

Approach

This case employs an innovative approach to healthcare education using authentic learning as a guiding framework, and Google Drive as an implementation platform. We used ten characteristics of authentic tasks (Herrington, Reeves, Oliver, & Woo, 2004), as a framework to guide the module design, and students used Google Drive to create their own content, assisted by a team of facilitators.

A description of how each element of authentic task design aligned in the course is given below.

1   *Have real-world relevance, matching as nearly as possible the tasks of professionals in practice.* The cases provided to students were based on common conditions that they would encounter in the clinical environment, and were designed to encourage ways of thinking that would be necessary for the management of patients. Instead of simply giving students the content to learn, conditions were presented in the classroom in the same way they would be found in the clinical context.

2   *Are ill-defined, and problems are open to multiple interpretations rather than easily solved by the application of existing algorithms.* The cases were complex, requiring students to find associations between variables that were not explicitly related. They needed to create research questions after identifying gaps in their knowledge, conduct research and then collaboratively create their own notes in Google Drive, summarising and synthesising the information they had found.

3   *Comprise complex tasks to be investigated by students over a sustained period of time.* Each case ran over a three-week period, with students and facilitators meeting in class for face-to-face contact three times a week. Interaction on Google Drive was used to supplement these classroom discussions. The clinical case was not an isolated activity, with Google Drive being used both in class while students engaged in research and content creation, and afterwards when facilitators and peers gave feedback on the students' notes.

4   *Encourage students to examine the task from different theoretical and practical perspectives, using a variety of resources that require them to critically evaluate information.* Facilitators reviewed students' online case notes weekly, providing feedback by asking questions about missing information, unsubstantiated claims, and dubious sources. Students were able to respond within the comments, asking their own questions or clarifying their understanding.

5   *Require collaboration, which is integral to the task, so that success is dependent on it.* Case notes were developed collaboratively by the student groups, and all notes were available to all other groups, as well as to facilitators. Each week, students created summaries of their case using the slideshow component of Google Drive, presented this in class, and then shared the summary with everyone. Google Drive also features an instant messenger, which allowed students to discuss aspects of the case notes while working on the document together, even when they were in different locations.

6   *Provide the opportunity to reflect on learning, both individually and with others.* Facilitators provided feedback to students within their case notes in the form of comments and questions, encouraging them to reflect on their assumptions and reasoning. Students were challenged on their statements and encouraged to articulate their understanding, as the questions were not asked to elicit information, but rather to stimulate further thinking.

7 *Authentic activities can be integrated and applied across different subject areas and lead beyond domain-specific outcomes.* Each case was designed to integrate research, ethical reflection, legal aspects of healthcare, and knowledge from other modules such as anatomy. The case was designed so that it was not an isolated activity that was separate from other modules.

8 *Are seamlessly integrated with assessment in a manner that reflects real-world assessment.* Formative assessment was an inherent part of the activity, with peers and facilitators regularly challenging statements and assumptions that arose during the classroom sessions, and in the online notes. This is more like the kind of formative assessment and learning that happens in the real world of clinical practice.

9 *Create polished products valuable in their own right rather than as preparation for something else.* The notes that students created in Google Drive constituted their learning content for the module, making them an important product of the task. The questions for the tests at the end of each term were derived from both the students' notes and the facilitators' guides, which meant that the student notes had real value as they were used as the foundation for their work in the clinical context.

10 *Allow multiple solutions and diversity of outcome, rather than having a single correct response obtained by the application of rules and procedures.* Each groups' online case notes were different, reflecting the questions they answered after exploring their own understanding of the case. While facilitators ensured that the major concepts were addressed, students could take their own routes to achieving the case objectives.

The adapted module was implemented and focus groups were held at the end of the first semester. All 61 students in the second-year class were asked if they were prepared to participate in a focus group, and 22 responded positively. Twelve students were invited to participate and were selected from both high and low ends of scales measuring their age, levels of online participation and their average marks in the module, in order to include as diverse a sample as possible. Based on the major changes in the module, participants were asked to discuss the move from lectures to case-based learning in small groups, and the use of Google Drive for students to collaboratively develop content.

The discussions were recorded and the audio files sent for independent transcription, and then sent to participants for verification. The transcripts were analysed inductively to determine themes that emerged from participant responses (Elo & Kyngäs, 2008). Words and phrases with similar meanings were identified, coded and then organised into categories that best represented the emergent themes.

Findings and discussion

The major themes that emerged during the analysis included: changes in student perceptions of their roles in the learning process, personal empowerment through self-directed learning, the development of critical thinking, and the changing of power relationships in the classroom.

Changing perceptions of learning roles (personal empowerment and self-directed learning)

The use of authentic task elements to develop cases that we implemented in Google Drive enabled us to help change how students perceive their own role in the learning process. As part of this process, students had to create their own research questions after identifying gaps in their understanding, through discussion with peers and facilitators. Rather than being given content and told what to learn, the process required them to evaluate their own needs and respond appropriately, thereby empowering students to take control of their learning (Veletsianos, 2011). Using Google Drive afforded students a platform to develop the processes and skills they needed for the independent exploration of concepts and facts (Justice et al., 2009). This critical interaction with information helped them to move towards autonomous learning, empowering them to control where, what and how they learn.

Development of critical thinking

This approach enabled students to change how they think about learning, relationships and content, in ways that led to critical thinking. If teaching is about "moving minds" to develop independent thinkers who will not bend to the will of teachers (Laurillard, 2012, p. 5), then these students did not simply accept the voice of authority. They grasped that knowledge is distributed and that the teacher is not the sole source of information (Veletsianos, 2011).

Changing power relationships

We used interaction in the online and physical space to intentionally change power relationships between teachers and students, guided by principles of authentic learning. Power relationships are well established in medical education, with teachers often using their power to "motivate" students with fear and shame (Jarvis-Selinger, Pratt, & Regehr, 2012). By intentionally changing these relationships we created a safe space, where both students and facilitators could normalise "not knowing" the answer. By liberating students from the necessity of being "right", they could explore their own understanding without fear of being exposed and shamed. The changing power relationship and reduction of authority can play a role in changing students' beliefs about who controls their learning, with an open environment helping them take on that responsibility (Bergström, 2010). This movement of authority away from the facilitators led to the development of personal empowerment among the students, enabling them to direct their own learning.

The major findings of the case were that students' perceptions of teaching and learning changed as a result of the approaches used in the module. Many acknowledged their own roles in learning, as well as showed evidence of a critical view of content, the profession, and authority figures in the course. It was clear that the power relationships in the module had changed, with students taking more responsibility for learning, and were moving towards independent thinking and self-directed learning. This move towards thinking about learning is significant in that it represents a departure from traditional conceptions of learning, where students simply get on with it, without putting much thought into what it means to learn (Ovens, Wells, Wallis, & Hawkins, 2011).

The use of Google Drive was therefore demonstrated to fundamentally change teaching and learning practices in ways that went beyond simply increasing the efficiency of information distribution. However, it should be noted that this approach required more time to develop and implement, and suggests the need for increased resources. Attempts to modify teaching practices in this way may have far-reaching consequences for other staff members, and should be approached with the understanding that they may resist the process. In this respect, educators considering innovative approaches to teaching and learning may need institutional support in order to drive the process (Bozalek & Dison, 2013).

Recommendations for future use/advice for practitioners

We used Google Drive as a collaborative authoring platform to implement authentic learning tasks in the form of clinical cases, and used features of the online service to encourage interaction and discussion in order to develop critical thinking. We demonstrated that students' ways of thinking about learning were transformed during the module. This was evident in their changing perceptions of their own role in the learning process, a movement of power away from teachers as students took control of their learning, and the emergence of critical attitudes towards knowledge and authority. If clinical educators aim to develop critical thinking within their students, they should consider the use of authentic tasks that are integrated across physical and online spaces, using appropriate technology platforms that are informed by sound theoretical perspectives.

CASE STUDY 14.3 USING WIKIS AND BLOGS TO MEDIATE AUTHENTIC LEARNING: A CASE OF TEACHING SPORT SCIENCE EDUCATION

Simone Titus

Context

Student engagement as a predictor of student success can be defined by two key components (Kuh, 2007). First, "what students do (the time and energy they devote to educationally purposive activities) and second, what institutions do (the extent to which they employ effective educational practices to induce students to do the right things)" (Strydom & Mentz, 2010, p. 3). Given the diverse nature of students in South Africa, student engagement may differ across cultures. Nagda and Zúñiga (2003) proposed that cross-group interactions, when structured with a collaborative process, can play a role in building multicultural communities. To this end, the classroom reflects the multicultural diversity of the country, which should provide a space for meaningful engagement. However, fruitful engagement is hindered because students gravitate towards peers of the same cultural background and do not always engage with peers from other cultures.

This study reports on an authentic task that was designed to enhance student engagement. In 2011, when a new academic first offered the module, students submitted an online assignment as a Word document. At this time, the module only used the learning management system (LMS) to support downloading class notes, uploading assignments, posting announcements and using the discussion forum. In 2012, the assignment was redesigned as an authentic learning task that students had to complete in the form of a wiki, using the Wikispaces platform. Authentic learning typically focuses on real-world, complex problems and their solutions within a learning environment similar to real-world disciplines (Herrington & Oliver, 2000; Lombardi, 2007). The authentic task for this module was designed to represent sport psychology activities that they would encounter in the real world. Students also had to contribute a reflective summary on the class blog using the Blogger tool.

The course included 14 weeks of instruction and 14 weeks of tutorial assistance split by a mid-term break. In both terms students attended a one-hour lecture and a one-hour tutorial. Sixty per cent of their final mark was comprised of their coursework marks obtained over the 14 weeks. Over the past four years, the number of students who registered for this compulsory module increased from 65 in 2009 to 83 in 2012.

This case study explores how emerging technologies were used to complete a collaborative authentically designed task in sport science education in order to foster student engagement.

Background

Over the past few decades, it has become increasingly challenging to teach using only didactic methods (Moll, Adam, Backhouse, & Mhlanga, 2007; Scott, Yeld, & Hendry, 2007). In many university faculties, this method of instruction is slowly fading as technological innovations are changing our teaching approach in health science education (Rowe, Frantz, & Bozalek, 2013; Republic of South Africa, 2012). Health science education includes practical activities infused into modules to demonstrate techniques that should be used in the workplace. Sport science education is no different. In order to demonstrate practical competence, students should be critically engaged with theoretical and practical content.

This study argues that activities can be designed by taking a constructivist approach to teaching and learning practices using educational technologies to foster engagement by facilitating meaningful collaboration. Vygotsky and Piaget contributed remarkably to constructivist and social-constructivist schools of thought (Ilyas, Rawat, Bhatti, & Malik, 2013). The focus of social constructivism is the attention placed on the social arenas within which knowledge is created. Therefore, the aim of a constructivist approach is to understand particular issues through the application of prior knowledge and experience using reasoning and critical thinking skills (Ilyas, Rawat, Bhatti, & Malik, 2013). Thus, for this study students were able to construct knowledge through their personal experiences being engaged in emerging technologies and personal interaction with peers. Vygotsky (1978) believed that objects are meaningless unless perceived socially. This means that students are able to give meaning to content through their interaction with their peers by designing a task that allows for meaningful engagement. Therefore, for the purposes of this study, Engeström's (1987) activity theory was used as a heuristic to examine whether wikis and blogs can explicitly mediate authentic learning in sport science education in order to improve student engagement.

The mediating tools used in this study were wikis and blogs. While explicitly, these technology tools were used to complete an authentic task as a means to an end, the implicit mediation was far more meaningful. The implicit mediation allowed for the manifestation of the nine elements of authentic learning to be realised. To this end, implicit mediation allowed for collaboration, engagement, co-construction of knowledge, meaningful interaction and reflection. For many learners, wikis are particularly appealing, providing instant, any time, any place access to a dynamic and ever building a digital repository of user-specific knowledge and a voice in a live community of practice (Wheeler, Yeomans, & Wheeler, 2008). In line with social constructivist thinking, wikis support collaboration among peers where they can work together to construct knowledge and share ideas (Neumann & Hood, 2009). This bodes well for this study where students were able to construct knowledge by doing a wiki task and contributed to a blog for reflective learning.

Question

How do wikis and blogs mediate authentic learning in sport science education in order to foster student engagement?

Approach

Using emerging technology tools like wikis and blogs has the potential to transform student-learning experiences (Wheeler et al., 2008). Wikis, as an emerging technology tool for educational purposes, have been used for the purposes of knowledge building, teamwork and increased participation (Calabretto & Rao, 2011). These techniques promote student learning, understanding, student engagement and knowledge construction. Blogs allow for the co-construction of knowledge on specific topics (Boulos, Maramba, & Wheeler, 2006).

For the purpose of this study, an authentically designed sport psychology wiki task, based on the nine elements of authentic learning outlined in Chapter 5, was completed by students to assist with student engagement, content and knowledge generation and collaboration with peers. The authentic tasks entailed students developing a psychological profile of a student athlete (in their own class) and developing or recommending activities these athletes could use to enhance their performance. The task was completed in the form of a wiki using the Wikispaces platform. Alongside this, a blog was used as a reflective tool in order to document students' experiences with using emerging technologies. Blog posts were used to allow students to reflect on their learning experiences and to engage in discussions about sport psychology topics.

Such an approach to learning is not overtly practised in sport science education and is worth academic scrutiny, as engagement through active collaboration is not easily achieved. Using a qualitative methodological approach, this case study draws on students' reflective experiences of completing an authentic task using emerging technologies in an attempt to improve student engagement and collaborative construction of knowledge. To this end, 67 student blog posts were analysed using a thematic analysis.

Findings and discussion

An analysis of the reflective summaries as posted by students on the class blog revealed that all nine authentic learning elements as outlined by Herrington, Reeves and Oliver (2010) were manifested in the learning activity (Figure 14.2).

As a result of the implementation of an authentically designed wiki-based assignment, the use of these technology-mediated tools transformed students' learning experiences in a number of ways.

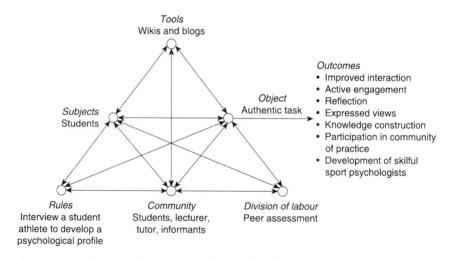

Figure 14.2 Activity of students' participation in a blogging and wiki activity

Students reported that while this task (object) had real-life relevance, emerging technology tools used in this educational exercise provided a valuable space for them to voice their opinions while interacting in an online space. What became even more relevant was that within the online space, students were able to interact with peers with whom they would not normally interact within the classroom setting. By interacting in the online space, students were able to engage (outcome) with one another in a rich and flexible space and learned from one another while collaboratively completing a task.

Previously, students would sit through face-to-face instruction and submit individual assignments. Through this process students moved from being passive recipients of learning to being active participants in a live community of practice. This implicit transformation allowed students to move from a space of discomfort when using these tools, because it was the first time they had received an assignment of this nature, to a space where they felt comfortable in doing so. Students were able to rely on expert performance from peers where more knowledgeable students assisted their peers through the exercise.

What can be concluded from this is that the design of the task provided a space for interaction with each other. This led to more meaningful engagement within an online space. As a result of this engagement, students became active participants in their own learning and were open to learning from one another. In turn, this led to better engagement through active collaboration.

Recommendations for future use/advice for practitioners

The use of technology tools such as wikis and blogs have been successful in mediating an authentic learning task as it had transformed student learning. Irrespective of discipline, task design is crucial if specific outcomes are to be met. Furthermore, keeping in mind both the elements of authentic learning and the affordances of the technology tools is of utmost importance in facilitating the development of successful and engaging learning activities.

Conclusion

The cases described here demonstrate that authentic learning environments and tasks require the investment of significant time and effort by students. They result in the creation of meaningful and polished products, as students translate their learning into visible constructs. Designing learning environments and tasks that enable often substantial parts of course curriculum is no easy task. Some educators question whether such an approach could be detrimental, by encouraging students to focus solely on the completion of the task and ignore the rest of the curriculum. However, a well-crafted task in a well-supported authentic learning environment can help to ensure that the completion of the task becomes the curriculum. A complex task can indeed form the focus of a meaningful learning experience, as is demonstrated so well in the cases presented in this chapter.

References

Barnett. R., & Coate, K. (2005). *Engaging the higher curriculum in higher education.* London: SRHE & Open University Press.

Bergström, P. (2010). Learning in higher education: Perspectives on the student-teacher relationship. *International Review of Research in Open and Distance Learning, 11*(2).

Boulos, M., Maramba, I., & Wheeler, S. (2006). Wikis, blogs and podcasts: A new generation of Web-based tools for virtual collaborative clinical practice and education. *BMC Medical Education, 6*(1), 41.

Bozalek, V., Carolissen, R., Leibowitz, B., Nicholls, L., Rohleder, P. & Swartz, L. (2010). *South African Journal Higher Education, 24*(6), 1021–1035.

Bozalek, V. & Dison, A. (2013). Using the human capabilities approach as a normative framework to evaluate institutional teaching and learning interventions at UWC. *South African Journal of Higher Education, 27*(2), 383–400.

Bozalek, V. & Matthews, L. (2009). E-learning: A cross-institutional forum for sharing socio-cultural influences on personal and professional identity. *International Social Work, 52*(2), 235–246.

Brown, J. S., Collins, A., & Duguid, P. (1989). Situated cognition and the culture of learning. *Educational Researcher, 18*(1), 32–42.

Calabretto, J., & Rao, D. (2011). Wikis to support collaboration of pharmacy students in medication management workshops: a pilot project. *The International Journal of Pharmacy Education and Practice, 7*(2), 1–12.

Dall'alba, G., & Barnacle, R. (2007). An ontological turn for higher education. *Studies in Higher Education, 32*(6), 679–671.

Elo, S., & Kyngäs, H. (2008). The qualitative content analysis process. *Journal of Advanced Nursing, 62*(1), 107–115.

Engeström, Y. (1987). *Learning by expanding: An activity-theoretical approach to developmental research.* Helsinki: Orienta-Konsultit.

Frenk, J., Chen, L., & Bhutta, Z. et al. (2010). Health professionals for a new century: Transforming education to strengthen health systems in an interdependent world. *The Lancet, 376*, 1923–1958.

Herrington, J. (2014). Introduction to authentic learning. In *Activity theory, authentic learning, and emerging technologies: Towards a transformative higher education pedagogy.* London: Routledge.

Herrington, A., Herrington, J., & Mantei, J. (2009). Design principles for mobile learning. In J. Herrington, A. Herrington, J. Mantei, I. Olney, & B. Ferry (Eds.), *New technologies, new pedagogies: Mobile learning in higher education* (pp. 129–138). Wollongong: UOW. Retrieved from: http://ro.uow.edu.au/.

Herrington, J. (2014). Introduction to authentic learning. In *Activity theory, authentic learning, and emerging technologies: Towards a transformative higher education pedagogy.* London: Routledge.

Herrington, J., & Kervin, L. (2007). Authentic learning supported by technology: 10 suggestions and cases of integration in classrooms. *Educational Media International, 44*(3), 219–236.

Herrington, J., & Oliver, R. (2000). An instructional design framework for authentic learning environments. *Educational Technology Research and Development, 48*(3), 23–48.

Herrington, J., Reeves, T. C., & Oliver, R. (2010). *A guide to authentic e-learning.* New York: Routledge.

Herrington, J., Reeves, T., Oliver, R., & Woo, Y. (2004). Designing authentic activities in web-based courses. *Journal of Computing and Higher Education, 16*(1), 3–29.

Ilyas, B. M., Rawat, K. J., Bhatti, M. T., & Malik, N. (2013). Effect of teaching of algebra through social constructivist approach on 7th graders' learning outcomes in Sindh (Pakistan). *International Journal of Instruction, 6*(1), 151–164.

Jarvis-Selinger, S., Pratt, D. D., & Regehr, G. (2012). Competency is not enough: Integrating identify formation into the medical education discourse. *Academic Medicine, 87*(9), 1185–1190.

Justice, C., Rice, J., Roy, D., Hudspith, B., & Jenkins, H. (2009). Inquiry-based learning in higher education: administrators' perspectives on integrating inquiry pedagogy into the curriculum. *Higher Education, 58*(6), 841–855.

Kneebone, R. (2002). Total internal reflection: An essay on paradigms. *Medical Education, 36*, 514–518.

Kuh, G. D. (2007). What student engagement data tell us about college readiness. *Peer Review, 9*(1), 4–8.

Laurillard, D. (2012). *Teaching as a design science: Building pedagogical patterns for learning and technology.* New York: Routledge.

Lombardi, M. M. (2007). Authentic learning for the 21st century: An overview. *EDUCAUSE Learning Initiative, 1*(May), 1–12. Retrieved from: http://net.educause.edu/ir/library/pdf/eli3009.pdf.

Mennin, S. (2010). Self-organization, integration and curriculum in the complex world of medical education. *Medical Education, 44*, 20–30.

Mitchell, V. (2012). The curriculum in medical education: A case study in obstetrics related to students' delivery experience. Master's thesis (Unpublished). University of Cape Town.

Mitchell, V. (2013). *Probing professionalism towards positive practice.* Retrieved from: http://opencontent.uct.ac.za/Health-Sciences/Probing-Professionalism-Towards-Positive-Practice.

Moll, I., Adam, F., Backhouse, J., & Mhlanga, E. (2007). *Status report on ICTs and higher education in South Africa: Prepared for the Partnership on Higher Education in Africa.* Johannesburg: South African Institute for Distance Education.

Nagda, B. A., & Zúñiga, X. (2003). Fostering meaningful racial engagement through intergroup dialogues. *Group Processes & Intergroup Relations, 6*(1), 111–128.

Neumann, D. L., & Hood, M. (2009). The effects of using a wiki on student engagement and learning of report writing skills in a university statistics course. *Australasian Journal of Educational Technology, 25*(3), 382–398.

Ovens, P., Wells, F., Wallis, P., & Hawkins, C. (2011). *Developing inquiry for learning: Reflecting collaborative ways to learn how to learn in higher education.* London: Routledge.

Reeves, T. C. (2006). Design research from a technology perspective. In J. van den Akker, K. Gravemeijer, S. McKenney, & N. Nieveen (Eds.), *Educational design research* (pp. 52–66). London: Routledge.

Republic of South Africa (2012). *Green paper for post-school education and training.* Pretoria: Department of Higher Education and Training.

Rowe, M., Frantz, J., & Bozalek, V. (2013). Beyond knowledge and skills: The use of a Delphi study to develop a technology-mediated teaching strategy. *BMC Medical Education, 13*(1), 51–59.

Ruch, G. (2002). From triangle to spiral: Reflective practice in social work education, practice and research. *Social Work Education, 21*(2), 199–216.

Savin-Baden, M. (2009). Liquid learning and liminal universities? Shifting academic complicit-ness in the processes of disempowerment. Paper presented at DPR8: Power and the Academy. Manchester Metropolitan University, 6–8 April 2009.

Retrieved from: http://cuba.coventry.ac.uk/learninginnovation/files/2009/04/mmu-paper.pdf.

Scott, I., Yeld, N., & Hendry, J. (2007). *Higher education monitor: A case for improving teaching and learning in South African higher education.* Pretoria: Council on Higher Education. Retrieved from http://www.che.ac.za/documents/d000155/17-HE_Monitor_6_ITLS_Oct2007.pdf.

Strydom, J. F., & Mentz, M. (2010). *South African survey of student engagement: Focusing the student experience on success through student engagement.* Pretoria: CHE. Retrieved from: http://www.che.ac.za/sites/default/files/publications/SASSE_2010.pdf.

Taylor, C. & White, S. (2000). *Practising reflexivity in health and welfare: Making knowledge.* Buckingham: Open University Press.

Veletsianos, G. (2011). Designing opportunities for transformation with emerging technologies. *Educational Technology, 51*(2), 41–46.

Vivian, L., Naidu, C., Keikelame, J., & Irlam, J. (2011). Medical students' experiences of professional lapses and patient rights abuses in a South African health sciences faculty. *Academic Medicine, 86,* 10.

Vygotsky, L. S. (1978). *Mind in society: The development of higher psychological processes.* Cambridge, MA: Harvard University Press.

Wheeler, S., Yeomans, P., & Wheeler, D. (2008). The good, the bad and the wiki: Evaluating student-generated content for collaborative learning. *British Journal of Educational Technology, 39*(6), 987–995.

Zembylas, M. (2013). Critical pedagogy and emotion: Working through 'troubled knowledge' in posttraumatic contexts. *Critical Studies in Education, 54*(2), 176–189.

15 The case studies

Emerging technologies

Dick Ng'ambi, Vivienne Bozalek, Daniela Gachago,
Jolanda Morkel, Eunice Ivala, Anita Campbell,
Sibongile Simelane, Dorothea Mathudi Dimpe,
Patient Rambe and Aaron Bere

This chapter reports on how educators at higher education institutions can appropriate emerging technologies to transform pedagogical practices with varying degrees of success. Through these case studies, the chapter illustrates how technologies, not necessarily new technologies, are being used to address teaching and learning challenges. In Case study 15.1, a closed Facebook group, accessible through students' mobile phones, is used to mediate articulation and reflection aimed at scaffolding architectural students' acquisition of skills to justify design decisions. In Case study 15.2, an anonymous Q&A tool of an institutional LMS, accessible through Short Message Services (SMS) is used in an extended degree programme to support student learning. These students suffered from low self-confidence, anxiety and reluctance to engage because they were all repeating a course, having failed mathematics the previous year. In Case study 15.3, micro-biology students use a closed Facebook group, accessed using students' mobile phones, to post Rhizopus stolonifer (bread mould) and club fungi (mushroom), hence engaging in an authentic learning task. In the final case study, Case study 15.4, a mobile-Instant Messaging (IM) tool, WhatsApp, is used to mediate question-based interactions to support learning of academically-at-risk third year students. One of the common threads in the four case studies is the co-construction of knowledge through inter-subjective interactions as seen in Case Studies 15.1 and 15.3 where Facebook mediated the interactions. The mobile phone is a material tool and cognitive signs include Internet connectivity, social networking and social construction of knowledge. These case studies illustrate how emerging technologies alter pedagogical designs, choice of tools to either mediate higher cognitive function or authentic learning tasks. Although learning maybe mediated by cultural tools (such as mobile phones), which are both readily available to users and in daily use, albeit for social purposes, transformative learning requires high levels of student–student, teacher–student, and student–content interactions. The case studies show that design of authentic learning activities that exploit the co-construction of inter-subjective interaction of human subjects (actors) are most likely to lead to higher-order cognitive or qualitative outcome. Designing such educational activities and tasks can produce qualitative outcomes, use authentic principles, make optimal use of tool mediation, and operate at the nexus of an individual learner's Zone of Proximal Development (ZPD) and ubiquitous emerging technologies. Although these case studies are not exhaustive, we hope they will inspire those exploring the intersection of emerging technologies, authentic learning and tool mediation.

CASE STUDY 15.1 USE OF FACEBOOK AS A COGNITIVE TOOL TO MEDIATE STUDIO-BASED LEARNING IN AN ARCHITECTURE COURSE

Jolanda Morkel, Daniela Gachago and Eunice Ivala

Context

This case study reports on the use of social media to mediate studio-based learning of final year undergraduate architectural students at the University of Technology in South Africa. One of the challenges of teaching architectural education is how to use design crit (critique) sessions of physically designed artefacts for deep and meaningful learning experiences. Architectural education is predominantly studio-based facilitated through project- and problem-based methods. The students formulate design proposals focusing on given complex architectural problems or challenges through an iterative process that relies heavily on formative feedback, also referred to as the design crit, review or tutorial. The design crit is a conversation through which students are supported by peers and lecturers (or tutors) to develop their thinking and building arguments to justify their design decisions. Final proposals – part of their portfolios – are presented in graphic and, to lesser extent, written formats, and are defended or justified verbally.

This case study reports on how a Facebook group mediates articulation and reflection whereby providing a virtual design crit that encourages students to think and build arguments to justify their design decisions.

Question

The architecture studio as a collaborative learning environment is at a crossroads. It is currently situated between its 'ICT-free' past and its 'ICT-aware future' (Laurillard, 2008). Class sizes are expanding and the student–lecturer ratio is under pressure. Because of the increasing use of the computer as a visualisation and documentation tool in Architecture Education, students are spending more and more time on campus in computer labs, and less time in the design studio. The physical set-up of traditional computer labs is not conducive to interaction, collaboration or to rich and meaningful learning conversations that happens in the design studio, and as a result, the vibrant community of practice – the trademark of architecture and design studios globally – is fast becoming a dead and deserted space.

There is a need to find new ways of facilitating student–lecturer, but also student–student interactions. The basic premise of social cultural theory is that higher-order learning does not happen alone and in isolation, but in a social context and needs to be mediated, be it through a slightly more knowledgeable other, or a technological tool. For our study, we explored the potential of a tool, i.e. a closed Facebook group, which was easily accessible through students' mobile phones, and used to support and expand studio-based learning and learning in the labs. It provided additional spaces for informal and formal communication during the period of developing their portfolios, which is one of the most stressful assessments in a student's career.

Approach

In 2010, students approached lecturers to set up a Facebook group, a tool familiar to students and which they used regularly in their social lives. It was envisaged that this group would help to improve communication among students and lecturers, in particular, communication around organisational issues, during the period preceding the portfolio assessment. Private Facebook groups are closed spaces in which group members can communicate, share content and discuss issues (Minocha, 2009), without having to be Facebook 'friends', one of the perceived barriers for academics to use Facebook as a learning tool (Ivala & Gachago, 2012).

This study explores the use of a closed Facebook group as a tool to mediate articulation and reflection in the design learning conversation. The two course lecturers involved in this study were interviewed and a thematic analysis of 511 students' asynchronous consecutive postings was done between 6 August and 23 October 2010 (covering the time of interim portfolio assessment). Data was categorised along Gabriel and Maher's (1999) conversational framework, in order to explore the kind of communications (informal or formal) the Facebook group mediated, whether and how it changed the object in the studio learning activity system, the portfolio assessment process.

Gabriel and Maher's (1999) conversational framework categorises communication into four areas, i.e. communication control, communication technology, academic communication and social communication. In a traditional face-to-face only studio, these categories would translate as follows: "communication control" would refer to the rules and methods of engagement through conversation. These categories relate to the traditional crit groups, e.g. "communication technology" in a face-to-face studio learning context refers to sketching, drawings overlays, the verbal and related gestures and facial expressions. Sometimes reference would be made to precedent studies (good built examples of designed work) on the Internet, or in e-book or pdf format, accessed via student laptop, tablet or smartphone. "Learning communication" in this context refers to "formal" communication through which knowledge construction occurs; communication related to the subject matter, which is architectural design. Finally, "social communication" refers to the non-academic interactions through informal conversations that are not directly linked to the academic project.

Thus, the teaching approach draws on social constructivist learning theory, which argues that learning occurs in a social and collaborative context (Clark & Maher, 2001). It therefore means that learning is a continuous conversation with the external world and its artefacts, with oneself, and also with other learners and teachers (Ivala & Gachago, 2012).

Findings and discussion

We will first report on the areas of communication and interactions, articulation and reflection that the closed Facebook group mediated using Gabriel and Maher's (1999) conversational framework. Then we will discuss the lecturers' perceptions on benefits and challenges of the Facebook group in transforming the portfolio assessment project.

Students' conversations in the Facebook group

In analysing the students' postings in the Facebook group, using Gabriel and Maher's conversational framework, it was found that:

- A large number of postings (29 per cent) were classified as 'social communication':

     Tchaikovsky playing, ArchiCAD kicking, caffeine ingesting, mildly amusing evening. How you guys doing? Ing ing ing.

- Twenty four per cent of the postings were related to 'communication control', the intended purpose of the tool:

     I just read . . . that we need to have R25 entry fee into Kirstenbosch. I would like to know why the department cannot cover that cost. Are these site visits not part of our course . . .??

- Only 5 per cent of postings focused on "communication technology", suggesting the relative ease of use of the tool:

     Hi there! Please look under info tag for updated online portfolio list . . .

- Interestingly, the largest number of postings (42 per cent) were classified as "design learning communication", discussing issues directly related to the curriculum content, in this case, the development of students' portfolios, thus confirming the application of Facebook as a mediating tool that changed the object of knowledge construction:

> You guys HAVE to check this out. Amazing visual method of explaining the development of design, although quite a mission to do it . . . But awesome, nonetheless.

Lecturers' perceptions of the Facebook group

In analysing the lecturers' perceptions of the use of the Facebook group, further useful insights emerged related to the expansion of teaching and learning spaces, crossing the boundaries between formal and informal learning, and the various roles and interpersonal relations of parties involved in the learning process. These insights are discussed in detail below.

Communication control and learning communication

The lecturers reported that Facebook *expanded the teaching and learning space*, allowing students to engage with them and with each other throughout the week and not just during the contact sessions, supporting the multiple roles and conversations necessary to affect design learning and development.

> The course really takes over their life; it's a very demanding programme. And for them it's been great to know – you know, that sense of feeling of helplessness – "it's the middle of the night, I have a hand-in tomorrow, I don't know what to do, I'm not sure." They can go on Facebook – because they're not in the physical studio through the night, they work at home or wherever they work.

The Facebook group provided a highly informal, democratic learning space, which served as an important source of *peer support* among students, supporting collaboration and interaction with fellow students beyond the classroom:

> They can get an answer, not from us, we deliberately try and step back, so the students could answer them. It's not as if they're posing us a question and we have to respond. Sometimes I actually have to restrain myself and say I'm not going to respond to this – somebody in the class should. I mean, questions about where to print or what time the class starts, or about this assignment or that – there's a lot of communication that's happening. I think that's actually empowering students to feel that they – You know, you need that reassurance: "I'm not the only one or I am doing the right thing" – all of those things.

Students' feedback on the course improved as well. The lecturers reported that Facebook gave the students *a safe space to engage with them and give feedback*, both on positive and negative experiences with the course:

> We got amazing feedback. In fact, feedback is always there, for us on record. But they feel more free to put things out there . . .

Social communication / learning

Facebook facilitated *more personal interaction* between lecturers and students, which allowed them to know their students better, and to also know them "differently". They gained insights in their students' thinking and feelings, which they wouldn't have been able if not for the Facebook group:

> Sometimes at night I'm on Facebook and then [the students] see the green dot and they're there and they will chat with you. They always start with how are you, what are you doing and this is what I'm busy with – which is not about their work. So you get a sense of what they're busy with before you actually get into discussion . . .

Crossing boundaries between social and academic learning

Barron (2006) argues that students create learning contexts for themselves within and across settings. Facebook facilitated *the crossing of these informal and formal learning boundaries*, as the following quote shows:

> The informal learning that happens on the social media is very, very valuable. But because students don't see it as now I'm entering the academic domain or the serious mode – they can chat about what they did last night and by the way, and that kind of coincidental learning is something that we don't always realize the value of . . .

Discussion

This case study explored the use of a closed Facebook group, to mediate studio-based learning in an Architectural Technology course. Although the Facebook group was introduced to primarily improve communication around organisational and course management issues, it proved highly useful in not only mediating social communication and support among students and lecturers, but also the academic project. It also, most importantly, expanded the learning space beyond the classroom and crossed the boundaries between academic and social learning.

CASE STUDY 15.2 USING MOBILE PHONES TO MEDIATE LEARNING OF MATHEMATICS AMONG REPEATING STUDENTS AT A SOUTH AFRICAN HIGHER EDUCATION INSTITUTION

Anita Campbell

Context

This case study is set in an extended degree programme in the engineering faculty of a prestigious South African university. The participants were students who had failed their first semester of mathematics and were repeating the course. Entrance into engineering programmes is highly competitive and all the students who failed were high achievers at school. The experience of failure in university mathematics is likely to have provoked feelings of low self-confidence, embarrassment, anxiety and a reluctance to engage with mathematics. The interventions we used took into account these anticipated feelings and aimed to engage students in non-threatening ways, potentially creating good experiences with mathematics to counterbalance their recent bad experience. It was also likely that students held misconceptions that needed to be gently exposed and addressed in ways that encouraged student participation.

Background

South Africa's past race-based educational policies privileged white students at the expense of other race groups. The disadvantage this gave to the majority of South African children is still evident two decades after the removal of race-based policies. The extended degree programme in engineering at the University of Cape Town was designed for students who are thought to have the potential to succeed at university but are likely to need support due to disadvantaged school and/or social conditions. The support in this programme takes the form of smaller classes (typically 80 students compared to 500 mainstream students), a reduced load in the first two years of the five year engineering programme, near double timetabled contact time for mathematics and physics, a communication course, and caring staff who follow up on students who seem to need intervention.

The repeat course where this case study takes place has two sets of students: those who were in the extended degree programme in the first semester but failed mathematics and those who were in mainstream for the first semester and have chosen to move into the extended degree programme because they have failed mathematics and other courses. The teaching approach in the repeat course takes into account that all students have already sat through lectures and have some familiarity with the content, making it a useful space to try innovative methods to engage students.

The course design also takes into account a common perception among students that the extended degree programme is for inherently weak students as opposed to students who have not reached their potential due to their previous education. Although many new students are initially resistant to being placed in the extended degree programme, this usually changes once they start to feel part of the programme's community and notice how students in the main-stream classes struggle with the heavier load. Students who join the programme are often more motivated by the reduced minimum credits required to avoid exclusion from university than a desire to join the programme. The majority of the students in this case study entered the programme only after they had already failed and this may add to their impression that the extended programme is for weak students.

The students in this case study were all young and possessed a personal mobile phone. Selwyn (2003) describes young people as experiencing time and space differently because of mobile technology. The choice of interventions using devices which are already integral to students' daily lives brought the benefit of adding interest and enthusiasm to students who had recently failed.

The interventions

Mobile phones were used to engage students in two ways: by interacting with the learning management system via anonymous text messages, and by making video explanations of mathematics questions.

The anonymous Q&A tool

The first application was an anonymous forum for posting questions and answers via text messages on a learning management system, called the Q&A tool. The Q&A tool was designed to have features that protect the users' privacy, such as not revealing names or mobile phone number and the option to unsubscribe from receiving text messages sent from the learning management system (LMS). Anonymity was intended to make students feel safe in asking questions without feeling exposed or embarrassed. Without the social discomfort of giving criticism face-to-face, this platform could make it easier for them to give honest feedback about their understanding of content in the course as well as the administration of the course. Using a personal device increases the level of privacy of students' comments and this might encourage participation.

A disadvantage of anonymity is that a lecturer cannot give verbal feedback in class to an individual unless users choose to identify themselves. Giving verbal feedback to the whole class based on a question posed on the Q&A tool has the risk of boring some students. Another disadvantage of anonymity was experienced in a class session where student responses were projected for all to see. Humorous but offensive comments were displayed and read by all students before the lecturer was able to delete them.

How the Q&A tool works

The Q&A tool provides a platform for collaborative, interactive and socially engaging learning. Table 15.1 shows examples of specific questions posed by students (for example, question 9256) or a more general question to stimulate discussion on content posed by the lecture (for example, question 9020). A class decision on how to spend a Friday afternoon was reached by projecting all anonymous contributions for the class to view. This allowed all students to have their opinion heard and a quick decision to be reached.

The Q&A tool could be used for real-time feedback on learning activities. For example, when the Q&A tool was used during a class session, a student asked for more information on a topic that had just been explained, which led to a change in the lesson plan. Using the tool in this way requires lecturers to be comfortable with adapting their teaching in response to student feedback.

Compared to question responses via email and in face-to-face discussions, questions and answers on the Q&A tool have the advantage that they can be viewed at any time throughout the duration of a course. Relevant questions and responses can also be made available to future cohorts of students in a course.

A constraint of the Q&A tool, particularly for students with little or no financial resources, was the cost of sending text messages to the Q&A tool, which was typically about R0.75 per message. The tool was introduced to students in a computer laboratory session so that students could experience the tool without incurring personal cost. Students were able to access the tool using simple mobile phones or devices that could connect to the Internet. In order to allow students to participate freely with the tool, investigations were made for ways in

Table 15.1 Some Q&A questions with number of answers and frequency of views

Question ID	Question	Answers	Views
8875	Why are radians preferred to degrees?	4	68
9020	Physicists often just use x as an approximation to sinx. Are they mad?	24	158
9021	Question 80 in the workbook asks for an estimate of ln 1.2 and ln 0.8. How do you know what point to use to find the equation of the straight tangent line?	6	108
9023	What can you say about average rates of change?	12	83
9256	How do you do question 38.c intergration by parts (the big weird S Is the interggral sign) i get it up to hre = 0.5x2arctanx − 0.5 Sx2/1+x2 dx. i dnt get how you get S1 − 1/1+x2 please explain this step	2	3

Table 15.2 Students' responses to a question on the Q&A tool

Q9020: Physicists often just use x as an approximation to sinx. Are they mad?

2011–08–31 09:11 no they are not mad, x is a good approximation to sinx for x = 0, but it does not seem to be like that for other x values

2011–08–31 09:12 nope theyre not mad:)

f(x) = sinx
f'(x) = cosx
f'(x) = cos(0)
so, m = 1
y – o = 1(x – 0)
y = x
:D

which the cost of sending text messages to the tool could be transferred to the university. However, it was not possible to allow reverse-charged text messages or establish a toll-free site, nor was it possible to provide each student with R10 credit for text messages on any of the three South African mobile service providers, due to the inflexible pricing of pre-paid bundles and contracts. Sending messages to the Q&A tool by accessing the LMS through an Internet-connected computer that students could connect for free to the university's wifi system was the preferred way of engaging with the tool for most students.

The management of the tool by the lecturer was made easier by establishing the rule that the tool was only for posing questions relating to the course or responding to questions that were posed. There was a chat room on the LMS site where students could have social conversations or ask for administrative details such as test times. The lecturer could also delete or edit questions and responses on the Q&A tool that were inappropriate or unclear. Table 15.2 shows some responses to a question.

Video explanations of mathematics questions

The second application involved students working cooperatively to make short video explanations of tutorial problems on BlackBerry Torch devices sponsored by Research in Motion. The main advantage of making video explanations was that it reduced the possibility of a student gaining credit for an answer they did not fully understand, which sometimes happened with written submissions of answers. Although a number of students had personal devices that could record videos, using the sponsored devices had two advantages: not incurring a cost to the students through sending videos from their devices and a high-quality video was produced.

An additional feature afforded by video submissions was to credit students for making videos in different languages. This was affirming for multilingual students who were learning in an English-dominated environment for the first time. Students were given the option to share their videos with future students through a multilingual database and almost all students agreed to this, suggesting that they felt pleased to be able to contribute to mathematics learning.

Students were grouped in pairs or groups of three and assigned roles of presenter, producer and checker, the third role being shared in the case of a pair. For the first two hours of the weekly tutorial, students worked at solving all problems on a handout given at the start of the tutorial. In the last hour, each group was assigned a selection of questions to prepare as video explanations. They were allowed to make up the required number by submitting answers for the same question in different languages, e.g. if they had to make four videos, they could submit answers to two questions in two different languages.

Discussion

The mobile phone technology used in this case study enhanced co-constructed inter-subjective interactions. A major advantage of capturing questions and explanations is that they can be viewed repeatedly, unlike a live interactive session that is not recorded. The higher-order functioning that these interventions are designed to stimulate occurs more in the production of comments and videos rather than in their viewing.

Future developments of the use of mobile phones for the purpose of building confidence with repeat mathematics students may include the integration of mastery quizzes with the videos, similar to the development of personalized learning platforms such as the Khan Academy (www.khanacademy.org). It would be interesting to know what the barriers are that prevent students from using the Q&A tool and what the limitations are regarding the effectiveness of text messages for communicating mathematics. If students posted photographs of their calculations or drawings, there may be a loss of anonymity from being able to identify handwriting, particularly in a small class.

Criticisms of the use of technology in education include the idea that learning involves a personal change in a learner's identity (Hughes, 2009). It may be that the use of technology does not remove the barriers to effective learning that exist in failing students. A deeper look at work on identity relating to learning would be helpful.

CASE STUDY 15.3 USE OF FACEBOOK TO PROMOTE AUTHENTIC LEARNING: A CASE OF TEACHING MICROBIOLOGY

Sibongile Simelane and Dorothea Mathudi Dimpe

Context

The Department of Student Development and Support at a university of technology in South Africa identified Microbiology as a challenge to students at first-year level due to the lack of sufficient background in Microbiology at high school level. Technology-enhanced learning and interactive activities have the potential to enhance interactive engagement, collaboration and authentic learning. This case study reports on the use of a Facebook group as an example of technology-enhanced learning to support authentic learning in Microbiology. The objective of the study was to investigate the design and implementation of technology engagement and interactive activities using Facebook as a mediating tool for student engagement. Participants in this study were 86 students registered for the National Diploma in Environmental Health. Microbiology is a prerequisite for the course. This implies that students can proceed to the second year without passing the subject but they will not be allowed to register for Food and Meat Hygiene and Epidemiology, which are major subjects in their programme. Data was collected by means of a pre-survey questionnaire, an orientation test and a post-survey questionnaire. Furthermore, activities that were posted on the Facebook group were analysed.

Background

Recently, the advances brought about by social networking services (SNSs) like Twitter, Facebook and LinkedIn have implied that SNSs are easily accessible on mobile phones and personal digital assistance (PDA) devices (Chuang & Ku, 2010). Users do not need a computer or laptop with Internet access to use these tools. In fact, Facebook is the most recognisable network in the education sector, because it was initially developed for university students (Cain & Fox, 2009). Oradini and Saunders (2007) state that social networking systems have the capability to deliver a learning platform where the students are at the centre of activities.

The current study was based on constructivist theory and authentic learning using Facebook. Anderson (2010) argues that technology-enhanced learning should be used with good theories. Good theories are useful because they assist us in understanding and acting properly. Students today are driven by the epistemic engagement view of learning (Anderson, 2010). Engagement and interaction are most closely associated with constructivist learning theory. The authentic learning framework also informs constructive theory.

It is pointed out by Herrington (2006) that authentic learning environments are process-driven and not content-driven, and they require students to complete complex real-world tasks over an extended period in collaboration with others, as they would in a real workplace. Herrington further mentions that authentic activities are driven by constructivist theory because they encourage and support student engagement, and involvement in a cognitive real environment can enable self-directed and independent learning. A framework of authentic learning was applied in this study to guide the design of authentic learning using Facebook by considering the nine key factors of authentic learning design (Herrington & Oliver, 2000). These factors are: an authentic context that reflects the way the knowledge will be used in real life, authentic tasks, access to expert performances and the modelling of processes, multiple roles and perspectives, collaborative construction of knowledge, reflection, articulation, coaching and scaffolding, and authentic assessment. Hence, this study investigated the pedagogical application of Facebook to promote authentic learning in Microbiology.

Questions

1 How can Facebook be integrated into teaching and learning to enhance engagement, interaction, collaboration and authentic learning?
2 What are the experiences and perceptions of participating in Facebook for learning?

Approach

The current case study investigated the effective use of a Facebook group to support authentic learning in Microbiology. The Facebook group was designed and developed in teaching and learning to promote engagement, interaction, collaborative construction of knowledge, and communication between lecturer and student, as well as between student and student to improve authentic learning. In order to determine what students already knew about microbiology and for the lecturer to distinguish the background knowledge of microbiology that students had gained from high school. The orientation test was conducted before any teaching of the year had taken place. The results show that 72 students (86.7 per cent) taking part in the study passed the orientation test and 11 (13.3 per cent) failed the test. The students who failed this test raised concerns about the study.

For this study, a pre-survey questionnaire was administered before any teaching of Microbiology had taken place. This was done in order to determine students' biographic information, to establish students' knowledge of Facebook and to ascertain whether they possessed Facebook accounts. Findings revealed that 67 of the students (80.7 per cent) had a Facebook account while 16 (19.3 per cent) did not have a Facebook account. About the use of Facebook in teaching and learning, results showed that 72 participants (86.7 per cent) said Facebook could be used for teaching and learning, while 7 participants (8.4 per cent) denied that Facebook could be used for teaching and learning and 4 participants (4.8 per cent) did not reply to this question.

The results of the orientation test and the pre-survey questionnaire led to the design and development of the Microbiology I Facebook group, guided by the factors of authentic learning framework. Lombardi (2007) defines authentic learning as learning-by-doing. Smith and Parker (2012) state that authentic learning engages students by allowing them to create meaningful, useful and shared outcomes of the learning. Authentic learning involves real-life tasks, or simulated tasks that provide the students with opportunities to connect to the real world.

In this case study, authentic learning in the subject was applied in order to incorporate Facebook in delivering the subject. The closed Microbiology I group was created on Facebook, which students could access on their mobile technologies, particularly cell phones, which are Internet-enabled. In South Africa, mobile technologies such as cell phones with Internet access and social networks are the emerging technologies currently gaining popularity in teaching and learning in higher education.

Only students who were registered for the particular subject participated in the group. The group created a personal learning environment for students to reflect, feel free to raise questions and comments, share the outcomes of their learning, and engage in real-life activities or simulations, unlike in a classroom environment where some of the students might be intimidated due to language barriers and a lack of acclimatisation to a new environment at a tertiary institution.

Operationalisation of Facebook and authentic learning

The Facebook group was implemented in order to promote engagement interaction, collaboration communication, self-directed learning and authentic learning among students. This was accomplished by various learning activities that were conducted on the Microbiology I Facebook group in order to establish the changes in students' academic performance. The lecturer began facilitating the group by posting open-ended questions on the work covered in class on a weekly basis. Students were engaged by inviting them to participate in the group and to respond to questions in their own time using their personal learning environment. For example, the lecturer posted a question on a chapter dealing with Prokaryotic structure and function on the major component of the Prokaryotic cell wall termed 'Peptidoglycan'. We observed students engaging in the real-life activities when responding to this question in their attempt to answer the questions. Activities in the form of graphics and simulations were used to explain the topic. Relevant YouTube videos were also posted through the collaboration of the instructional designer and the lecturer to assist the students. It was pointed out that Facebook is capable of supporting several characteristics of authentic learning including collaboration, multiple sources and perspectives, reflections and sharing of results (Bozalek et al., 2013; Lombardi, 2007).

Results showed that students did not rely on the lecturer's questions only, but they took full control of their learning by further posting relevant graphics for each chapter to assist each other in the subject. For example, after presentation of a chapter on fungi, most students were motivated about their discovery of edible and non-edible fungi. Students posted graphics of Rhizopus stolonifer (bread mould) and club fungi (mushroom) while they were interacting with each other. We observed personal learning environments, collaboration and self-directed learning promoted among students. The students were posting questions on their own, they were learning by doing and interacting with one another. The Internet and a variety of emerging communication, visualisation, and simulation technologies now make it possible to offer students authentic learning experiences ranging from experimentation to real-world problem solving (Smith & Parker, 2012).

During the implementation of Facebook activities, we saw the role of the lecturer changing from lecturer-based teaching method to that of a facilitator and guide. The lecturer monitored the communication and discussions in order to channel students in the right direction if there were deviations and also to provide clarity. Lombardi (2007) argues that it is the lecturer's role to design suitable comprehension checks and feedback loops into the authentic learning exercise. We also observed how the lecturer constructed a flexible, interactive and engaging student personal learning environment that would support students' transition to the workplace.

What was interesting in this group was that students would even say how they felt about the tasks covered in class, how they engaged more in order to understand the concepts better and how they were learning from one another. The Microbiology I Facebook group aided communication between the lecturer and the students as all messages and updates related to the subject were posted and this generally created a harmonious environment of teaching and learning through mobile technology.

Findings and discussion

Findings indicated that students were able to use Facebook group to engage in self-motivated and engaged collaborative activities. Students supplemented the textbook and the lecturer's notes with Facebook interactions. These self-motivated activities included the sharing of graphics, YouTube videos and relevant websites. This case study concludes that participants took full control of the Facebook group, posted questions, answered questions from peers, and shared resources that they considered having potential value for other students.

Lessons learnt

In this case study, we learnt that the lecturer took advantage of students' use of technology (mobile phone with Internet connection) to integrate Facebook effectively in order to promote teaching and learning. A closed group on Facebook was created and this provided a safe and secure environment and personal learning space. We also learnt that Facebook could be incorporated effectively in teaching and learning, but comprehensive planning and time are required. Facebook gave students an opportunity to reflect on the way their knowledge will be used in real life and on ways to find more information on their own and to share it with other participants.

Recommendations for future use/advice for practitioners

It is recommended that lecturers in higher education take advantage of Facebook and integrate it into their teaching practices in order to complement the knowledge of students of the twenty-first century. It is crucial to ensure that all students have access to the relevant technology before technology can be implemented. It is important too that lecturers familiarise themselves with the appropriate teaching and learning theories in order to implement mobile technologies successfully. We recommend that higher education take advantage of social networks in order to meet the demands and the challenges that higher education practitioners encounter in their teaching practices. Facebook has created the opportunities for more flexible and easily accessible learning environments in higher education, therefore we advise lecturers to take advantage of this opportunity.

CASE STUDY 15.4 FOSTERING SEAMLESS LEARNING THROUGH MOBILE DEVICES: A CASE OF STUDENT WHATSAPP POSTINGS

Patient Rambe and Aaron Bere

Context

This study was conducted at a South African University of Technology (UoT), a contested site where a disjuncture persists among policy directives that emphasise the central role of emerging technologies in educational transformation, educators' hesitation to adopt mobile technologies and students' social immersion in such technologies. To address this implementation gap, the study examines the potential of an emerging technology – a mobile instant messaging application, WhatsApp, to support seamless learning among academically-at-risk Third Year Information Technology students. Cultural-Historical Activity Theory (CHAT) and educator-student and peer-based engagements via WhatsApp were drawn upon to investigate student experiences of seamless learning in mobile environments. The research question investigated the evidence of seamless learning embedded in WhatsApp postings by students. Herrington's authentic learning framework served as an analytical heuristic for unravelling seamless learning that unfolded in individual and collective activities on WhatsApp. Findings suggest that though some semblance of seamless learning manifested in student task-focused en-gagements and appropriation of peer-generated content, a lack of systematic organisation and theoretical depth of peer-generated content as well as student difficulties in downloading pictorial and graphical content were the result. Lessons learnt include the need for increased synchronisation of the traditional learning management system (LMS) and the utilisation of mobile applications including the need for progression from physical access to educational resources to critical engagement with collectively generated mobile resources. The study recommends strategic academic development of students' digital skills, honing of their critical engagement skills and aligning of engagements across learning platforms (LMS and MIM).

The current study was conducted with third-year Information Technology students at the Central University of Technology (CUT) in South Africa. Du Pré (2010) states that Universities of Technology (UoTs) are a consequence of the major reconfiguration of the higher education landscape in South Africa involving the merger or division of former Technikons, which took place from 2004 onwards. Although the credentials and constitution of UoTs are heavily contested terrains (Brook, 2000; Winberg, 2004; Du Pré, 2010), one of their widely shared defining characteristics is the interweaving focus and interrelation between technology and the nature of these universities (Du Pré, 2010). However, the irony with regard to the academic identity of most UoTs in South Africa, including that of CUT, however, is the peripheral role of technology in the mediation of meaningful pedagogical strategies and learning activities. This subsidiary essence of technology is a cause for concern, given the manifold of challenges that current beset South African higher education such as the difficulty of developing inclusive learning environments that celebrate the differences in student identities and demographic traits (Swart & Pettipher, 2011), broadening equitable access and ameliorating drop-out rates for potentially at-risk students (Scott, 2007), improving student effective participation and success, regardless of markers of differences especially for learners from vulnerable groups (Artiles and Kozleski, 2007; Swart and Pettipher, 2011).

The peripheral location of technology in UoTs manifests in the technology adoption schism that persists among institutional policy-makers who seem to foreground emerging technologies as drivers of transformative pedagogy, combined with the limited familiarity and hesitance of CUT educators (as technology laggards) to adopt emerging technologies, and their students who have embraced emerging technologies they bring into the university (digital natives). Yet the literature respects the value of aligning institutions' policy imperatives that acknowledge the central place of technology in pedagogical delivery and educators' commitment to productively appropriate emerging technologies (Bozalek, Ng'ambi, & Gachago, 2013). Mindful of the aforementioned technological disjuncture, the current study sought to bridge this gap by exploring the potential of an emerging technology, i.e. a popular mobile instant application (WhatsApp), to enhance seamless learning among students. Seamless learning describes a learning style where a student can learn in a variety of contexts and can shift to different contexts (formal, quasi-formal and informal) easily and quickly drawing on the affordances of a mediating device (Chan et al., 2006).

Background

To explore the potential of mobile instant messaging (MIM) application, WhatsApp, to support seamless mobile learning among academically challenged third-year IT students, Cultural-Historical Activity Theory and Herrington, Reeves and Oliver's (2010) authentic learning framework were adopted as the theoretical and analytical lenses for the exploration of seamless learning, design of learning activities, tasks and technological supports on WhatsApp. Activity Theory draws on systems theory to unravel how artefact-mediated action shapes human interaction with the object to attain pre-determined outcomes. Activity system components include the *hierarchical structure of activity, object-orientedness, internalization/*

externalization, tool mediation and *development* (Kaptelinin, Kuutti, & Bannon, 1995). These activity elements are elaborated below.

The *hierarchy of activity* involves *activities*, *actions* and *operations* aimed at reinforcing goal-oriented behaviour and outcomes. WhatsApp-mediated interaction constitutes the *activity* and *actions* describe goal-directed-processes that must be undertaken in pursuit of a defined objective (Nardi, 1996). On WhatsApp, *actions* denote all social practices that students engage in which are directed at enhancing seamless learning like texting, conversing, arguing, questioning, responding and critical reading. *Operations* involve the automated routines geared at perfecting the art of WhatsApp-mediated engagements, such as logging on, viewing postings, tracking conversations and supporting feedback loops. The interaction between the three-tier *hierarchy of activity* enables the transactional exchanges between individuals, groups and community to give effect to activity outcomes.

Object-orientedness considers the value of goal-oriented action in support of pre-conceived motives in real-world contexts. The *object* constitutes meaningful WhatsApp-mediated interaction between students, peers and educators in their online learning community. In activity systems, *internalisation* involves the conversion of external processes into internal ones, a consequence of the subject's direct interactions with external reality without manipulating the physical objects (e.g. mental modelling, conceptualisation). *Tools* are the artefacts that mediate subjects' interaction with the object to achieve some predetermined outcomes. WhatsApp constitutes the tool that mediates student interactions with the object of seamless learning and contributes to the assimilation, negotiation and transformation of collectively generated knowledge. In WhatsApp interactions, *development* involves the shifting of mental schema and changes in psychological functioning activated by technology-mediated actions and activities. The study thus examined WhatsApp (*tool*)-mediated interaction among students (*subjects*), educators and guest lecturer (*community*) in situated mobile contexts (*socio-cultural contexts*) to unravel the potential of mobile applications to enhance seamless learning (*object*) and engender meaningful participation in higher education (*outcome*).

Question

What evidence in educator-student and peer-based engagements via WhatsApp suggests the potential of WhatsApp to support seamless learning?

Approach

In terms of the design of learning activities, the current work drew on Herrington et al,'s (2010) nine design elements namely:

1   *An authentic context* realised through the use of WhatsApp, which most students had traditionally adopted to realise their communicative needs and social networking desires.

2   An *authentic task*, which comprised educators' requirement for students to download WhatsApp, to accept the educator's expectation for them to join eight engagement clusters created for them. Other tasks included consulting peers using questions, responding to peers' queries, knowledge sharing within clusters and engaging with supplementary educational materials provided by the educator.

3   *Access to expert performances.* The educator requested an online lecturer (a lecturer from another South African traditional university) provide additional IT-related information and some hints on critical IT problem solving to students during WhatsApp consultations. Students were also connected to the institutional LMS to access additional educational resources (lecturer slides, readings, course guides).

4   *Multiple perspectives.* Diverse student perspectives were enabled by the multiple engagements with peers, educators, guest educator and by access to peer and educator-generated learning resources.

5   *Collaboration.* Every day after hours, the educator posted a practical IT problem, question or diagram that tested student understanding and required their soliciting of peer guidance and involvement in devising its solution.

6   *Reflection.* Students critically reflected on peer-generated queries and questions before responding to ensure meaningful contributions and critique.

7   *Articulation* was promoted through question-based consultations, peer critique and student engagement with supplementary information supplied on WhatsApp.

8   *Coaching and scaffolding* unfolded through the educators' hints and practical guidance in IT problem solving.

9   *Authentic assessment* involved educators' informal review of student postings on their respective WhatsApp clusters and recapping of complex IT problems in class.

Findings and discussion

The analytical framework examined students' WhatsApp postings using AT concepts as shown in Table 15.3.

Subjects' agency

Students demonstrated academic agency by drawing on task-focused engagements and question-based consultation to share collectively-generated resources. They engaged in seamless learning by discussing IT concepts and seeking peers' and educators' guidance on complex tasks that they struggled to execute in class, across university contexts and beyond the classes. The discursive affordances of WhatsApp enhanced students' epistemological access to educators, peers and extended learning community, thus enhancing context-free access to educational resources.

Table 15.3 Analysing WhatsApp artifacts using Activity Theory

Activity Theory concepts	*Original artifacts*	*Research comments*
Subject	Guys I got a Q . . . wen creatn a composite entity u include PKs of both reltd entinties as FKPK in da entity u retain ? [Student posting] I have a question Mr Bere on the derived attributes do we have to knw the calculations for calculating the derived attribute or w jct hv 2 identify the derived attribute [Student posting]	Subject employs question-based consultation to access peers' knowledge outside formal learning spaces WhatsApp enables seamless learning through context-free access to the educator
Instrument/Tool (*Tool mediation*)	Sir..will you be going through the same questions you gonna do tomorrow on ethutho on this WhatsApp group? [Student posting] I am using ethutho only because i want to accommodate other students without WhatsApp. I know that you guys with WhatsApp can also use ethutho [Lecturer posting]	WhatsApp mediates question-based interaction between students and educators Institutional LMS complements WhatsApp-enabled consultation
OBJECT (*Object-orientedness*)	Thank u very much sir for helping us to revise da tests [via WhatsApp]. The discussions helped us to analyze da questions u posted . . . [Student posting]	Questions are useful tools for scaffolding students and sustaining seamless learning
Community (*Internalisation*)	So will this chatroom dissolve now that we wrote? Or will it continue till June? [Student posting] Why shud we dsslv it? . . . its vry hpfl [Student posting] Guys cn u please explain the concept of mandatory and optional for me frm that EERD [Student posting]	Student acknowledges the academic support of the WhatsApp community Student recognises the collectivity of an online community

Tool-mediated action

WhatsApp complemented the institutional LMS, eThutho, by supporting academically-at-risk students who could not normally access learning resources (supplementary academic materials, peer-generated queries, questions, comments) through the LMS after hours and vice versa. Therefore, WhatsApp enhanced inclusive learning by recruiting student attention to academic tasks and supporting their task-focused engagement, thus compensating for their limited access to eThutho.

Object-orientedness

The direct alignment of curricular goals of collaborative interaction to WhatsApp-mediated engagement (questions, answers, queries) and learning tasks enhanced the student orientation towards seamless learning. The intersection of critical questioning, reflective reading of peers' posts, informed responses, collaborative discussions, educator and peer support enhanced the realisation of the object of seamless learning.

Internalisation

Students openly acknowledged the academic value of their affinities on the WhatsApp learning community. The fact that they accessed on-demand academic support and belonged to a cohesive academic community triggered a sense of collective identity that propelled the involvement of different clusters.

Contradictions

The pressure to realise seamless learning through robust discussions and meaningful contributions exposed the contradiction between WhatsApp (*tool*) and the *object*. While sustained meaningful interaction necessitated timeous responses to peers' posts (*role*), WhatsApp's random organisation of posts (*tool*) directed at different questions militated against systematic flow of discussions.

Another contradiction emerged between students' lack of theoretical depth (*subject*) and educator's expectation for objective, scholarly engagements (*role*). Lastly, students (*subject*) expressed some difficulties with downloading pictorial and graphical content posted by the educators and peers via WhatsApp (*community*).

Recommendations for future use/advice for practitioners

Mindful of student challenges with the downloading online content, the study recommends academic development programmes aimed at sharpening students' digital skills and competencies by connecting skill-based training to academic curricula goals. The fragmented nature of WhatsApp postings necessitates the development of applications for systematic organisation of postings by topics. Students also need additional academic scaffolding in task-based discussions, argumentation and critical engagement with content. Lastly, student discussions across different learning platforms (LMS and MIM) need to be synchronised to sustain the critical mass of collective engagements within the WhatsApp community that guarantee seamless learning. These recommendations are summarised as follows:

- Let sharpening of students' digital skills and competencies be an outcome of an academic development programme.
- Focus academic scaffolding on task-based discussions, argumentation and critical engagement with content.
- Sustain a critical mass of collective engagements within the WhatsApp community to guarantee seamless learning.

References

Anderson, T. (2010). Theories for learning with emerging technologies. In G. Veletsianos (Ed.), *Emerging technologies in distance education*. Edmonton: Athabasca University Press.

Artiles, A.J., & Kozleski, E.B. (2007). Beyond convictions: Interrogating culture, history and power in inclusive education. *Language Arts, 84*(4), 351–358.

Barron, B. (2006). Interest and self-sustained learning as catalysts of development: A learning ecology perspective. *Human Development, 49*(4), 193–224.

Bozalek, V., Gachago, D., Alexander, L., Watters, K., Wood, D., Ivala, E. & Herrington, J. (2013). The use of emerging technologies for authentic learning: A South African study in higher education. *British Journal of Educational Technology, 44*, 629–638.

Bozalek, V., Ng'ambi, D., & Gachago, D. (2013). Transforming teaching with emerging technologies: Implications for Higher Education Institutions. *South African Journal of Higher Education, 27*(2), 419–436.

Brook, D. (2000). The making of a university of technology. In L. O. K. Lategan (Ed.), *Technikon free state studies in higher education*, 3, Bloemfontein.

Cain, J. & Fox, B. I. (2009). Web 2.0 and pharmacy education. *American Journal of Pharmaceutical Education, 73*, 1–11.

Chan, T-W., Roschelle, J., Hsi, S., Kinshuk, Sharples, M. et al. (2006). One-to-one technology enhanced learning: An opportunity for global research collaboration. *Research and Practice in Technology Enhanced Learning, 1*(1), 3–29.

Chuang, H. Y., & Ku, H. Y. (2010). Users' attitudes and perceptions toward online social networking tools. In D. G. B. Dodge (Ed.), *Proceedings of Society for Information Technology & Teacher Education International Conference 2010*. AACE, pp. 1396–1399.

Clark, S., & Maher, M. L. (2001). The role of place in designing a learner centered virtual learning environment. In B. De Vries, J. van Leeuwen, & H. Achten (Eds.), *CAAD Futures Conference* (pp. 187–200). Eindhoven, The Netherlands: Kluwer Academic Publishers.

du Pré, R. (2010). Universities of Technology in the context of the South African higher education landscape. *Kagisano Issue No. 7 Universities of Technology: Deepening the debate*. Pretoria: Council on Higher Education (CHE).

Gabriel, G., & Maher, M. L. (1999). Coding and modeling communication in architectural collaborative design. In O. Ataman & J. Bermudez (Eds.), *ACADIA '99*, ACADIA, pp. 152–166.

Herrington, J. (2006). Authentic e-learning in higher education: Design principles for authentic learning environments and tasks. In *Proceedings of World Conference on E-Learning in Corporate, Government, Healthcare, and Higher Education, 2006* (pp. 3164–3173). Honolulu.

Herrington, J., & Oliver, R. (2000). An instructional design framework for authentic learning environments. *Educational Technology Research and Development, 48*, 23–48.

Herrington, J., Reeves, T., & Oliver, R. (2010). *A guide to authentic learning.* London: Routledge.

Hughes, G. (2009). Social software: New opportunities for challenging social inequalities in learning? *Learning, Media and Technology, 34*(4), 291–305.

Ivala, E., & Gachago, D. (2012). Social media for enhancing student engagement: The use of Facebook and blogs at a University of Technology. *South African Journal for Higher Education (SAJHE), 26*(1), 152–167.

Kaptelinin, V., Kuutti, K., & Bannon, L. (1995). Activity Theory: Basic concepts and applications. In B. Blummenthal, J. Gornostaev, & C. Unger (Eds.) *Human–computer interaction: Lecture notes in computer science.* Berlin: Springer.

Laurillard, D. (2008). Technology enhanced learning as a tool for pedagogical innovation. *Journal of Philosophy of Education, 42*, 521–533.

Lombardi, M. M. (2007). Authentic learning for the 21st century: An overview. *EduCause Learning Initiative.* ELI paper 1 Online. Retrieved from: http://alicechristie.org/classes/530/EduCause.pdf.

Minocha, S. (2009). A study of the effectiveness use of social software to support student learning and engagement. *JISC.* Retrieved from: http://www.jisc.ac.uk/whatwedo/.

Nardi, B. (Ed.). (1996). *Context and consciousness: Activity Theory and human-computer interaction.* Cambridge, MA: MIT Press.

Ng'ambi, D., Bozalek, V., & Gachago, D. (2013). Empowering educators to teach using emerging technologies in higher education: A case of facilitating a course across institutional boundaries. In *Proceedings of the 8th International Conference on e-Learning* (pp. 292–300). The Cape Peninsula University of Technology Cape Town, South Africa.

Oradini, F., & Saunders, G. (2007). *The use of social networking by students and staff in higher education.* London: University of Westminster.

Scott, I. (2007). Addressing diversity and development in South Africa: Challenges for educational expertise and scholarship. Council on Higher Education for the Improving Teaching and Learning for Success Project, Cape Town. Unpublished.

Selwyn, N. (2003). Schooling the mobile generation: The future for schools in the mobile-networked society. *British Journal of Sociology Education, 24*(2), 131–144.

Smith, T., & Parker, J. (2012). Designing an authentic blend: Development of a 'real-life' learning environment for higher education. In *Creating an inclusive learning environment: Engagement, equity, and retention. Proceedings of the 21st Annual Teaching Learning Forum,* 2–3 February 2012. Perth: Murdoch University. Retrieved from: http://otl.curtin.edu.au/tlf/tlf2012/refereed/smith.html.

Swart, E. & Pettipher, R. (2011). A framework for understanding inclusion. In E. Landsberg, D. Krüger, & E. Swart (Eds.), *Addressing barriers to learning: A South African perspective.* Hatfield, SA: Van Schaik Publishers.

Winberg, C. (2004). Becoming a University of Technology. *Sediba sa Thuto, 1*, 38–54.

16 Conclusion

Towards a transformative higher education pedagogy

Vivienne Bozalek, Dick Ng'ambi, Denise Wood, Jan Herrington, Joanne Hardman and Alan Amory

This edited collection provides a vision for the reconceptualization of higher education pedagogy. It provides many examples of the use of Cultural-Historical Activity Theory (CHAT) as an analytical tool and heuristic for the design of authentic learning activities, through the effective use of emerging technologies. The use of CHAT is central to this vision, in particular, Engeström's articulation of CHAT in his systems model has been exemplified in the chapters of this edited collection, particularly in Part I, as well as in the case studies of effective practices that demonstrate expansive learning. The chapters on authentic learning (AL) in Part II, and related case studies, also show how CHAT can be used as a theoretical foundation underpinning the principles of AL. Thus, the interaction between CHAT and AL is well illustrated in the chapters of this edited collection. The usefulness of the principles of AL to evaluate and to inform the design of pedagogical practices is also illustrated with reference to a variety of disciplines (such as health science education, women's and gender studies, entrepreneurship, and innovation), and across different higher education institutions in a range of locations.

In addition to the interactions of Cultural-Historical Activity Theory (CHAT), and authentic learning (AL), the chapters and case studies in this book have also discussed in different ways the potential of emerging technologies (ET) to be used in more effective ways to achieve transformative practice. The combination of these foci suggests that all three are important for transformative pedagogy. Part III of the book focuses more specifically on emerging technologies, and how – with reference to the theoretical perspectives provided by CHAT and AL – they can be used to mediate learning to achieve transformative outcomes.

Thus, these relationships of a connected world are changing the ways students *learn*, but the changes to how most academics teach continue to be marginal, as a number of authors have pointed out in the book (see Ng'ambi and Brown, in Chapter 4, for example). However, this sensitivity to learning needs is not sufficient in and of itself – the responses also need to be well theorized, located in authentic contexts, and the affordances of emerging technologies need to be harnessed.

CHAT provides a lens through which the contradictions and conflicts that may occur between different elements of the activity system can be viewed. The idea that teachers learn along with students who teach one another, heralds a change in traditional roles that is useful in assessing the potential effect of emerging technologies in higher education. The affordances of emerging technologies – such as social networking, mobile learning, e-books, blogs and podcasting – introduce contradictions into the activity of teaching with technology that, if understood, could lead to innovative pedagogical designs.

This edited collection has shown that the use of emerging technologies in teaching can require new and innovative approaches that require teachers to rethink the use of technologies. Instead of providing teacher-created learning environments, which students inhabit only within the parameters set for them, emerging technologies can instead be viewed as powerful cognitive tools used by learners to solve problems and create products. Alternatively, teachers can choose to use – or possibly create – more complex virtual environments and simulations that require the development of tasks, the training of students and other associated processes. Although students ultimately realise the benefits of using such tools for making learning more realistic, collaborative and active, there are real implications for teachers. The difference between enthusiastic intentions and plans, and the actual realities of the teachers' situations, where time may be limited in an ever-increasing pressurized higher education environment, means that one or more key pedagogical or theoretical considerations may suffer. However, the CHAT framework is particularly useful in that it includes a holistic view in which all aspects of the context are considered. The teachers' fears, beliefs and current teaching practices need to be taken into account when implementing changes – as is demonstrated in Chapter 10, "Twenty-first-century pedagogies: Portraits of South African higher educators using emerging technologies". An important conclusion of this study, which is revealed by the CHAT framework, is the role that the structural context, in terms of the unique circumstances of the historical, economic and cultural location, plays in the mediational means and new implied object of the activity. In this case, the lack of access to technology both in and outside of the classroom necessitated the selection of student-owned and controlled tools and technologies to support students' learning beyond the classroom to achieve transformative learning.

Towards a transformative pedagogical framework

The reality of increased connectivity and, even in relatively under-resourced areas, the increasing use of emerging technology as a tool for teaching and learning, provided the empirical impetus for the studies that are reported in this book. For example, despite continuing inequities in the distribution, access to and use of emerging technologies (see in particular the AnTEP programme located in a remote region of South Australia, discussed by Wood et al. in Chapter 3, and the reference to South African resource-constrained areas by Bozalek, Gachago, and Watters in Chapter 10), it is evident that an increasing number of students attending higher education institutions are using emerging technologies to get and stay connected in authentic ways for their learning needs. Students are engaging in ways that make these technologies enabling for their learning, they are choosing to connect with who and what matters to them, and are continuously responding to their changing context. Thus, these relationships of a connected world are changing the ways that students learn, but the changes in how most academics teach have remained marginal, as several authors have pointed out (see Ng'ambi and Brown's and Rowe's contributions in Chapters 4 and 14, for example). It is therefore important for higher educators to think about how best to harness these practices to transform teaching and learning in higher education.

The contributors to this edited collection have all, in one form or another, been motivated by the following question: *How does emerging technology transform teaching and learning in higher education settings?* This then is the empirical basis for the book. Cultural-Historical Activity Theory (CHAT) is applied as the theoretical basis for understanding how introducing a novel tool (in this instance, new and emerging technologies) into an existing activity (teaching/learning in higher education settings) *must* alter that activity. Moreover, CHAT's acknowledgement of the cultural and historical embeddedness of activity is essential in trying to understand the cases reported here, which are drawn from different geopolitical and multicultural contexts. This concluding chapter draws on Engeström's (1987) systems model as an heuristic framework with which to analyse the various cases reported throughout the book. The generative power of this model lies in its focus on contradictions, or double binds, as sites of dynamic change. The authors of this chapter therefore draw primarily on this framework in order to show how pedagogical transformation can be tracked through an empirical engagement with contradictions that emerge in the data.

Thus, in this final section, we develop a *transformative pedagogical framework* which can be used to analyse situations where emerging technologies are introduced into higher education to alter pedagogy (object of activity) from traditional pedagogy (a transmission model) to transformative pedagogy whose object is authentic learning (Amory, 2012).

Located within the broad field of CHAT, the book draws on activity system framework to examine pedagogical change with emerging technology. The CHAT-informed understanding that introducing a novel tool into an existing activity must, necessarily alter that activity, whether regressively or progressively, is a central point of departure for our analysis in this chapter. For Engeström, contradictions alter activities and are therefore sites of potential dynamic change; and this change can be progressive or regressive – such as when a primary contradiction in the object (for example, obsessive concern about curriculum coverage versus developing deep conceptual learning) narrows the object. Contributions in this edited collection give indications about how the introduction of emerging technologies into higher education institutions may play a role in transforming pedagogy in South Africa, Australia and New Zealand. The premise of this book, then, is that introducing emerging technologies into higher education institutions can alter the object (pedagogy) from a traditional trans-mission mode of pedagogy, whose object in turn, is the transmission of knowledge rather than the development of students' cognitive capacity (see for example,

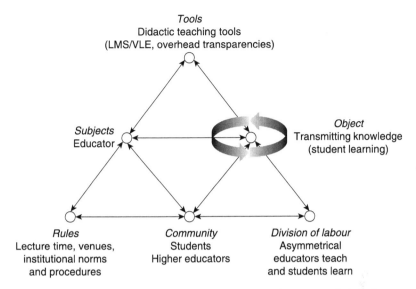

Figure 16.1 Activity System: Use of didactic tools to reinforce transmission of knowledge

Engeström, 2003; Hardman, 2005) to transformative pedagogy where the object is authentic student learning. Figure 16.1 represents the traditional, transmission mode of pedagogy still prevalent in the academy.

The subject of the system is a higher educator who acts on the object, students' acquisition of a body of knowledge (often, however, the object is nothing more than curriculum coverage, as noted by Hardman, 2008), using traditional tools, such as notes and didactic teaching. In these contexts, most educators use technologies such as Learning Management Systems (LMS) or other technological tools to mediate the transmission of knowledge. Power relations are asymmetrical and the division of labour is set, with the educator teaching and the students 'learning'. The community is narrow, generally encompassing only the educator and the students. The rules, too, are firmly defined by the institution and also by the educator (for example, times and venues of lectures are set and cannot be changed).

Figure 16.2 illustrates the starting point of this book. What we can see in Figure 16.2 is that the tools have altered to include emerging technologies.

The object of this activity in Figure 16.2 is different to Figure 16.1. Here we are concerned with acting on *pedagogy* to transform it from transmission mode to transformative pedagogy. Connectivity and mobile devices that enable anywhere, anytime engagement, influence the definition of rules. These rules are therefore loose, unregulated and foster creation of Personal Learning Environments (PLE). Social networks widen the community and the division of labour is more

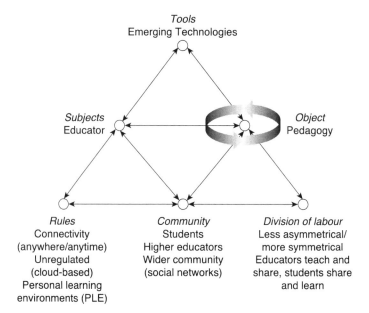

Figure 16.2 Activity System: Use of emerging technologies to transform pedagogy

symmetrical as both educators and students fulfil their roles but are inclined to share with each other and with the community. In Case study 13.1, students learning singing collaborate, engage in co-construction of knowledge with peers and the teacher; similarly, Case study 14.1 shows how obstetric students construct collaborative critical insights with peers. Figure 16.3 illustrates how the outcome of this activity (illustrated in Figure 16.2) becomes a novel tool (transformative pedagogy) that can now be used to act on the new object: authentic student learning, that is, the creation of complex and genuinely useful outcomes and products capable of transforming students cognitively. What we can see in Figure 16.3 is that the new tool, transformative pedagogy, which ideally uses principles of authentic learning, alters the object of the activity as well as the power relations in the teaching activity.

In this activity system it is evident that students are not simply students; they can inhabit the role of an educator as well as student. The educator, too, is no longer acting solely in the role of educator: s/he can become a learner and co-creator of knowledge. The use of emerging technologies as tools has altered the rules of the activity too: times and venues are no longer rigidly controlled by the institution.

The democratization of knowledge and the affordances of emerging technologies have propelled the organic formation of virtual communities and teams in higher education contexts. However, the increasing use of emerging technologies in these

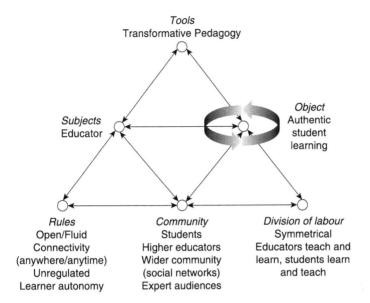

Figure 16.3 Activity System: Use of transformative pedagogy for authentic student learning

contexts has led to sporadic uses of these tools, with sparse attention to the theoretical foundations upon which the pedagogical approaches rest. These general uses have tended to focus on technology per se rather than a careful theoretical conception of what underpins the use of teaching and learning with technology. This book has shown that theory informs critique – and informs the design – of guidelines for transformative pedagogy (as illustrated conceptually in Figure 16.4).

In a *transformative pedagogical framework* as depicted in Figure 16.4, educators use didactic teaching tools to reinforce transmission of knowledge. The word reinforce is used to suggest that the goal is not necessarily to alter pedagogy. While emerging technologies may be appropriated to support transmission of knowledge, it has potential to alter pedagogy (i.e. disruptive or transformative) hence the outcome is dependent on the design of an activity system. The case studies reported in this book exemplify how educators designed learning activities that exploited the affordances of emerging technologies to *transform* pedagogical practices. Rather than use didactic teaching tools, these transformative pedagogies are enabling student learning in authentic contexts. It can be inferred from this *transformative pedagogical framework* that increasing uses of emerging technologies in higher education is changing traditional approaches to teaching and learning (object of activity) to a transformative pedagogy whose object is authentic learning.

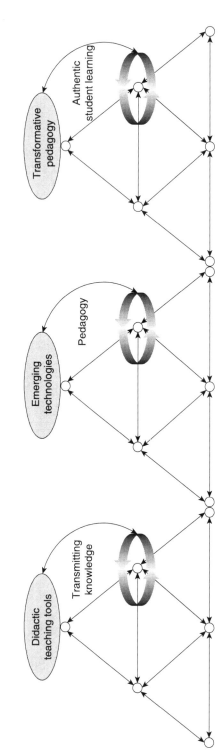

Figure 16.4 Transformative pedagogical framework

Didactic teaching tools

Transmitting knowledge

Emerging technologies

Pedagogy

Transformative pedagogy

Authentic student learning

References

Amory, A. (2012). Tool-mediated authentic learning in an educational technology course: a designed-based innovation. Retrieved from: http://www.tandfonline.com/doi/abs/10.1080/10494820.2012.682584.

Engeström, Y. (1987). *Learning by expanding: An activity-theoretic approach to developmental research.* Helsinki: Orienta-Konsultit Oy.

Engeström, Y. (2003). The horizontal dimension of expansive learning: Weaving a texture of cognitive trails in the terrain of health care in Helsinki. Paper presented at the international symposium New Challenges to Research on Learning, Helsinki, Finland, March.

Hardman, J. (2005). Activity Theory as a potential framework for technology research in an unequal terrain. *South African Journal of Higher Education, 19*(2), 378–392.

Hardman, J. (2008). New technology, new pedagogy? An activity theory analysis of pedagogical activity with computers. Unpublished doctoral thesis. University of Cape Town.

Index